On Good and Evil
and the Grey Zone

By the same author

Very Special Relationship (Brassey's, 1986)
Establishing the Anglo-American Alliance (Brassey's, 1990)
International Perspectives on the Falklands Conflict (ed.) (Macmillan, 1992)
The Franks Report: The Falkland Islands Review (ed.) (Pimlico, 1992)
Oliver Franks (Clarendon, 1993)
International Perspectives on the Gulf Conflict (ed.) (Macmillan, 1994)
Fin de Siècle: The Meaning of the Twentieth Century (ed.) (Tauris, 1995)
International Perspectives on the Yugoslav Conflict (ed.) (Macmillan, 1996)
On Specialness (Macmillan, 1998)
Alchemist of War: The Life of Basil Liddell Hart (Weidenfeld & Nicolson, 1998)
War Diaries: Field Marshal Lord Alanbrooke (ed.) (Weidenfeld & Nicolson, 2001)
The Iraq War and Democratic Politics (ed.) (Routledge, 2005)
Georges Braque (Hamish Hamilton, 2005)
Picasso Furioso (Dilecta, 2008)
On Art and War and Terror (Edinburgh University Press, 2009)
100 Artists' Manifestos (Penguin, 2011)
Cézanne: A Life (Profile, 2012)
The Letters of Paul Cézanne (ed.) (Thames & Hudson, 2013)

ON GOOD AND EVIL
AND THE GREY ZONE

Alex Danchev

EDINBURGH
University Press

Edinburgh University Press is one of the leading university presses in the UK. We publish academic books and journals in our selected subject areas across the humanities and social sciences, combining cutting-edge scholarship with high editorial and production values to produce academic works of lasting importance. For more information visit our website: www.edinburghuniversitypress.com

© Alex Danchev, 2016, 2017

Edinburgh University Press Ltd
The Tun – Holyrood Road
12 (2f) Jackson's Entry
Edinburgh EH8 8PJ
www.euppublishing.com

First published in hardback by Edinburgh University Press 2016

Typeset in Sabon by
Servis Filmsetting Ltd, Stockport, Cheshire,
and printed and bound in Great Britain by
Printed and bound by CPI Group (UK) Ltd, Croydon, CR0 4YY

A CIP record for this book is available from the British Library

ISBN 978 1 4744 1031 1 (hardback)
ISBN 978 1 4744 2800 2 (paperback)
ISBN 978 1 4744 1032 8 (webready PDF)
ISBN 978 1 4744 1033 5 (epub)

The right of Alex Danchev to be identified as author of this work has been asserted in accordance with the Copyright, Designs and Patents Act 1988 and the Copyright and Related Rights Regulations 2003 (SI No. 2498).

Contents

Figures

Acknowledgements

This book is a collection of published and unpublished work. An earlier version of Chapter 1 appeared in the *Journal of European Studies*. Chapter 2 is unpublished. Earlier versions of Chapters 3, 4 and 5 appeared in *International Affairs*. Chapter 6 is unpublished in this form. Elements of it appeared as the introduction to *Let a Thousand Flowers Bloom* (Hong Kong: White Cube, 2012), by Anselm Kiefer, and in *Times Higher Education*. Chapter 7 is unpublished. Earlier versions of Chapter 8 appeared in the *Review of International Studies* and in *Iraq and the Vietnam Syndrome* (New York: Free Press, 2007), edited by Lloyd Gardner and Marilyn Young. An earlier version of Chapter 9 appeared in the *British Journal of Politics and International Relations*. An earlier version of Chapter 10 appeared as the introduction to *100 Artists' Manifestos* (London: Penguin, 2011). An earlier version of Chapter 11 appeared as the epilogue to *Cézanne: A Life* (London: Profile and New York: Pantheon, 2012). An earlier version of Chapter 12 appeared in *International Affairs*.

Anna Steinmann, a model of efficiency, has been a tremendous help in the assemblage of the work, the presentation of the text, and the sourcing of the illustrations.

For intellectual and moral support in realizing this project, which is in a certain sense an on-going project, I am grateful to Roland Bleiker, Bernadette Buckley, Craig Burnett, Paul Edson, Patrick Finlay, Andrew Gordon, Christopher Hill, Bruce Hunter, Anthony King, Andrew Linklater, Debbie Lisle, Tim Marlow, Adelheid Scholten, Caroline Soper, Paul Stoop, Charles Trueheart, and my colleagues in the School of International Relations at the University of St Andrews, in particular Richard English and Nicholas Rengger.

I am grateful to Chloe Dewe Mathews, John Keane, Anselm Kiefer and Reinhard Mucha for generously allowing their work to be reproduced here. For Tim Hetherington's photographs, I thank the Magnum Agency; for Paul Klee's painting, the Israel Museum. For their part in making this happen, I much appreciate the help of Waltraud Forelli at Atelier Kiefer, Jochen Arentzen at Sprüth Magers, Jonathan Bell at Magnum Photos, and Rachel Laufer at the Israel Museum.

In art as in life, Dee Danchev has been a full partner in this enterprise.

For Xan

'Good and evil are the prejudices of God' – said the snake.

Friedrich Nietzsche*

It was granted to me to carry away from my prison years
on my bent back, which nearly broke beneath its load, this
essential experience: *how* a human being becomes evil and
how good. In the intoxication of youthful successes I had felt
myself to be infallible, and I was therefore cruel. In the surfeit
of power I was a murderer, and an oppressor. In my most
evil moments I was convinced that I was doing good, and I
was well supplied with systematic arguments. And it was only
when I lay there on rotting prison straw that I sensed within
myself the first stirrings of good. Gradually it was disclosed to
me that the line separating good and evil passes not through
states, nor between classes, nor between political parties
either – but right through every human heart – and through all
human hearts. This line shifts. Inside us, it oscillates with the
years. And even within hearts overwhelmed by evil, one small
bridgehead of good is retained. And even in the best of all
hearts, there remains . . . an unuprooted small corner of evil.

Alexander Solzhenitsyn[†]

---

* Friedrich Nietzsche, trans. Josefine Nauckhoff, *The Gay Science* [1882] (Cambridge: Cambridge University Press, 2001), p. 150.
† Alexander Solzhenitsyn, trans. Thomas P. Whitney, *The Gulag Archipelago* (London: Fontana, 1976), parts III and IV, p. 597.

Introduction
Blasphemers and Others

In ways that I do not pretend to understand fully, painting deals with the only issues that seem to me to count in our benighted time – freedom, autonomy, fairness, love.

Andrew Forge[1]

So we have to revise Adorno's famous phrase, according to which art is impossible after Auschwitz. The reverse is true: after Auschwitz, to show Auschwitz, art is the only thing possible, because art always entails the presence of an absence; because it is the very job of art to reveal something that is invisible, through the controlled power of words and images, connected or unconnected; because art alone thereby makes the inhuman perceptible, felt.

Jacques Rancière[2]

The time has come to realize that we are also capable of inventing emotions, perhaps even basic emotions comparable in power to love or hate.

Paul Nougé[3]

This book is conceived as a sequel or successor to an earlier collection, *On Art and War and Terror*, not merely in the scansion of the title, but in its nature and purpose and mode of address. It seeks to engage important ethical and political questions in the modern world through the medium of works of the imagination – works of art – painting and writing, photography and film. At the same time it tries to fathom what artists of various stripes are up to, in order to come to some assessment of their endeavours, and the consequences of their actions. To do that – not an easy task – it pays close attention to what the artists themselves have to say. In other words, it takes painters and others seriously as thinkers – philosophers, even – not to mention public intellectuals. It also treats them as moral agents. More particularly, it treats the art, and the artist, as a witness of our current discontents; indeed, the essential moral witness of the terrible twentieth century, as Winston Churchill called it, and the torturous twenty-first.

It may be objected that this is to place excessive faith in a broken reed, or at any rate an unthinking one. Seamus Heaney, the author of the credo and manifesto of this collection and the last, tackled the issue head-on in *The Government of the Tongue*, a brilliant conceit, playing on (among other things) Shelley's celebrated contention that poets are the unacknowledged legislators of the world:

> Here is the great paradox of poetry and of the imaginative arts in general. Faced with the brutality of the historical onslaught, they are practically useless. Yet they verify our singularity, they strike and stake out the ore of self which lies at the base of every individuated life. In one sense the efficacy of poetry is nil – no lyric has ever stopped a tank. In another sense, it is unlimited. It is like the writing in the sand in the face of which accusers and accused are left speechless and renewed. . . .
>
> This is what gives poetry its governing power. At its greatest moments it would attempt, in Yeats's phrase, to hold in a single thought reality and justice. Yet even then its function is not essentially supplicatory or transitive. Poetry is more a threshold than a path, one constantly approached and constantly departed from, at which reader and writer undergo in their different ways the experience of being at the same time summoned and released.[4]

Heaney is an unimpeachable witness – an unannullable witness, in Paul Celan's idiolect.[5] His own credo is worth attending to in this context. When asked by his interrogator and comrade-in-words Dennis O'Driscoll, 'What has poetry taught you?', he replied, magnificently, 'That there's such a thing as truth and it can be told – slant; that subjectivity is not to be theorized away and is worth defending; that poetry itself has a virtue, in the first sense of possessing a quality of moral excellence and in the sense also of possessing inherent strength by virtue of its sheer made-upness, its *integritas*, *consonantia* and *claritas*.'[6] The three qualities knowingly deployed here appear as the three things needed for beauty in 'another pennyworth of wisdom from Aquinas' in *A Portrait of the Artist as a Young Man* (1916), by James Joyce, where they are translated as wholeness, harmony and radiance. I am not sure about Aquinas, but I think a hap'orth of Heaney is something to hang on to.

So much for beauty. As for truth, I should like to adduce three more qualities, *diligentia*, *subtilitas* and *sobrietas*, which I propose to encapsulate as exactitude, with its sympathetic cognates of exactness, exacting and exaction. The exaction of art for the maker is what Celan had in mind, I think, when he said that 'with art you go into very selfmost straits', and when he added: 'And set yourself free.' The exaction of art for the spectator or reader has to do with the requirement to pay attention, as we might say, to bring to bear a combination of openness and attentiveness which issues in a state of mindfulness. Celan himself urged the need to be mindful, of days and dates, and others.

> The poem is lonely. It is lonely and underway. Whoever writes one stays mated with it.

> But in just this way doesn't the poem stand, right here, in an encounter – *in the mystery of an encounter?*

> The poem wants to reach an Other, it needs this Other, it needs an Over-against. It seeks it out, speaks toward it.

> For the poem making toward an Other, each thing, each human being is a form of this Other.

> The attentiveness a poem devotes to all it encounters, with its sharper sense of detail, outline, structure, colour, but also of 'quiverings' and 'intimations' – all this, I think, is not attained by an eye vying (or conniving) with constantly more perfect instruments. Rather, it is a concentration that stays mindful of all our dates.

> 'Attentiveness' – allow me here to quote a saying by Malebranche from Walter Benjamin's Kafka essay – 'Attentiveness is the natural prayer of the soul.'[7]

According to the great Polish poet Zbigniew Herbert (who supplemented his income by selling his blood, one exacting year), 'Writing must teach men soberness: *to be awake.*'[8]

These insights into what art can offer, it seems to me, serve to indicate a tremendous potential for ethical and political inquiry. The essays gathered here are an attempt to show how.

It is possible that a work entitled *On Good and Evil and the Grey Zone* is itching to prospect for moral excellence, wherever it may be found, a little like panning for gold – notwithstanding the compelling moral cogency of 'the grey zone', as adumbrated in Primo Levi's last testament, *The Drowned and the Saved* (see Chapter 1). The reverse applies. Execration is a sore temptation, especially for the rascally in public office, in particular the rascalliest. There is a strain of that, no doubt, in the pages that follow. Nevertheless, I side with Solzhenitsyn. 'So let the reader who expects this book to be a political exposé slam its covers shut right now.' In the gargantuan edifice that is *The Gulag Archipelago*, the author returns time and again to the deceiving and self-deceiving simplicities of the old dichotomies, as if worrying at a bone. One such passage, late in the work, stands as an epigraph to *On Good and Evil and the Grey Zone*. There is another outburst early on in *The Gulag Archipelago*:

> If only it were all so simple! If only there were evil people somewhere insidiously committing evil deeds, and it were necessary only to separate them from the rest of us and destroy them. But the line dividing good and evil cuts through the heart of every human being. And who is willing to destroy a piece of his own heart?
>
> During the life of any heart this line keeps changing place; sometimes it is squeezed one way by exuberant evil and sometimes it shifts to allow enough space for good to flourish. One and the same human being is, at various ages, under various circumstances, a totally different human being. At times he is close to being a devil, at times to sainthood. But his name doesn't change, and to that name we ascribe the whole lot, good and evil.

Solzhenitsyn had something more to say, of capital importance for the subject. 'To do evil,' he writes, 'a human being must first of all believe that what he's doing is good, or else that it's a well-considered act in conformity with natural law. Fortunately, it is in the nature of the human being to seek a *justification* for his actions.'

> Macbeth's self-justifications were feeble – and his conscience devoured him. Yes, even Iago was a little lamb too. The imagination and the spiritual strength of Shakespeare's evildoers stopped short at a dozen corpses. Because they had no *ideology*. . . .
>
> Thanks to *ideology*, the twentieth century was fated to experience evildoing on a scale calculated in the millions. This cannot be denied, nor passed over, nor suppressed. How, then, do we dare insist that evildoers do not exist? And who was it that destroyed these millions? Without evildoers there would have been no Archipelago.[9]

Like its predecessor, *On Good and Evil and the Grey Zone* repudiates binary thinking – good and evil, black and white, us and them, civilization and barbarism. It does not shrink from skewering evildoers – telling truth, slant as it may be – but it also strives to keep its distance from self-deception, and to practise a degree of humility and self-scrutiny, as artists do. 'Western societies are not, even now, the paradise of scepticism and rationalism that they believe themselves to be,' as Teju Cole reminds us.

> The West is a variegated space, in which both freedom of thought and tightly regulated speech exist, and in which disavowals of deadly vio-

lence happen at the same time as clandestine torture. But, at moments when Western societies consider themselves under attack, the discourse is quickly dominated by an ahistorical fantasy of long-suffering serenity and fortitude in the face of provocation. Yet European and American history are so strongly marked by efforts to control speech that the persecution of rebellious thought must be considered among the foundational buttresses of these societies. Witch burnings, heresy trials, and the untiring work of the Inquisition shaped Europe, and these ideas extended into American history as well and took on American modes, from the breaking of slaves to the censuring of critics of Operation Iraqi Freedom.[10]

In the wake of the *Charlie Hebdo* murders in Paris, in January 2015, blasphemy was widely extolled as Western virtue. ('*Je suis Charlie.*') And yet it has been argued that Chelsea Manning and Edward Snowden are blasphemers, too, and 'they have not been universally valorized', as Cole delicately puts it. One person's blasphemer is another person's traitor. Snowden himself seems to me less a blasphemer than a troublemaker – an honourable profession or avocation, and a historically necessary function, as A. J. P. Taylor pointed out with some glee (see Chapter 5). As for Manning, on 2 December 2014 the prophetic J. M. Coetzee wrote him a birthday letter:

> I'm sure it is not much fun spending your birthday behind bars, but I want to let you know that there are thousands and millions of people in the wider world who are thinking of you and wishing you well. We admire you for the steps you took in the service of democracy – that is to say, of the right of the people to govern themselves – and we respect you for the fortitude with which you have carried yourself since you were arrested, times when you must have felt very lonely and isolated.
>
> I myself am in my 70s, so I don't expect to be around when you regain your freedom (unless your president comes to his senses and offers you a pardon), but I want you to know that I am confident there will come a day when your image, and the image of Edward Snowden, will appear on postage stamps of the US Postal Service.[11]

Whatever we may think of whistleblowers, the characterization is a suggestive one. Artists themselves are blasphemers of a kind, perhaps, a soubriquet some of them might welcome. *On Good and Evil and the Grey Zone* is a book of blasphemers, troublemakers, world menders, hallowed mentors, do-gooders, God-botherers, bystanders, banalizers, torturers, and turbulent priests of every persuasion.

Notes

1. Andrew Forge, 'Painting and the Struggle for the Whole Self', *Artforum* 14 (September 1975), p. 49.
2. Jacques Rancière, trans. Julie Rose, *Figures of History* (Cambridge: Polity, 2014), pp. 49–50.
3. Paul Nougé, 'La Conférence de Charleroi' (1929), in *Histoire de ne pas rire* (Lausanne: L'Age d'Homme, 1980), p. 211.
4. Seamus Heaney, *The Government of the Tongue* (1986), in *Finders Keepers* (London: Faber, 2002), pp. 189–90. See also the introduction to Alex Danchev, *On Art and War and Terror* (Edinburgh: Edinburgh University Press, 2011). 'Poets are the unacknowledged legislators of the world' is the conclusion of Shelley's essay, *A Defence of Poetry* (1840).
5. See Chapter 2 below. Apropos Celan, Heaney observed, 'It's not impossible to write a poetry of tragic recognition, which recognises the whole weight and burden of the suffering of the world and at the same time doesn't either fly into bits or go into enigma.' Think of Zbigniew Herbert, he added, felicitously. Dennis O'Driscoll, *Stepping Stones: Interviews with Seamus Heaney* (London: Faber, 2008), p. 452.
6. O'Driscoll, *Stepping Stones*, p. 467.
7. Paul Celan, trans. John Felstiner, 'The Meridian: speech on the occasion of the award of the Georg Büchner Prize' (1961), in *Selected Poems and Prose of Paul Celan* (New York: Norton, 2001), pp. 409–11. See Chapter 6.
8. John and Bogdana Carpenter, 'Interview with Zbigniew Herbert' (1984), in Charles Simic, 'The Philosophy of 3AM', *New York Review of Books*, 26 April 2007. See Chapter 2.
9. Alexander Solzhenitsyn, trans. Thomas P. Whitney, *The Gulag Archipelago* (London: Fontana, 1976), parts I and II, pp. 168, 173–4.
10. Teju Cole, 'Unmournable Bodies', *The New Yorker*, 9 January 2015. Cf. Pankaj Mishra, 'Time for a new Enlightenment', and Christopher de Bellaigue, 'Stop saying it's time for a Muslim Enlightenment', *Guardian*, 20 January and 19 February 2015.
11. Coetzee to Manning, 2 December 2014, in *Guardian*, 16 December 2014. See Chapter 5.

1

'Good? But what is good?'
Ethics after Ikonnikov

Good men and bad men alike are capable of weakness. The difference is that a bad man will be proud all his life of one good deed – while an honest man is hardly aware of his good acts, but remembers a single sin for years on end.

Vasily Grossman[1]

The hero of this tale is a former Tolstoyan called Ikonnikov-Morzh, who is surely destined to find his place as one of the great characters of world literature. He might be called a Shakespearian character, if he were not so intimately associated with Vasily Grossman. Ethically and politically, his works and days are of the first importance.

He is given an outline biography in Grossman's great novel, *Life and Fate* (published in English in 1985), a kind of Second World War and Peace. His forebears had all been priests, but Ikonnikov received a lay education. In his final year at the Petersburg Institute of Technology he was converted to the teachings of Tolstoy. He left the institute to become a people's teacher in a village to the north of Perm. After eight years he quit the village and went to Odessa. There he was taken on as an engine-room mechanic in a merchant ship. He voyaged to India and Japan; he lived for a while in Sydney. After the Revolution he returned to Russia and joined a peasant commune. He believed that Communist agricultural labour would bring about the Kingdom of Heaven on earth, but he found that was not to be. He lived through collectivization, depopulation, starvation. He was no stranger to famine. He began preaching the Gospel; he became a little unhinged. He spent a year in a prison psychiatric hospital. After his release he went to live with his elder brother, a professor of biology, in Byelorussia. In 1941, Byelorussia was invaded. Ikonnikov knew something of the war of annihilation on the Eastern Front. He also knew what was happening to the Jews. He begged people to give them sanctuary; he tried to save women and children himself. Miraculously, he escaped the gallows.

He is first encountered as a prisoner of war in a German concentration camp, in a hut with several others 'of special interest to the Gestapo', including Mikhail Sidorovich Mostovskoy, an Old Bolshevik; an assortment of Russian officers; and Gardi, an Italian priest. In this company, the greybeard Ikonnikov, 'a strange man who could have been any age at all', is at the same time a genuine oddity and a recognizable type.

> He slept in the worst place in the whole hut: by the main door, where there was a freezing draught and where the huge latrine pail or *parasha* had once stood. The other Russians referred to him as 'the old parachutist'. They looked on him as a holy fool and treated him with a mixture of disgust and pity.
>
> He was endowed with the extraordinary powers of endurance characteristic of madmen and simpletons. He never once caught cold, even though he would go to bed without taking off his rain-soaked clothes. And surely only the voice of a madman could be so clear and ringing.

He introduces himself by walking up to Mostovskoy and staring intently into his face. 'What's the good news then?' enquires the Old Bolshevik sardonically. 'Good? But what is good?' replies Ikonnikov, immediately establishing his signature theme.[2]

It is the holy fool who voices Grossman's ethics. In fact he personifies them. By word and deed, the ethics of *Life and Fate* are embodied in Ikonnikov, whose very name seems to be an invitation to wonder.

The Russian prisoners are set to do some hard labour in the marshland not far from the camp. It is construction work; and soon enough it becomes clear that what they are constructing is a gas chamber. For Ikonnikov this realization triggers a crisis of conscience posed as an agonizing dilemma – to carry on working, and helping; or to refuse, and condemn himself to death? One day, in his torment, he reaches out and grasps the bare foot of the priest, sitting on the second tier of bunks in their hut, and in scrambled French, German and Italian asks this anguished question: '*Que dois-je fais, mio padre? Nous travaillons dans una Vernichtungslager.*' ['What am I to do, father? We are working in an extermination camp.'][3]

The question hangs in the air of the totalitarian century. Forty years earlier, in Joseph Conrad's *Heart of Darkness*, Kurtz had scrawled his answer: 'Exterminate all the brutes!' That answer in its chilling simplicity tickles the ear of any exterminator. 'All of Europe contributed to the making of Kurtz,' as Conrad took care to remind us.[4] All of Europe contributes to Ikonnikov's life and fate and utterance – and to his salvation. For he is resolute, it turns out, in spite of his anguish. He has seen what the century has to offer. He has seen the Terror. He has seen the killing squads. He has seen the mass graves. Significantly, he has witnessed the massacre at Berdichev, Grossman's birthplace (unnamed in the novel). 'Don't make fun of me,' he admonishes Mostovskoy. 'I didn't come over here just to make you laugh. On the fifteenth of September last year [1941] I watched twenty thousand Jews being executed – women, children and old men. That day I understood that God could not allow such a thing and that therefore he did not exist.'[5]

Like his creator, Ikonnikov is a moral witness (see Chapter 2). In the camp, unwittingly, he has become an accomplice. He has poured the concrete for the gas chamber. But he is not prepared to acquiesce in such a fate. Not for him the fathomless existence of domination, degradation and dehumanization that Giorgio Agamben calls 'bare life'.[6] For Ikonnikov, bare life is intolerable. His spirit has rebelled. The priest's passivity sparks a magnificent dissent:

> Gardi's coal-black eyes looked round at the three men. '*Tout le monde travaille là-bas. Et moi je travaille là-bas. Nous sommes des esclaves,*' he said slowly. '*Dieu nous pardonnera.*' ['Everyone works there. I myself work there. We are slaves. God will forgive us.']
>
> '*C'est son métier,*' added Mostovskoy. ['That's his job.']
>
> '*Mais ce n'est pas votre métier,*' said Gardi reproachfully. ['But it's not your job.']
>
> 'But that's just it, Mikhail Sidorovich, you too think you're going to be forgiven,' said Ikonnikov, hurrying to get the words out and ignoring Gardi. 'But me – I'm not asking for absolution of sins. I don't want to be told that it's the people with power over us who are guilty, that we're innocent slaves, that we're not guilty because we're not free. I *am* free! I'm building a *Vernichtungslager*; I have to answer to the people who'll be gassed here. I can say "No." There's nothing can stop me – as long as I can find the strength to face my destruction. I *will* say "No!" *Je dirai non, mio padre, je dirai non!*'[7]

Ikonnikov gives an irrefutable answer to his own momentous question. Having done so, he quits the scene. He is taken away for interrogation, never to return, but his eloquence is not stilled by his disappearance.[8] Like Kurtz, he leaves a kind of testament. In keeping with Conrad's voracious irony, Kurtz has been writing a report for the International Society for the Suppression of Savage Customs, 'for its future guidance'.[9] Ikonnikov has been writing for himself, and possibly for his ideological foil, Mostovskoy, for his edification, and ours. 'Ikonnikov's scribblings' are reproduced in full in *Life and Fate*, where they take up nearly a whole chapter.[10] In them beats the ethical heart of the work.

Ikonnikov does not believe in Good. He believes in human kindness.

> Yes, as well as this terrible Good with a capital 'G', there is everyday human kindness. The kindness of an old woman carrying a piece of bread to a prisoner, the kindness of a soldier allowing a wounded enemy to drink from his water flask, the kindness of youth towards age, the kindness of a peasant hiding an old Jew in his loft. The kindness of a prison guard who risks his own liberty to pass on letters written by a prisoner not to his ideological comrades, but to his wife and mother.
>
> The private kindness of one individual towards another; a petty, thoughtless kindness; an unwitnessed kindness. Something we could call senseless kindness. A kindness outside any system of social or religious good. . . .
>
> Even at the most terrible times, through all the mad acts carried out in the name of Universal Good and the glory of States, times when people were tossed about like branches in the wind, filling ditches and gullies like stones in an avalanche – even then this senseless, pathetic kindness remained scattered throughout life like atoms of radium.

The holy fool has lost his faith. Or rather he has lost one faith and found another. For Ikonnikov the battle of good and evil is a delusion. He clings instead to 'what is human in human beings', to the human qualities that persist, 'even on the edge of the grave, even at the door of the gas chamber'.

> My faith has been tempered in Hell. My faith has emerged from the flames of the crematoria, from the concrete of the gas chamber. I have seen that it is not man who is impotent in the struggle against evil, but the power of evil that is impotent in the struggle against man. The powerlessness of kindness, of senseless kindness, is the secret of its immortality. It can never be conquered. The more stupid, the more senseless, the more helpless it may seem, the vaster it is. Evil is impotent before it. The prophets, religious teachers, reformers, social and political leaders are impotent before it. This dumb, blind love is man's meaning.

Ikonnikov expounds an ethics of small acts of senseless kindness. *Life and Fate* is among other things a serial demonstration of such ethics applied, in the most extreme circumstances. Three episodes echo down the decades.

The first is the encounter between Sofya Osipovna Levinton, a doctor, and a little boy called David, who shares many of Grossman's childhood memories as well as his birthday. They are thrown together in a transport to Auschwitz. As they begin to suffer from hunger and thirst, Sofya has the inspiration of tearing a strip of cloth from the hem of her shirt and pushing it through a chink in the cattle-wagon, so that it absorbs rain water. She offers the wet cloth to the boy, for him to suck; she also gives him some bread. Once they reach their destination, she takes him by the hand. When the cry goes up for doctors and surgeons, Sofya does not respond: she chooses to remain with the boy. As they process towards the bath house, a man in front of them attacks an SS guard. Sofya tries to follow suit, momentarily forgetting about David, but she stumbles and falls. The others pick her up and restore her to her place in the line. Once more she takes the boy by the hand. 'David saw how clear, fierce and splendid human eyes can be when – even for a fraction of a second – they sense freedom.'

They enter the bath house and then the gas chamber. Sofya holds David tightly to her. High up, behind a rectangular metal grating in the wall, a fan begins to turn. The boy becomes aware of a faint sweet smell.

> Sofya Levinton felt the boy's body subside in her arms. Once again she had fallen behind him. In mineshafts where the air becomes poisoned, it is always the little creatures, the birds and mice, that die first. This boy, with his slight, bird-like body, had left before her.
>
> 'I've become a mother,' she thought.
>
> That was her last thought.[11]

The second episode is the encounter of Semyonov, an Army driver, and an old woman called Khristya Chunyak. Semyonov is taken prisoner at the same time as Mostovskoy and Sofya Levinton. He is held for ten weeks in a camp near the front, and then sent by train towards the western border, together with other captured Red Army soldiers. For ten days he is shut in another cattle wagon. On the eleventh day he is hauled out, unconscious, and left for dead. After ten weeks and eleven days of near starvation, Semyonov is not worth the trouble of shooting. 'Let him crawl to the village,' says the local commandant, echoing Regan's cruel dismissal of the blinded Gloucester in *King Lear*: 'Go thrust him out at gates, and let him smell/ His way to Dover.'

Semyonov drags himself to the village. At the first hut he is turned away. At the second there is no answer. The door to the third is half-open. He walks in, feels dizzy, and lies down on a bench near the door. A woman appears, catches sight of him, and screams. Yet she lets him stay. 'That day his life and fate was decided not by the merciless forces of warring States, but by a human being – old Khristya Chunyak.' Khristya Chunyak takes him in. She gives him a mug of milk; she undresses him and bathes him; she makes up a bed on top of the stove, and lifts him on to it, 'as easily as if he were a chicken'. She asks no questions. He comes to think of her as 'the mistress of the good hut'.[12]

The third episode is perhaps the most arresting. In the ruins of Stalingrad, some German prisoners are bringing out Russian corpses from the cellar of a building that used to be the headquarters of the Gestapo. As they lay out the bodies on the frozen ground, the prisoners are watched by a crowd of women and boys and old men. These people are angry. Their anger focuses on the only one of the prisoners who shows any sign of being affected by this gruesome work: 'a young man in an officer's greatcoat, who had tied a handkerchief round his mouth and nose and was shaking his head convulsively like a horse stung by gadflies. The expression of torment in his eyes seemed close to madness.'

> 'So you're trying to look away, are you?' muttered a squat woman who was holding a little boy by the hand.
> The officer could sense the weight of emotion in the woman's slow, penetrating look. The air was full of hatred that needed to be discharged; it was like the electrical energy in a storm-cloud that strikes blindly and with consuming power at one of the trees in the forest.

The next corpse to be brought out is that of an adolescent girl. Her body is shrivelled; only her blond hair has kept its life, falling in disorder around the blackened face. The sight of her produces an instant reaction in the crowd.

> The squat woman let out a shrill cry. Her voice cut through the cold air like a blade. 'My child! My child! My golden child!'
> The crowd was shaken by the way the woman had cried out for a child who wasn't even her own. The woman began tidying the girl's hair; it looked as though it had only recently been curled. She gazed at her face, at her forever-twisted mouth, at her terrible features; in them she could see what only a mother could have seen – the adorable face of the baby who had once smiled at her out of its swaddling clothes.

The woman got to her feet and strode towards the officer. Everyone was struck by the way she kept her eyes fixed on him and yet at the same time managed to find a brick that wasn't part of a great frozen heap – a brick that even her poor hand could pick up, her poor weak hand that had been deformed by years of labour, that had been scalded by boiling water, icy water and lye.

The guard sensed what was about to happen and knew there was nothing he could do to stop the woman; she was stronger than his tommy gun. The prisoners couldn't take their eyes off her; the children watched her avidly and impatiently.

The woman could no longer see anything at all except the face of the German with the handkerchief round his mouth. Not understanding what was happening to her, governed by a power she had just now seemed to control, she felt in the pocket of her jacket for a piece of bread that had been given to her the evening before by a soldier. She held it out to the German officer and said: 'There, have something to eat.'[13]

These episodes are parables of senseless kindness. The acts they describe are at once individual and universal, great and small. Not even their perpetrators can make sense of them.[14] We had been warned. Ikonnikov's potted biography concludes: 'The ideas of this dirty, ragged old man were a strange hotchpotch. He professed a belief in an absurd theory of morality that – in his own words – "transcended class".'[15]

How is this 'absurd theory' derived?

Grossman had been pondering the phenomenon of human kindness for some time – even as he bore witness to the bottomless depths of man's inhumanity to man. A seminal short story, 'The Old Teacher' (1943), turns on another encounter, between an eighty-two-year-old teacher, Boris Isaakovich Rosenthal, and a little girl, Katya, in a sort of role reversal of the relationship between Sofya Levinton and David. The story is set in an unnamed town that bears some resemblance to Berdichev. It begins with the old teacher sunning himself in the yard, a small volume of Chekhov on his knee, when the girl appears:

Then six-year-old Katya, the daughter of Weissman, the lieutenant who had been killed, came up to him in her torn dress, shuffling along in galoshes that were falling off her dirty, scratched little feet. Offering him a cold, sour pancake, she said, 'Eat, teacher!'

He took the pancake and began to eat it, looking at the little girl's thin face. . . . Rosenthal dropped his book and did not try to pick it up – he was looking at the little girl's huge eyes, which were intently, even greedily, watching him as he ate. Once again he felt the urge to understand a wonder that never ceased to amaze him: human kindness. Perhaps the answer was there in the child's eyes. But her eyes must have been too dark, or maybe what got in the way were his own tears – once again he saw nothing and understood nothing.

The atmosphere is oppressive; events move fast. The Jews are rounded up and marched towards a ravine outside the town. Along the way, Katya is separated from her mother and grandmother. She hangs on to the old teacher's jacket. With some difficulty, he picks her up and carries her – to the very edge of the ravine. His constitution is weak; his legs are shaking and his ears are ringing from the effort. 'His breathing became laboured, but the old man went on holding the little girl in his arms. Thinking about her was a distraction.'

> 'How can I comfort her? How can I deceive her?' the old man wondered, gripped by a feeling of infinite sorrow. At this last minute too, there would be no one to support him, no one to say what he had longed all his life to hear – the words he had desired more than all the wisdom of books about the great thoughts and labours of man.
>
> The little girl turned towards him. Her face was calm; it was the pale face of an adult, a face full of tolerant compassion. And in a sudden silence he heard her voice.
>
> 'Teacher,' she said, 'don't look that way, it will frighten you.' And, like a mother, she covered his eyes with the palms of her hands.[16]

The emphasis on the mother in these episodes is not accidental. Grossman had a consuming personal interest in the events he recounted. There can be little doubt that his strongly felt sense of duty to speak on behalf of the dead, 'on behalf of those who lie in the earth', was in part filial – towards his mother – fed by a sense of guilt.[17] After his own death, in 1964, an envelope was found among his papers. In it were two letters he had written to his dead mother, in 1950 and 1961, together with two photographs. One was a family snap: it shows him with his mother when he was still a child in a sailor suit. The other was a trophy picture, confiscated from a dead SS officer: it shows hundreds of dead women and girls, naked, in a pit. Grossman's mother, Yekaterina Savelievna, perished in a pit, in Berdichev, in 1941. 'I have tried, dozens, or maybe hundreds of times, to imagine how you died, how you walked to your death,' he wrote to her in the earlier letter. 'I tried to imagine the man who killed you. He was the last person to see you. I know that you were thinking about me a great deal – all this time.'[18] What he tried to imagine was her look. To his everlasting sorrow, he failed. We who come after him strain to catch it in her passport photograph. She is small, dwarfed by the number plate above her head. She is slightly blurred, and a little off-centre. Her head is heavy; the face is worn; the eyes are black and dull. Passport holder 35116 has seen enough already.

Not only did he fail to imagine her, he failed to save her. He might have succeeded; discouraged by his wife, he did not try. Ikonnikov was there. Grossman was not. Afterwards, that must have been a heavy burden. It is tempting to speculate that self-examination and self-criticism fed his reflections on human kindness. Year after year he reread his mother's letters. 'I cry over these letters, because you are present in them,' he wrote to her on the twentieth anniversary of her death. 'Your kindness is there in them, and your purity, and your bitter, bitter life, and your nobility, and your sense of justice, your love for me, your concern for others, and your wonderful mind.' She was his model of human kindness. 'To me you represent all that is human, and your terrible fate is the fate of humanity in an inhuman time.'[19] *Life and Fate* is dedicated to her; she haunts its pages. Embedded in the novel is the last letter that Anna Semyonovna writes to her beloved son Viktor – a letter smuggled out of the ghetto, the way station to destruction. It is in itself a remarkable feat of imagining, and a source of more clues.[20]

As her neighbours fight over her furniture, the only ones to treat Anna Semyonovna like a human being are the yard dog Tobik, who is very affectionate, and (much to her surprise) a former patient called Shchukin, who carries her belongings, gives her 300 roubles, and promises to come to the fence once a week and bring her some bread. Anna Semyonovna's belongings consist of a pillow, some bedclothes, a cup, a spoon, a knife, two forks, a few medical instruments, Viktor's letters, a photograph of her late mother and Uncle David, and another of Viktor and his father – 'Do we really need so very much?' – and some books: a volume of Pushkin; Daudet's *Lettres de mon moulin* (1869), of which her favourite is 'Les Vieux'; a volume of Maupassant containing *Une vie* (1883); and of course some Chekhov, including 'A Boring Story' and 'The Bishop'.[21]

Books are survivors. Anna Semyonovna was permitted to take fifteen kilograms of belongings to the ghetto. These volumes were worth their weight in prose – prose more precious than we might think. For Grossman, books were a kind of touchstone. Against the advice of his closest friends, he submitted the manuscript of *Life and Fate* to the Soviet authorities in 1960. What he had written was in many ways heretical, but at the time of the Khrushchev 'thaw' he clearly believed that the novel was publishable. He was sadly mistaken. The book itself was arrested, as the author said; the KGB raided his apartment and confiscated not only the manuscript but also the carbon paper and typewriter ribbons. Grossman continued to petition for its release. Undaunted, he wrote to Khrushchev himself: 'There is no sense or truth in my present position, in my apparent freedom, while the book to which I have given my life is in prison. For I have written it, and I have not renounced it and am not renouncing it,' he concluded, Ikonnikov-like. 'Twelve years have passed since I began work on this book. I still believe that I have written the truth, and that I wrote this truth out of love and pity for people, out of faith in people. I ask for freedom for my book.'[22]

He received no reply. In the fullness of time he was summoned to an audience with the chief ideologue of the Central Committee, the notorious Mikhail Suslov, who coolly informed him that his book could not be published for another 200 years. ('Why should we add your book to the atomic bombs that our enemies are preparing to launch against us? Publishing your book would only increase the number of victims.') For Grossman this was a crushing blow. 'They strangled me in a dark corner,' he said.[23] However, he was not completely bereft. He had taken the precaution of making two clandestine copies of the manuscript. For a while they disappeared; at length one of them was found and microfilmed, with the help of the most eminent microfilmers in all Russia, Andrei Sakharov and Yelena Bonner, and smuggled out to the West by the dissident writer Vladimir Voinovich. It was eventually published, in French, in Switzerland in 1980, then in English in the United Kingdom and the United States in 1985, and finally in Russian, in the last days of the USSR in 1988 – too late for Vasily Grossman.

Books appear in his work as themselves. The early novel *The People Immortal* (1942) chronicles the destruction of an ancient city in an air raid. In the street is the body of an old man, a retired legal expert, killed by a bomb. 'Beside him lay the scattered, torn and blood-spattered books carried by the old man. Apparently at the moment of explosion he had sat up, looking out of the shallow slit. Bogarev read the title of the book which lay next to the body: *Annals*. Tacitus.'[24] Grossman set himself to reading and annotating the *Annals* during the Terror of 1936–8. Absorbed in the reigns of Tiberius, Claudius and Nero, he lived through the reign of Stalin. It must have been an enthralling and disquieting experience. The *pièce de résistance* is the account of Tiberius, depicted as deeply complex, fundamentally deceptive, irredeemably corrupted, and finally depraved. 'Ordinary human interaction had been destroyed by the power of fear,' writes Tacitus, 'and with the growth of the savagery came the exclusion of pity.' His summation is a devastating moral reckoning:

> [Tiberius's] character also saw different phases. The period he spent as a private citizen, or upholding various commands under Augustus, was, both for his life and his reputation, a noble one. The interval while Germanicus and Drusus remained alive was one of secrecy and hypocrisy as he affected virtue. While his mother still lived he was a mixture of good and bad. He was atrocious in his brutality, but his lechery was kept hidden while he loved, or feared, Sejanus. In the end, he erupted into an orgy of crime and ignominy alike, when, with all shame and fear removed, he simply followed his own inclinations.[25]

Parallels with the Soviet present were difficult to ignore. From Grossman's notes on his reading: 'Beautiful soul – Tacitus admires courage, nobility, intelligence, just decisions, truthful speeches, spousal fidelity, filial love, firm friendship. He condemns lying, denunciations, flattery, cowardice, cruel murders, corruption, incest, weakness, servility.'[26]

On this account, Tacitus sounds a little like Chekhov's cultured person. In *Life and Fate*, Chekhov comes into his own.

> Viktor looked at his wife, wondering what the two of them would be like in ten or fifteen years.
>
> 'Do you remember Chekhov's story "The Bishop"? The mother used to take her cow out to graze and tell the other women how her son had once been a bishop. No one believed her.'
>
> 'No, I don't remember,' said Lyudmilla. 'I read it when I was a little girl.'
>
> 'Well, read it again,' said Viktor irritably. He had always resented Lyudmilla's indifference towards Chekhov; he suspected that she hadn't even read most of his stories.[27]

Indifference to Chekhov is always a cause for reproach. Grossman adored Chekhov. In her last letter Anna Semyonovna recalls that 'the one play which reduced me to tears, together with the whole audience – a congress of village doctors – was Stanislavsky's production of *Uncle Vanya*'. Another character is said to prefer 'the tendentious novels of a Dreiser or a Feuchtwanger' to 'The Bishop' or 'A Boring Story', a preference at once mysterious and alienating.[28] Despite its Tolstoyan scale and structure, *Life and Fate* is a surprisingly

Chekhovian work. As the translator Robert Chandler has pointed out, many individual chapters are like Chekhov's short stories. Much of it can be read as a series of miniatures, just as Grossman himself thought that the short stories could be read as a single epic.

One of the characters in the novel launches into a disquisition on Chekhov's teaching. 'He said – and no one had said this before, not even Tolstoy – that first and foremost we are all of us human beings. Do you understand? Human beings! . . . He said that first of all we are human beings – and only secondly are we bishops, Russians, shop-keepers, Tartars, workers. Do you understand? Instead of saying that people are good or bad because they are bishops or workers, Tartars or Ukrainians, instead of this he said that people are equal because they are human beings.' 'Chekhov said: let's put God – and all those grand progressive ideas – to one side. Let's begin with man; let's be kind and attentive to individual man – whether he's a bishop, a peasant, an industrial magnate, a convict in the Sakhalin Islands or a waiter in a restaurant. Let's begin with respect, compassion and love for the individual – or we'll never get anywhere. That's democracy, the still unrealized democracy of the Russian people.'[29]

The democratic insistence on the individual, on what is human in human beings, chimes with an influential interpretation of Chekhov's plays that emphasizes 'prosaics' – the prosaic decencies and the prosaic lives that were close to his heart. 'Chekhov's characters imagine that they are heroes or heroines in a genre suffused with romance, heroism, great theories, and decisive action, or else they try to play the lead roles in tragic tales of paralyzing disillusionment and emptiness. They consider themselves to be either heroes or "heroes of our time". But their search for drama unfolds in Chekhov's universe of prosaics.'[30] Tell me what you want and I will tell you what you are, he wrote in one of Anna Semyonovna's treasured volumes. 'And now, too, I examine myself: what do I want? I want our wives, our children, our friends, our students to love not our name, our firm, our label, but ourselves, ordinary human beings.'[31] Invited to join a circle of the *intelligentsia*, he responded with a restatement of his most cherished beliefs: simple acts of kindness for which 'you've got to be not so much the young literary figure as just a plain human being. Let us be ordinary people, let us adopt the same attitude *toward all*, then an artificially overwrought solidarity will not be needed.' In the universe of prosaics, the everyday is truly meaningful. For Chekhov as for Reinhard Mucha (see Chapter 7), greatness resides in smallness. Cultured people are sincere, 'and dread lying like fire', he instructed his wayward brother Nikolai. 'They don't lie even in small things.' Small is a serviceable discriminator. Chekhov extolled 'good habits, good manners, and small acts of consideration'.[32]

Ordinary people have ordinary virtues. Ordinariness speaks to common-or-garden goodness, and ordinary virtues consort well with senseless kindness. They begin at home; they are small-scale, low-level, commonly recognizable, essentially personal – petty, thoughtless and unwitnessed, in Ikonnikov's idiom. Their ordinariness consists in such unheroic acts as caring and looking – *Life and Fate* is all about looking. War is a realm of chance and contingency. Anything can happen, as Seamus Heaney memorably said:

> Anything can happen, the tallest towers
> Be overturned, those in high places daunted,
> Those overlooked regarded.[33]

Ordinary virtues are associated with the writings of the most celebrated moral witness of the age of the gulag and the *Vernichtungslager*, Primo Levi. Thirteen have been derived from his *œuvre* by Robert Gordon – a rather arbitrary number. The list is ill-sorted and intriguing: looking; memory; discretion, or language and silence; use; measure, or a sense of limit; practice, or trial and error; perspective, or looking again; invention, or first things; common sense; friendship; storytelling; irony, or wit revisited; and play. Gordon's account is indebted to 'the affirmation of ordinary life' in Charles Taylor's *Sources of the Self*, a wonderfully suggestive work which sets out to map our moral world. 'This sense of the importance of the everyday in human life, along with its corollary about the importance of suffering, colours our whole understanding of what it is truly to respect human life and integrity.'[34]

Primo Levi was a survivor. His guilt was greater. If Grossman was strangled, Levi was drowned, slowly, over many years. Survival is a life sentence. His own reflection is definitive:

> I must repeat: we, the survivors, are not the true witnesses. This is an uncomfortable notion of which I have become conscious little by little, reading the memoirs of others and reading mine at a distance of years. We survivors are not only an exiguous but also an anomalous minority: we are those who by their prevarications or abilities or good luck did not touch bottom. Those who did so, those who saw the Gorgon, have not returned to tell about it or have returned mute, but they are the 'Muslims' [*Muselmänner*], the submerged, the complete witnesses, the ones whose deposition would have a general significance. They are the rule, we are the exception.[35]

Ethically, Grossman and Levi are in the same key. As artists, there is a certain dissonance. The literary quality of Levi's writing is concealed in a scientist's report. The tone is cool. The distinction of his work lies in its precision and its concision, to borrow his own words, and its scrupulous restraint: 'Death begins with the shoes.' Grossman blows hot by comparison, but for compelling immediacy, gravity and veracity, coupled with moral clarity, he has no peer.

As moralists, these chemists are fiercely attached to the individual particle. Their unit of analysis is enunciated in the title of Levi's first book, *If This Is a Man* (published in English in 1959). They reject aggregates, as Grossman puts it, structural or ideological ('are not the terrible mechanics of Fascism founded on the principle of quantum politics, of political probability?').[36] They have no use for doctrines or systems. They deprecate binary thinking – us and them, black and white, good and evil, civilization and barbarism. Levi's refusal of the stark opposition between good and evil finds expression in 'The Grey Zone', the chapter he considered the most important in his last book, *The Drowned and the Saved* (published in English in 1988). There he speaks of the grey zone of *protekcja* (privilege) and collaboration, 'where the two camps of masters and servants both diverge and converge'. Levi's special subject is the universe of Auschwitz; he adduces as an 'extreme case of collaboration' the *Sonderkommando*, the Special Squad entrusted with the grisly privilege of running the crematoria. He offers a searching assessment of their choice, or their predicament, capped with a subdued admonition: 'Therefore I ask that we meditate on the story of "the crematorium ravens" with pity and rigour, but that judgement of them be suspended.' The conclusion of his discussion is masterly:

> We too are so dazzled by power and prestige as to forget our essential fragility. Willingly or not we come to terms with power, forgetting that we are all in the ghetto, that the ghetto is walled in, that outside the ghetto reign the lords of death, and that close by the train is waiting.[37]

In terms of international readership, and recognition, Primo Levi did not become Primo Levi until the success of *The Periodic Table* (published in English in 1984). Vasily Grossman experienced a somewhat similar time lag. Nonetheless he has found compelling expositors. Grossman's ethics have a long reach. Tzvetan Todorov, for one, is captivated. Todorov identifies three ordinary virtues – dignity; caring, or concern; and (oddly) the life of the mind. He stresses the point that acts of ordinary virtue are by definition personal: they target specific individuals. A small act of senseless kindness involves an agent and a beneficiary. The beneficiary is not necessarily deserving; like Khristya Chunyak, agents ask no questions. Such acts serve human beings rather than abstractions. As Todorov paraphrases Ikonnikov – overstating somewhat – Good with a capital G is 'the morality of principles, hardly distinguishable from evil itself'; human kindness is 'the morality of sympathy, the only commendable morality'.[38]

Todorov is not alone. In a striking case of intellectual discovery and spiritual affinity, Grossman's ethics had a tremendous impact on the philosopher Emmanuel Levinas.

According to Levinas, the ethical (and political) crux of the matter is our response and our responsibility to the other. The other appears to us as 'the face'. What he calls the face is not to be understood literally, or even metaphorically, but poetically. Strictly speaking, it is a rhetorical figure. Thus, in one characteristic formulation, 'the face is a hand in search of recompense, an open hand. That is, it needs something. It is going to ask you for something.' He is not content to stop there. For Levinas, the face is a demand – a demand, not a supplication – which calls for an ethical response. 'I think that the beginning of language is in the face. In a certain way, in its silence, it calls you. Your reaction to the face is a response. Not just a response, but a responsibility.' We are hostage to the other, Levinas liked to say, in his figurative fashion, as if harking back to Jean Fautrier's paintings (see Chapter 2). 'The tie with the other is knotted only as responsibility. To say "Here I am."'[39]

Levinas was profoundly affected by *Life and Fate*, 'a fundamental book of our time', which he appears to have read in Russian in 1983 or 1984. Certain episodes lived in his memory. He recalled the encounter of the squat woman and the German officer:

> Toward the book's end, when Stalingrad has already been rescued, the German prisoners, including an officer, are cleaning out a basement and removing the decomposing bodies. The officer suffers particularly from this misery. In the crowd, a woman who hates Germans is delighted to see this man more miserable than the others. Then she gives him the last piece of bread she has. This is extraordinary. Even in hatred there exists a mercy stronger than hatred.

Levinas considered that the essential message of the work was Ikonnikov's, 'There is neither God nor Good, but there is goodness.' He associated himself with that vision. He called it 'ethics without ethical system'.[40]

> Grossman's eight hundred pages offer a complete spectacle of desolation
> and dehumanization. . . . Yet within that decomposition of human rela-
> tions, within that sociology of misery, goodness persists. In the relation
> of one man to another, goodness is possible. There is a long monologue
> where Ikonnikov – the character who expresses the ideas of the author
> – casts doubt upon all social sermonizing, that is, upon all reasonable
> organization with an ideology, with plans. . . . Every attempt to organize
> humanity fails. The only thing that remains undying is the goodness of
> everyday, ongoing life. Ikonnikov calls that 'the little act of goodness'.[41]

One episode in particular made a deep impression on him, and became
almost a key to his thought: Yevgenia Nikolaevna Shaposhnikova's
visits to the Lubyanka, in search of information about her husband,
Nikolay Grigorevich Krymov, a staunch Communist but now a
political prisoner, accused of Trotskyism and links with the Gestapo
– serious crimes. A man found guilty of such crimes could disappear
forever. At the Lubyanka (where Grossman himself was interrogated in 1938), enquiries about cases of this sort elicited a standard response: 'Parcel not accepted.' Those words might be a death
sentence.

Yevgenia and Krymov are estranged. She has since found happi-
ness of a kind with another man, Colonel Pyotr Pavlovich Novikov,
the commander of a Tank Corps. Novikov appears to be an honourable man. And yet, given the charge of Trotskyism, Yevgenia raises
the possibility that he could have denounced Krymov to the NKVD,
repeating something that she herself had told him: that Trotsky once
complimented Krymov on an article he had written, with a singular
turn of phrase, 'Splendid, that's pure marble.' However that may
be, Krymov has been arrested, interrogated, tortured. Yevgenia
makes a fateful choice – she decides to abandon her lover and stand
by her husband. She writes Novikov 'a mercilessly truthful letter',
fully anticipating the inevitable break. She is committed. 'She would
follow Krymov,' come what may. 'What did it matter if he didn't
forgive her – she deserved his never-ending reproaches. She knew
that he needed her, that in prison he thought of her all the time.' For
Levinas, her decision is an act of senseless kindness, 'an act of goodness, absolutely gratuitous and unforeseen'.[42]

Day after day at the Lubyanka – like Anna Akhmatova – Yevgenia
joins the queue in front of the little information windows in the
drab reception room. As she waits her turn, she observes the people
in front of her. There follows one of the most remarkable passages
in the whole book. In Levinas's translation: 'Yevgenia had never

thought that the human back could be so expressive, and could convey states of mind in such a penetrating way. Persons approaching the counter had a particular way of craning their neck and their back, their raised shoulders with shoulder blades tensed like springs, which seemed to cry, sob, and scream.'[43]

Grossman thereby furnished Levinas with an illustration and encapsulation of his own ethical project. Throughout a long lifetime, he was often pressed to explain precisely what he meant by the face, in his rather abstruse usage. He provided no definitive answer. Towards the end, however, he found this. The face may be a face – a human face – but it may also be another part of the body, perhaps even a body part. In the queue, the face is the back, or the nape of the neck. For Levinas this was the crucial perception. 'Grossman isn't saying that the nape is the face,' he explained in one interview, 'but that all the weakness, all the mortality, all the naked and disarmed mortality of the other can be read from it.'

> The face requires you, calls you outside. And already there resounds the word from Sinai, 'thou shalt not kill', which signifies 'you shall defend the life of the other'. . . . It is the very articulation of the love of the other. You are indebted to someone from whom you have not borrowed a thing. . . . And *you* are responsible, the only one who could answer, the non-interchangeable and unique one. In this relation of the unique to the unique there appears . . . the original sociality.[44]

'*You* are responsible' seems to echo Ikonnikov's 'I *am* free.' The onus is on us. Whatever our condition, we are called to 'the extravagant generosity of the for-the-other', in Levinasian language, 'the commandment of a gratuitous act'.[45] Even the philosopher is not above a few variations on the original.

Life and Fate was for Levinas much more than an illustration. It was at once a confirmation and a revelation, for the character of its individual encounters, and above all for the message at its moral centre – Grossman's ethics.

> Vasily Grossman in *Life and Fate* – such an impressive book, coming right after the major crises of our century – goes even further. He thinks that the 'small goodness' from one person to his fellow man is lost and deformed as soon as it seeks organization and universality and system, as soon as it opts for doctrine, a treatise of politics and theology, a state, and even a church. Yet it remains the sole refuge of the good in being. Unbeaten, it undergoes the violence of evil, which, as small goodness, it can neither vanquish nor drive out. A little kindness going only from man

to man, not crossing distances to get to the places where events and forces unfold! A remarkable utopia of the good or the secret of its beyond.[46]

There is lyric poetry after Auschwitz. There is also senseless kindness.

Notes

1. Vasily Grossman, trans. Robert Chandler, *Life and Fate* (New York: NYRB, 2006), p. 824.
2. *Life and Fate*, pp. 10–11. His outline biography follows (pp. 12–13); later, Ikonnikov himself sums up what he has seen (pp. 390–1).
3. *Life and Fate*, p. 288.
4. Joseph Conrad, *Heart of Darkness* [1902] (Oxford: World's Classics, 2002), pp. 154–5.
5. *Life and Fate*, pp. 11–12.
6. See Giorgio Agamben, trans. Daniel Heller-Roazen, *Homo Sacer* (Stanford: Stanford University Press, 1998); and the sympathetic discussion in Judith Butler, *Precarious Life* (London: Verso, 2004), pp. 60ff.
7. *Life and Fate*, pp. 288–9. 'Dieu nous pardonnera. C'est son métier' are said to be Heine's last words, in exile, in Paris – a further 'Europeanization' of Ikonnikov's predicament.
8. Later on (p. 515), his fate is confirmed: he is executed for refusing to work on the construction of an extermination camp.
9. *Heart of Darkness*, p. 155. The ISSSC is a fiction, though possibly an allusion to the International Association for the Exploring and Civilizing of Africa, of which King Leopold II of Belgium was President.
10. *Life and Fate*, pp. 388–94.
11. *Life and Fate*, pp. 530, 538. Sofya and David's journey begins on pp. 180–4, and ends on pp. 521–38.
12. *Life and Fate*, pp. 540–7. In the course of his war reporting, Grossman had interviewed a real-life Khristya Chunyak, a forty-year-old peasant woman from the village of Krasilovka, in the Brovarsky district of the Kiev oblast. See Vasily Grossman, trans. Antony Beevor and Luba Vinogradova, *A Writer at War* (London: Harvill, 2005), p. 253.
13. *Life and Fate*, pp. 787–90. Is the golden hair an echo of Margareta in Paul Celan's 'Deathfugue' (first published in German in 1952)? See Chapter 6.
14. The squat woman in particular is at a loss to understand her own actions, as Grossman underlines. *Life and Fate*, p. 790.
15. *Life and Fate*, p. 13.
16. 'The Old Teacher', in Vasily Grossman, trans. Robert and Elizabeth Chandler, with Olga Mukovnikova, *The Road* (New York: NYRB, 2010), pp. 85, 113–14.
17. 'All the materials in our possession are accounts by people who

managed to escape death by some miracle,' said Grossman at a meeting of the Literary Commission, on 13 October 1944. 'But we also have the responsibility of speaking on behalf of those who lie in the earth and cannot speak for themselves. We must shed light on what happened to the 99% of those led off to Babi Yar, and not to the 5 people who escaped from Babi Yar.' This apropos *The Black Book*, a documentary account of the Shoah in the Soviet Union and Poland, compiled by Ilya Ehrenburg and Grossman between 1943 and 1946. Quoted in John and Carol Garrard, *The Life and Fate of Vasily Grossman* [1996] (Barnsley: Pen & Sword, 2012), p. 206.

18. Grossman to his mother, 15 September 1950, in *The Road*, p. 265. The family snap is reproduced in *The Road*, p. 260; the passport photograph in *Writer at War*, p. xii.

19. Grossman to his mother, 15 September 1961, in *The Road*, p. 268.

20. 'The last letter' has become a one-woman play (and film), staged in Moscow in 2005 on the centenary of Grossman's birth.

21. *Life and Fate*, pp. 64–77. All of these might yield lessons in human kindness. In *Une vie*, for example, the exquisitely named Baron Simon-Jacques Le Perthuis des Vauds: 'His great strength, and also his great weakness, was his kindliness, a kindliness that had not arms enough to caress or to give or to embrace, the kindliness of a creator, undiscriminating, as though some sinew of his will were paralysed, as though his motor-force lacked some essential element. It was almost a vice.' And Maupassant also refuses a black and white view of good and bad. The novel closes with the reflection of Rosalie the servant: 'You see, life's never as good or as bad as we think.' Guy de Maupassant, trans. Roger Pearson, *A Life* (Oxford: World's Classics, 2009).

22. Grossman to Khrushchev, 23 February 1962, extracted in *The Road*, p. 261. The letter is printed in full, in a different translation, in *The Life and Fate of Vasily Grossman*, pp. 354–7.

23. Grossman's account of his interview with Suslov, 23 July 1962, in *The Life and Fate of Vasily Grossman*, p. 358; Chandler, introduction to *Life and Fate*, p. xix, citing Semyon Lipkin.

24. Quoted in Frank Ellis, *Vasily Grossman* (Oxford: Berg, 1994), p. 117. Tacitus also figures in the play *If You Believe the Pythagoreans* (written before the German invasion of the Soviet Union in 1941, but not published until 1946), in which one character reads to another from the *Annals*.

25. Tacitus, trans. J. C. Yardley, *The Annals* (Oxford: World's Classics, 2008), pp. 194, 214.

26. Unpublished notes on his reading, 1938, in *The Life and Fate of Vasily Grossman*, p. 142.

27. *Life and Fate*, p. 745. Chekhov's requirements for a cultured person are set out in a famous letter to his brother Nikolai, in March 1886,

printed in Janet Malcolm, *Reading Chekhov* (London: Granta, 2003), pp. 99–100.

28. *Life and Fate*, p. 731. Theodore Dreiser was the author of *An American Tragedy* (1925); Lion Feuchtwanger was the author of *Der falsche Nero* [*The Pretender*] (1936), comparing the Roman upstart Terentius Maximus (who claimed to be Nero) with Hitler.

29. *Life and Fate*, p. 267.

30. Gary Saul Morson, 'Uncle Vanya as Prosaic Melodrama', in Robert Louis Jackson (ed.), *Reading Chekhov's Text* (Evanston, IL: Northwestern University Press, 1993), p. 217. This article cites other work on the same theme.

31. Anton Chekhov, trans. David Magarshack, 'A Boring Story' [1889], in *Lady with Lapdog and Other Stories* (Harmondsworth: Penguin, 1964), p. 101.

32. Chekhov to Leontiev-Shcheglov, 3 May 1888, cited in Morson, 'Uncle Vanya as Prosaic Melodrama', pp. 216–17 (emphasis in the original); Malcolm, *Reading Chekhov*, pp. 99, 110.

33. Seamus Heaney, 'Anything Can Happen', in *District and Circle* (London: Faber, 2006), p. 13.

34. Charles Taylor, *Sources of the Self* (Cambridge: Cambridge University Press, 1989), pp. 13–14; Robert Gordon, *Primo Levi's Ordinary Virtues* (Oxford: Oxford University Press, 2001). There is also Judith Shklar's *Ordinary Vices* (Cambridge, MA: Harvard University Press, 1984), which necessarily involves a covert account of ordinary virtues, as Peter Berkowitz has observed.

35. Primo Levi, trans. Raymond Rosenthal, *The Drowned and the Saved* [1986] (London: Abacus, 1989), pp. 83–4. In classical mythology, there were three Gorgons: Medusa, Stheno and Euryale. Their glance turned their victims to stone. For this reason, the face of the Gorgon was 'prohibited', as Agamben says; it was a non-face or 'anti-face'. See Giorgio Agamben, trans. Daniel Heller-Roazen, *Remnants of Auschwitz* (New York: Zone, 2002), pp. 53–4. Agamben in his turn borrows from Françoise Frontisi-Ducroux, *Du masque au visage* (Paris: Flammarion, 1995).

36. *Life and Fate*, p. 78. See also p. 825.

37. Levi, *The Drowned and the Saved*, ch. 2.

38. Tzvetan Todorov, trans. Arthur Denner and Abigail Pollack, *Facing the Extreme* (New York: Holt, 1996), pp. 112–18. Grossman is fundamental to this work (an inquiry into moral life in the camps), and is presented as an exemplary figure in his own right, alongside Primo Levi, Margarete Buber-Neumann, David Rousset, Romaine Gary and Germaine Tillion, in Todorov's *fin-de-siècle* 'reflections on the twentieth century', trans. David Bellos, *Hope and Memory* [2000] (London: Atlantic, 2003), pp. 48–73.

39. Tamra Wright et al., trans. Andrew Benjamin and Tamra Wright, 'The Paradox of Morality: An Interview with Emmanuel Levinas' [1986], in *The Provocation of Levinas* (London: Routledge, 1988), pp. 168–9. For an extended treatment of 'Auschwitz, Politics, and the Twentieth Century', see Michael L. Morgan, *Discovering Levinas* (Cambridge: Cambridge University Press, 2007).

40. Emmanuel Levinas, trans. Michael B. Smith, 'The Bible and the Greeks' [1986], in *In the Time of Nations* (Bloomington: Indiana University Press, 1994), p. 135; *Is It Righteous to Be?* (Stanford: Stanford University Press, 2001), pp. 81 and 89, citing in particular his own *magnum opus, Totality and Infinity* (1961).

41. Levinas, *Is It Righteous*, pp. 217–18.

42. *Life and Fate*, pp. 663, 731; Levinas, *Is It Righteous*, p. 89. Indicatively, perhaps, it is Novikov who is said to prefer a Dreiser or a Feuchtwanger to Chekhov.

43. Emmanuel Levinas, trans. Peter Atterton and Simon Critchley, 'Peace and Proximity' [1984], in *Basic Philosophical Writings* (Bloomington: Indiana University Press, 1996), p. 167. Cf. *Life and Fate*, p. 667.

44. Emmanuel Levinas, trans. Michael B. Smith and Barbara Harshav, 'The Other, Utopia, and Justice' [1998], in *Entre Nous* (London: Continuum, 2006), p. 201; *Is It Righteous*, p. 192. For a reading of the face *à la* Levinas in war photography, see Alex Danchev, *On Art and War and Terror* (Edinburgh: Edinburgh University Press, 2011), ch. 2.

45. Levinas, 'Peace and Proximity', p. 169; 'Paradox of Morality', p. 176.

46. Levinas, 'The Other, Utopia, and Justice', p. 230.

2

Our Brothers' Keeper:
Moral Witness

---

witness

Attestation of a fact, event, or statement; testimony, evidence; evidence given in a court of justice. . . .

Applied to the individual testimony of conscience; after 2 Cor[inthians] i. 12 ['For our rejoicing is this, the testimony of our conscience, that in simplicity and godly sincerity . . . we have had our conversation in the world'.] . . .

One who is or was present and is able to testify from personal observation; one present as a spectator or auditor (cf. eye-witness, ear-witness). . . .

Something that furnishes evidence or proof of the thing or fact mentioned; an evidential mark or sign, a token. . . .

One who testifies for Christ or the Christian faith, esp. by death; a martyr.

Oxford English Dictionary

For many of those who traffic in images, producers and consumers alike, witnessing is an essential part of the project. Witness testimony is evidence, and something more than evidence. The act of witness is not confined to the laws or the scriptures, though it smacks a little of both. Witnessing shapes history and memory. All over the world, society is saturated in images and image-makers clamouring to bear witness. What do pictures want?[1] To testify!

It is often remarked that artists bear witness. They have done so since the beginning of time. It is less often remarked that works of art themselves bear witness. The most celebrated example in recent memory may be Picasso's *Guernica* (1937), reproductions of which were worn as a badge of honour by anti-war protestors on the eve of the Iraq War in 2003: warning and witnessing at the same time. Another example is Klee's *Angelus Novus* (1920) – Walter Benjamin's 'angel of history' – a survivor who bears witness to the terrible twentieth century (see Chapter 3). Ironically, when it comes to witnessing, the testimony of the author of the act is not always to be trusted. Artists (and other makers of graven images) are rarely explicit or programmatic; often they obfuscate their purpose. Occasionally, someone makes a statement. The mottos of Goya's *Disasters of War* (1810–20) are legendary: 'One cannot look at this.' 'I saw it.' 'This is the truth.' In the Western canon, or the Western way of witness, Goya is the gold standard. He testifies from personal observation, as prescribed. His testimony is to all intents and purposes irrefutable; it is etched in the cultural memory of an entire continent. Goya is Paul Celan's Breathcrystal,

> your unannullable
> witness.[2]

Every war artist who came after him, every war photographer in particular, has Goya on his shoulder. Don McCullin, one of the best of them, made those mottos his own. In his autobiography he recalls coming on a father and two sons lying in a pool of their own blood in a stone house in Cyprus during the conflict of the 1960s. He is riveted by the scene, as much for the tableau as the tragedy. It is as if he has been called upon to act; that is to say, to witness. McCullin is an ethical professional, with an active conscience. Still rooted to the spot when the rest of the family return, he is suddenly conscious of trespassing with his camera. But the survivors are content for him to do what he has to do. 'When I realized I had been given the go-ahead to photograph,' he writes, 'I started composing my pictures in a very serious and dignified way. It was the first time that I had pictured something of this immense significance and I felt as if I had a canvas in front of me and I was, stroke by stroke, applying the composition to a story I was telling myself. I was, I realized later, trying to photograph in a way that Goya painted or did his war sketches.'[3]

McCullin's counterpart James Nachtwey is perhaps the most exacting ethical professional in the business. He is remorseless. At the beginning of his signature collection, *Inferno* (1999), he quotes Dante: 'Through me is the way to join the lost people.' Nachtwey has been to Hell on our behalf; he is intimately familiar with the place, all nine circles of it. He keeps going back to tell the tale – to bear witness – whether we like it or not. 'Nachtwey's photographs are an odd, compelling combination of misery and serenity, of horrible content and stylized form,' observes Susie Linfield. 'But the perfection of their compositions – their so-called beauty – should not deflect us: Nachtwey's photographs are brutal, and they show us more than we can bear. But not more than we need to see.'[4]

There are many ways of witnessing, and a degree of fuzziness to much of the thinking about it. Despite a vast outpouring of historical studies, cultural studies, memory studies, and even philosophical studies, it remains a rather elusive subject, as to the basics of who, and when, and how, and why, and larger questions of equal pertinence: to what end, and to what effect? Part of the problem may be its excess baggage – juridical, ethical and even spiritual – as the *Oxford English Dictionary* serves to reveal. 'Applied to the individual testimony of conscience', it records, citing the magnificent formulation from the Book of Corinthians, 'we have had our conversation in the world'. Witnessing may not change the world, but having that conversation marks it, tempers it, and occasionally rubs it red raw. The act of witnessing is not a neutral act. It does not leave things as the witness finds them. It does not spare feelings. The witness spares nothing and nobody, not even the witness. That is the idea – to prick the conscience, to lodge in the memory or stick in the throat. Here is where art finds its place. 'Art as freedom from moral narrowness and corner-perspectives,' as Nietzsche says, 'or as mockery of them.'[5] In this sense, the witness is more akin to an agitator than a bystander, but also more purposive, more principled, more pure. If the bystander is a deeply compromised figure, the witness is a profoundly elevated one. Put differently, the witness is an historical agent with a moral purpose and a militant faith, in Avishai Margalit's words, 'that in another place or another time there exists, or will exist, a moral community that will listen to their testimony'.[6]

Margalit's exposition of the 'moral witness' is a scrupulous and suggestive treatment, deservedly influential. His moral witness has a lot to live up to, however, being at once special case and ideal type. Margalit applies strict criteria for admission to this select company. The only ones who qualify are those who have direct, personal experience of radical evil and its consequences, those who have 'knowledge-by-acquaintance of suffering', as he puts it.[7] The paradigm case is probably a survivor of the camps, like Primo Levi or Elie Wiesel, or of the Terror and the Gulag (Vasily Grossman, Alexander Solzhenitsyn), or of sustained torture (Henri Alleg, Jean Améry).[8] Somewhat weaker cases might include those with knowledge-by-acquaintance of systemic persecution and incarceration in the Eastern Bloc in its Cold War heyday (Václav Havel, Adam Michnik), or the multiple degradations of military dictatorships (Ariel Dorfman, Wole Soyinka), or – bringing it all back home – Guantánamo (Moazzam Begg, Mohamedou Ould Slahi).[9] Astonishingly, Slahi wrote 122,000 words of his Guantánamo diary in a single-cell segregation hut in Camp Echo, in 2005, after he had been put through a 'special interrogation plan' personally approved by Donald Rumsfeld (see Chapter 12). The diary was published ten years later, after a prolonged legal battle. The author remained in captivity, but his book was free at last – though heavily redacted. Slahi's account is untutored, and surprisingly measured; often decoded by sympathetic editing, the redactions function as a kind of silent reinforcement. On one occasion, as the special interrogation plan is in full swing, he is undone by a kind word:

> 'How you been?' said one of the Puerto Rican escorting guards in his weak English.
>
> 'I'm OK, thanks, and you?'
>
> 'No worry, you gonna back to your family,' he said. When he said that I couldn't help breaking in [redacted].[10]

We supply the tears.

Slahi is insistent on only one thing: he must make himself heard. He must testify. 'Please,' he tells his Administrative Review Board, 'I want you guys to understand my story okay, because it really doesn't matter if they release me or not, I just want my story understood.'[11] As a witness, he has a conspicuous virtue: he is eminently capable of imagining a moral community that will listen to his testimony. He addresses that community in his summing up:

> I don't even know how to treat this subject. I have only written what I experienced, what I saw, and what I learned first-hand. I have tried not to exaggerate, nor to understate. I have tried to be as fair as possible, to the US government, to my brothers, and to myself. I don't expect people who don't know me to believe me, but I expect them, at least, to give me the benefit of the doubt. And if Americans are willing to stand for what they believe in, I also expect public opinion to compel the US government to open a torture and war crimes investigation. I am more than confident that I can prove every single thing I have written in this book if I am ever given the opportunity to call witnesses in a proper judicial procedure, and if military personnel are not given the advantage of straightening their lies and destroying evidence against them.[12]

The moral witness may be memorized and memorialized. The greatest poetic witness of the Terror was the majestic Anna Akhmatova:

the one who meant most to her country and culture; the one who kept the word, 'the great Russian word', alive for them; the one who outlasted her persecutors – who so exasperated them, she said, that they all died before her of heart-attacks. *Requiem*, the sequence of poems she composed during the late 1930s, but did not commit to paper, is reported to have survived only in the memories of the poet and a few of her most trusted friends: her own moral community. 'Eleven people knew *Requiem* by heart,' she recalled, 'and not one of them betrayed me.' It was first published in 1963, 'without the author's knowledge or consent', by the Society of Russian Émigré Writers, from a copy which had found its way to the West. It was prefaced by a brief note dated April 1957. The note itself became a legend:

> In the fearful years of the Yezhov terror I spent seventeen months in prison queues in Leningrad. One day somebody 'identified' me. Beside me, in the queue, there was a woman with blue lips. She had, of course, never heard of me; but she suddenly came out of that trance so common to us all and whispered in my ear (everybody spoke in whispers there): 'Can you describe this?' And I said: 'Yes, I can.' And then something like the shadow of a smile crossed what had once been her face.[13]

For Margalit, moral witnesses of this ilk are insiders rather than outsiders; they are inside the story they have to tell, unlike photographers or filmmakers or reporters, concerned or unconcerned, embedded or unembedded. They are 'special agents of collective memory', promoting 'thick identity' based upon 'thick relations', that is to say, a felt sense of shared ties, human and cosmopolitan. Their moral standing is assured, not only by their fortitude, but also by their resolve – the moral witness deliberately accepts the personal risk.

> No one
> bears witness for the
> witness.[14]

The notion of the moral witness is a compelling one. Undaunted by the excess baggage, it succeeds in capturing the ethical impulsion that is fundamental to the very idea of witnessing. The act of witness is linked axiomatically to the exercise of conscience. The moral witness is a kind of conscientious objector. But is she alone in that? The Margalit model of moral witness is persuasive enough, as far as it goes, but it appears to impose certain limitations on the subject, in particular, as to who and when and how.

The thrust of the argument about insider and outsider is surely right – witnessing is not a spectator sport, and witness tourism no more palatable than war tourism – but the distinction is not so simple to maintain. During the Occupation, for example, the artist Jean Fautrier moved in Resistance circles in Paris; his studio was a rendezvous. In 1943 he was arrested by the Gestapo and briefly imprisoned. After his release he went into hiding in a sanatorium on the outskirts of the city, where he began work on a series of abstract, head-like forms called *Hostages* (1943–5), a response to the sounds he could hear from his window: the screams of torture and the shots of executions. Fautrier was an ear-witness. Ostensibly, he had nothing to say – he was famously close-mouthed – but 'Fautrier l'enragé', as Jean Paulhan called him, was impelled to act. 'One can't be painting apples while heads are rolling,' he declared.[15] His testimony, in his own idiom, was as searing as any. The *Hostages* were exhibited in 1945, immediately after the Liberation; they achieved mythic status.[16] They testified eloquently to man's inhumanity to man. At the same time they were an attestation of human dignity, claimed by André Malraux as 'the most beautiful monument to the dead of the Second World War'.[17] They were also an affront, an outrage. Like 'the face' in the philosophy of Emmanuel Levinas (see Chapter 1), the *Hostages* demanded a response – an ethical response. 'How should we respond when confronted with the idea of the *Hostages?*' asked Francis Ponge. 'One might say that here is one of the fundamental questions of our time.'[18]

Fautrier was an insider of a kind. So, too, is Sebastião Salgado, the photographer of famine in the Sahel, and other battles in other wars. As Eduardo Galeano has written, in a brilliant appreciation, 'Salgado photographs people. Casual photographers photograph phantoms.'

As an article of consumption, poverty is a source of morbid pleasure and much money. Poverty is a commodity that fetches a high price on the luxury market. Consumer-society photographers approach but do not enter. In hurried visits to scenes of despair or violence, they climb out of the plane or helicopter, press the shutter release, explode the flash: they shoot and run. They have looked without seeing and their images say nothing. Their cowardly photographs soiled with horror or blood may extract a few crocodile tears, a few coins, a pious word or two from the privileged of the earth, none of which changes the order of their universe. At the sight of the dark-skinned wretched, forsaken by God and pissed on by dogs, anybody who is nobody confidentially congratulates himself: life hasn't done too badly by me, in comparison. Hell serves to confirm the virtues of paradise.

> Charity, vertical, humiliates. Solidarity, horizontal, helps. Salgado photographs from inside, from solidarity.[19]

Salgado's works of witness are humanitarian interventions. They are ethical and, inescapably, political. 'Like all politically effective images,' argues David Levi Strauss, 'the best of Salgado's photographs work in the fissures, the wounds, of the social. They cause those who see them to ask themselves: *Are we allowed to view what is being exposed?*'[20] This is the path to thick relations, the hallmark of moral witness, and the signature of the master photographer. 'It allows his subjects to be themselves and more than themselves at once.'[21]

Witnessing (moral or otherwise) may be done after the fact. Paradoxical as it may seem, the act of witness need not be instantaneous or contemporaneous. Robert Capa's celebrated dictum, 'If your pictures aren't good enough, you're not close enough,' does not apply, if the burden of that dictum is to prescribe a kind of action shot, a close-up in the moment. Unquestionably, 'I was there' can deliver a visceral charge. Capa's D-Day landings are sufficient proof of that; and McCullin's shell-shocked soldier returns to haunt us at regular intervals. But powerful witnessing happens after the battle – after the war – sometimes long after. Simon Baker has noted 'the capacity of photography to bear witness even (or especially) at removes of several decades'.[22]

This form of witness we might call 'post-witness', by analogy with 'post-memory', the term proposed by Marianne Hirsch to comprehend the folk memory (or family memory) of successor generations, whose connection to the original event or source is not through recollection, as she says, but through 'imaginative investment and creation'.[23] Post-witness is exemplified in a recent project, which is also an anniversary project, by Chloe Dewe Mathews (born 1982), *Shot at Dawn* (2014).[24] Arresting alike in its clarity and its humanity, *Shot at Dawn* is not immediately recognizable as an act of witness, or indeed as a morally cogent act at all. It is at first sight a suite of landscape photographs: bucolic scenes, for the most part, a path beaten through a field, a snow-covered wood, a stream. They are plainly titled, as if marked on the map: 'Vanémont, Vosges, Lorraine', 'Verbranden-Molen, West-Vlaanderen', 'Klijtebeek stream, Dikkebus, Ieper' – Ypres or 'Wipers' to the Tommies who had the misfortune to fetch up there. They are big – big enough for the viewer to lose himself, or his bearings, but not his moral compass. These are the sites at which

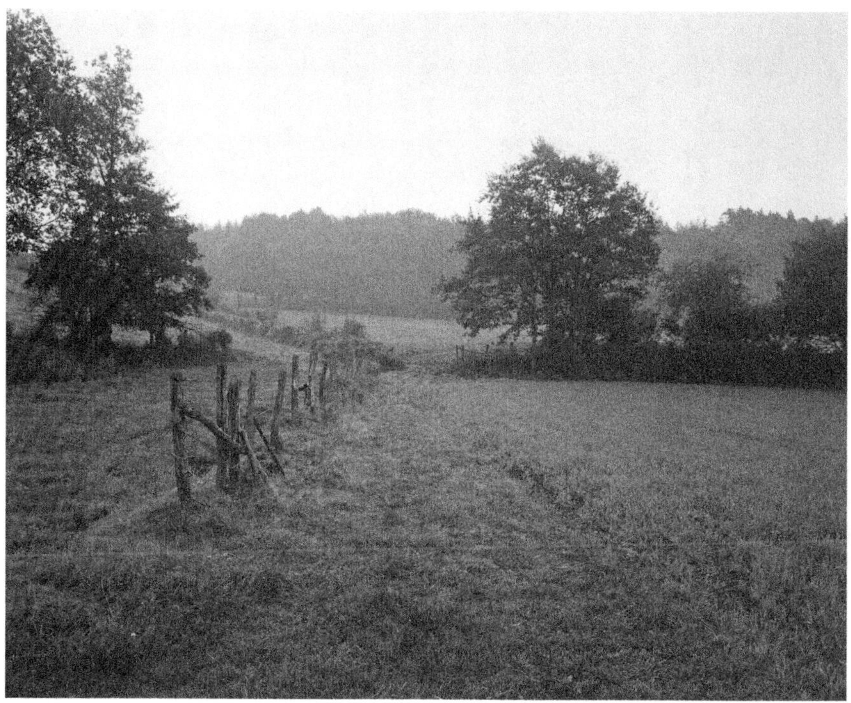

Figure 2.1
Chloe Dewe Mathews, *Shot at Dawn*, 2014

Soldat Eugène Bouret
Soldat Ernest Macken
Soldat Benoît Manillier
Soldat Francisque Pitiot
Soldat Claudius Urbain
Soldat Jean Ducarre
06:30 / 7.9.1914

Soldat Jules Berger
Soldat Gilbert Gathier
Soldat Fernand Inclair
07:45 / 12.9.1914

Vanémont, Vosges, Lorraine

Chloe Dewe Mathews: Shot at Dawn is commissioned by the Ruskin School of
Art at the University of Oxford as part of 14–18 NOW, WW1 Centenary Art
Commissions

British, French and Belgian soldiers were executed for cowardice and
desertion during the Great War.

The complete series comprises twenty-three photographs, of
which a sample may be inspected in various exhibitions. Inspection is

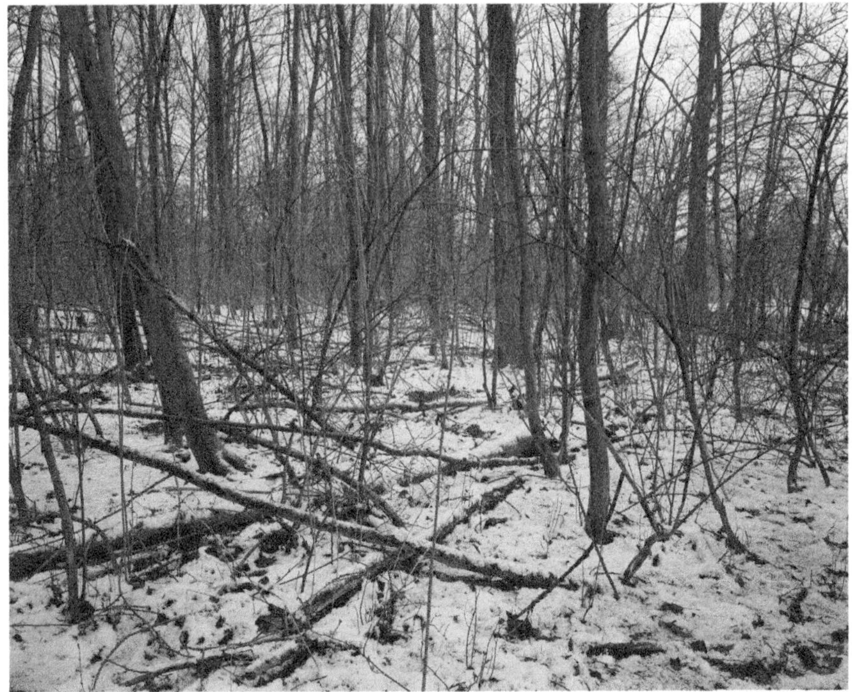

Figure 2.2
Chloe Dewe Mathews, *Shot at Dawn*, 2014

Soldat Ahmed ben Mohammed el Yadjizy
Soldat Ali ben Ahmed ben Frej ben Khelil
Soldat Hassen ben Ali ben Guerra el Amolani
Soldat Mohammed Ould Mohammed ben Ahmed
17:00 / 15.12.1914

Verbranden-Molen, West-Vlaanderen

Chloe Dewe Mathews: Shot at Dawn is commissioned by the Ruskin School of Art at the University of Oxford as part of 14–18 NOW, WW1 Centenary Art Commissions

invited, or incited, by a gnawing awareness of their back-story – the slow realization of their slow realization – and by the deadpan data accompanying each one.

In an era of the 'global war on terror', the naming itself is an act of witness. *Shot at Dawn*, it transpires, is a resurrection – not a body-snatching but a revisiting, an investigation of the record, an invitation to think again.

The record was deliberately concealed for a long period; the story remained untold until very recently. In 2006, the Ministry of Defence

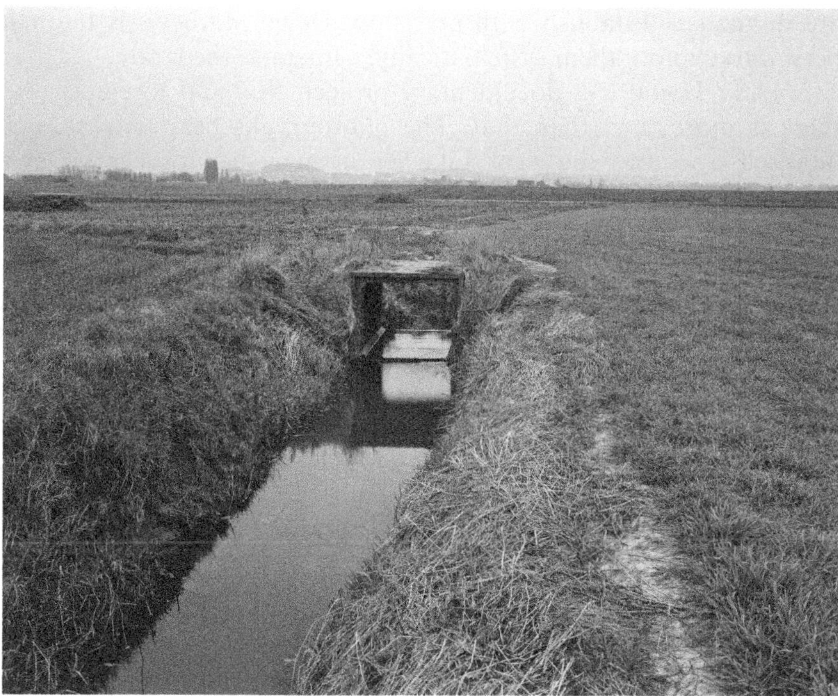

Figure 2.3

Chloe Dewe Mathews, *Shot at Dawn*, 2014

Private Henry Hughes
05.50 / 10.4.1918

Klijtebeek stream, Dikkebus, Ieper, West-Vlaanderen

Chloe Dewe Mathews: Shot at Dawn is commissioned by the Ruskin School of Art at the University of Oxford as part of 14–18 NOW, WW1 Centenary Art Commissions

announced that 306 soldiers convicted of desertion in the face of the enemy and executed during the Great War were to be posthumously pardoned. Each of the countries immediately involved is wrestling with its own painful history, though in each case the brutality of summary justice was leavened with a certain residual compassion (or caution). In Britain, the vast majority of those sentenced to death were pardoned at the time; of over 3,000 convictions for capital offences, 346 were carried out. In Belgium, the proportions were somewhat similar: of 220 convictions, eighteen were carried out. In France, of 412 convictions during a summer of mutinies in 1917, fifty-five were carried out. The names, dates and times of these executions appear in courts-martial proceedings. The locations, however, are difficult to establish with precision. Dewe Mathews is the first person to explore them systematically, camera at the ready.

Shot at Dawn is a documentary project, first and foremost, but there is more to it than that. The photographs bear witness, one hundred years after the event. Like her distinguished forebears, Dewe Mathews is not merely a shutter-operator but a thinker-photographer. 'These places have been altered by a traumatic event,' she reflects. 'By photographing them, I am reinserting the individual into that space, stamping their presence back onto the land, so that their histories are not forgotten.'[25] Every photograph is a certificate of presence, as Roland Barthes pointed out. Fundamentally, this is a moral position. Dewe Mathews is a moral witness. *Shot at Dawn* is excavatory, testamentary, perhaps even reparatory. In every sense, the plot is subject to scrutiny. Those bucolic scenes, soaked in meaning, are sites of memory, certainly, but also sites of self-examination, for spectators of all sorts. In the final analysis, these photographs are little histories of conscience – a centenary of conscience – inventories of its excitation and reinterpretation over time.

They are also examples of exactitude: an ethical attribute. Witnessing imposes its own exacting requirements. For Paul Celan, it was the date – he urged 'a concentration that remains mindful of all our dates'.[26] In the case of *Shot at Dawn*, an approximate location or an approximate time of day would nullify the core concept. *Shot at Dawn* is the very opposite of shoot and run. Similarly, for Simon Norfolk, a photographer who follows the wars and the massacres, inspecting the ground and the guilty secrets sown there, precise knowledge of the gravesites and the killing fields is of vital importance, for the credibility of the work and the veracity of the witness.[27] As Mr Cogito knew, in these matters accuracy is necessary. From 'Mr Cogito on the Need for Precision', in Zbigniew Herbert's *Report from a Besieged City* (1983), which is among other things a witnessing of Warsaw under martial law:

a spectre is haunting
the map of history
the spectre of indeterminacy
. . .
we count the survivors
and an unknown remainder
neither known to be alive
nor definitively deceased
are given the bizarre name

of the lost

. . .

how hard to establish the names
of all those who were lost
battling against inhuman power
the official data
diminish their number
once again mercilessly
decimating the fallen

. . .

eyewitnesses
blinded by gas
deafened by gun salvos
by fear and despair
are inclined to exaggerate

. . .

but in these matters
accuracy is necessary
one can't get it wrong
even in a single case
in spite of everything
we are our brothers' keepers
ignorance about those who are lost
undermines the reality of the world[28]

The work of witness stands against indeterminacy and ignorance. 'An evidential mark or sign,' offers the *OED*, 'a token'. On the battlefields of the Great War, the lost are still missing. The Thiepval Memorial to the Missing of the Somme (1928–32) is one such sign, inscribed with the names of the 72,195 officers and men who died there between 1915 and 1918, who have no known grave. Memorials, too, bear witness. Lost and found, we have need of this token. Witnessing does not right wrongs; it makes possible their reappraisal.

Witnesses seem to whisper among themselves. 'I should have liked to call you all by name,' recorded Akhmatova in *Requiem*, 'but they have lost the lists . . .'. Ingeborg Bachmann salutes Anna Akhmatova:

To create a single lasting sentence,
to persevere in the ding-dong of words.
No one writes this sentence
who does not sign her name.[29]

Zbigniew Herbert salutes Jean Améry:

> The torturers sleep soundly their dreams are rosy
> good-natured genocides – foreign and home-grown
> already forgiven by brief human memory[30]

Witnessing is intimately bound up with suffering. Loss is the common currency. 'And so they are ever returning to us, the dead,' as W. G. Sebald reminds us.[31] Bearing witness is good, it appears, but on occasion it is too much. After 9/11, public witness to the 'jumpers' from the World Trade Center was disallowed, and the photograph of the famous 'falling man' effectively suppressed; the deaths are recorded as homicide due to blunt trauma. Suicide (on our side) is indeed more than we can bear. The reality of the world is difficult to stomach. 'We cannot bear reality,' muses David Levi Strauss, 'but we bear images – like stigmata, like children, like fallen comrades. We suffer them. We idealize them. We believe them because we need what we are in them.'[32] Sometimes, we refuse them. Yet they have a way of getting under our skin. In the preamble to the remarkable work of witness to the lives of the poor sharecroppers of Alabama in the Great Depression, *Let Us Now Praise Famous Men* (1941), in collaboration with the photographer Walker Evans, the writer James Agee poses a series of unforgettable questions. 'Who are you who will read these words and study these photographs, and through what cause, by what chance, and for what purpose, and by what right do you qualify to, and what will you do about it?'[33]

Every act of witness asks the same.

Notes

1. A question famously posed by W. J. T. Mitchell, *What Do Pictures Want?* (Chicago: University of Chicago Press, 2005), subtitled 'The Lives and Loves of Images'.
2. Paul Celan, trans. John Felstiner, 'Etched Away', in *Selected Poems and Prose of Paul Celan* (New York: Norton, 2001), p. 247.
3. Don McCullin, *Unreasonable Behaviour* (London: Vintage, 2002), p. 47.
4. Susie Linfield, *The Cruel Radiance* (Chicago: Chicago University Press, 2010), p. 211.
5. Friedrich Nietzsche, trans. Walter Kaufmann and R. J. Hollingdale, *The Will to Power* (New York: Vintage, 1968), p. 435.
6. Avishai Margalit, *The Ethics of Memory* (Cambridge, MA: Harvard University Press, 2002), p. 155.
7. Margalit, *Ethics*, p. 149.

8. See Primo Levi, trans. Raymond Rosenthal, *The Drowned and the Saved* [1986] (New York: Vintage, 1989); Elie Wiesel, trans. Marion Wiesel, *Night* [1958] (London: Penguin, 2008); Vasily Grossman, trans. Robert Chandler, *Life and Fate* [1980] (New York: NYRB, 2006); Alexander Solzhenitsyn, trans. Thomas P. Whitney, *The Gulag Archipelago* [1973] (London: Fontana, 1976); Henri Alleg, trans. John Calder, *The Question* [1958] (Lincoln, NE: University of Nebraska Press, 2006); Jean Améry, trans. Sidney Rosenfeld and Stella P. Rosenfeld, *At the Mind's Limits* [1966] (Bloomington, IN: Indiana University Press, 1980). On Grossman, see Chapter 1.

9. See Moazzam Begg, *Enemy Combatant* (London: Free Press, 2006); Mohamedou Ould Slahi, *Guantánamo Diary* (Edinburgh: Canongate, 2015).

10. Slahi, *Guantánamo Diary*, pp. 228–9. The editor, Larry Siems, notes: 'It seems possible, if incredible, that the US government may have here redacted the word "tears".'

11. Slahi, *Guantánamo Diary*, p. xix.

12. Slahi, *Guantánamo Diary*, p. 369. Slahi's interrogation was led by Richard Zuley, a former Chicago detective with a long record of alleged brutal interrogation techniques. See Spencer Ackerman, 'Bad lieutenant', *Guardian*, 19 February 2015.

13. Anna Akhmatova, trans. D. M. Thomas, 'Requiem', in *Selected Poems* (London: Penguin, 1988), p. 87. Nikolai Yezhov was head of the NKVD from 1936 to 1938, at the height of the Terror.

14. Celan, 'Ash-Aureole', in *Selected Poems and Prose*, p. 261.

15. Brigitte Hedel-Samson, 'Les révoltes de Fautrier', in *Jean Fautrier* (Paris: RMN, 1996), p. 24. See Jean Paulhan, trans. Carol J. Murphy, 'Fautrier l'enragé' (1943), and Francis Ponge, trans. Vivian Rehberg, 'Note on the *Hostages*, Paintings by Fautrier' (1945), in Curtis L. Carter and Karen K. Butler (eds), *Jean Fautrier* (New Haven: Yale University Press, 2002), pp. 170–87.

16. A status undiminished (perhaps enhanced) by the paucity of documentary evidence on the precise circumstances of their creation. Even after the war, there does not appear to be any mention of the executions in Fautrier's personal correspondence. He seems to have given a detailed account to Palma Bucarelli, *Jean Fautrier* (Milan: Saggiatore, 1960), but to no one else.

17. André Malraux, in *Jean Fautrier* (Paris: Musée d'art moderne de la ville de Paris, 1989), p. 222. See also Malraux, trans. Karen K. Butler and Harry Cooper, 'The Hostages', preface to the 1945 exhibition catalogue, in Carter and Butler, *Fautrier*, p. 188.

18. Francis Ponge, 'Note sur les *Otages*, peintures de Fautrier' (1945), in *Atelier contemporain* (Paris: Gallimard, 1977), p. 23. Ponge's ruminations on Fautrier are celebrated ethical examinations (and

self-examinations); so much so, that they may perhaps be considered secondary acts of witness.

19. Eduardo Galeano, trans. Asa Zatz, 'Salgado, 17 Times', in *Sebastião Salgado: An Uncertain Grace* (New York: Aperture, 1990), p. 11.

20. David Levi Strauss, 'The Documentary Debate', in *Between the Eyes* (New York: Aperture, 2003), p. 7. The sentence in italics derives from Avital Ronell, who contends that every photograph poses itself as such a question.

21. Levi Strauss, 'Epiphany of the Other', *Between the Eyes*, p. 42, a propos Salgado.

22. Simon Baker, 'Armageddon in Retrospect', in Simon Baker and Shoair Mavlian (eds), *Conflict Time Photography* (London: Tate, 2014), p. 200.

23. Marianne Hirsch, *Family Frames* (Cambridge, MA: Harvard University Press, 1997), p. 21.

24. Chloe Dewe Mathews, *Shot at Dawn* (Madrid: Ivory Press, 2014).

25. Dewe Mathews conversation with Shoair Mavlian, 23 May 2014, in Baker and Mavlian, *Conflict*, p. 211.

26. John Felstiner, *Paul Celan* (New Haven: Yale University Press, 2001), p. 188. Cf. Celan, 'The Meridian', in *Selected Poems and Prose*, p. 408.

27. See his testimony in Paul Lowe, 'The Forensic Turn', in Liam Kennedy and Caitlin Patrick (eds), *The Violence of the Image* (London: Tauris, 2014), pp. 223–6.

28. Zbigniew Herbert, trans. Alissa Valles, 'Mr Cogito on the Need for Precision', from *Report from a Besieged City* (1983), in *The Collected Poems* (London: Atlantic, 2008), pp. 404–8.

29. Ingeborg Bachmann, trans. Peter Filkins, 'Truly', in *Darkness Spoken* (Brookline, MA: Zephyr, 2006), p. 615. Bachmann met Akhmatova in 1964 and published this poem the following year. For more on Bachmann see Chapter 6.

30. Zbigniew Herbert, trans. Alissa Valles, 'From an Unwritten Theory of Dreams', *New York Review of Books*, 20 June 2013.

31. W. G. Sebald, trans. Michael Hulse, *The Emigrants* (London: Harvill, 1997), p. 23.

32. Levi Strauss, 'The Highest Degree of Illusion', *Between the Eyes*, p. 185.

33. James Agee and Walker Evans, *Let Us Now Praise Famous Men* (London: Penguin, 2006), p. 7.

3

Angelus Novus:
The Angel of History

Proust says memory is of two kinds.
There is the daily struggle to recall
where we put our reading glasses

and there is the deeper gust of longing
that comes up from the bottom
of the heart

involuntarily.
At sudden times.
For surprise reasons.

Here is an excerpt from a letter Proust wrote
in 1913:

We think we no longer love our dead

but that is because we do not remember them:
suddenly
we catch sight of an old glove

and burst into tears.

Anne Carson[1]

We will remember them, as Laurence Binyon's threnody reminds us, each Remembrance Day.[2] But how will we remember? And what will we remember, now that they are all dead? How are we to understand the Great War? What was it for them and for those who came after them? What is it for us? What will it become?

Our conception of this war, and every war, has been profoundly shaped by works of art, of all kinds and conditions. Among the English-speaking peoples, 'war poetry' has been virtually synonymous with Great War poetry for several generations. In more than one sense, the war poets served to define the Western Front. Theirs is the last word on that unsurpassable place, which has come to epitomize the character of the conflict, to colour (or rather to black and white) its collective memory, and to instantiate its meaning, in the polity and the culture. The poetry has trumped the history, as historians never cease to complain.[3] The poetic voice is instantly recognizable. After the Somme, after Passchendaele, 'The Charge of the Light Brigade' no longer scans. It is 'the pity of war' that is the leitmotif and lightning conductor of strong feelings surrounding the political imperatives, the operational conduct, the moral calculus and the human cost of this war – and subsequent wars, right down to our own day. The voice carries, knowingly.

> The poets eat kahi and drink cardamon tea
>   in Baghdad, and it could be 1948
> or 2004, it could be British bombers
>   overhead, or the 173rd Airborne
> parachuting down from a metal-blue sky,
>   but these poets will soon be dead,
> and bridges will be blown all over Iraq . . .
> *Is it worth it? Can there be no other way?*[4]

Some desperate glory remains, perhaps, but the reckoning is severe. 'What passing-bells for these who die as cattle?'[5]

And yet the poetry (if not the pity) can be overdone. Every nation has its own Great War.[6] The war poetry of Wilfred Owen and Siegfried Sassoon and their brothers in arms may be deeply ingrained in the Anglo-Saxons, but it does not travel as far or as fast as is sometimes assumed. Owen and Sassoon were not translated into French until very recently; Paul Fussell's massively influential literary exegesis *The Great War and Modern Memory* (1975) has never been published in France. There is poetry aplenty, of course, but to take the measure of the artistic response to the Great War and its aftershocks, it is necessary to look elsewhere. One image in particular has come to haunt the European cultural imagination, offering a remarkable case study in the generative power of art – perhaps even the regenerative power of art – its capacity to nourish thought and sustain hope, its iconic properties, its fathomless quality, its uncanny futurity, its connective reach, its ethical freight, and its inspirational potential.

The image is not an image of the battlefield, or for that matter the war. It is an image of an angel – a new angel – *Angelus Novus* (1920) by Paul Klee. This little angel was Walter Benjamin's most treasured possession. He called it the angel of history. The ninth of

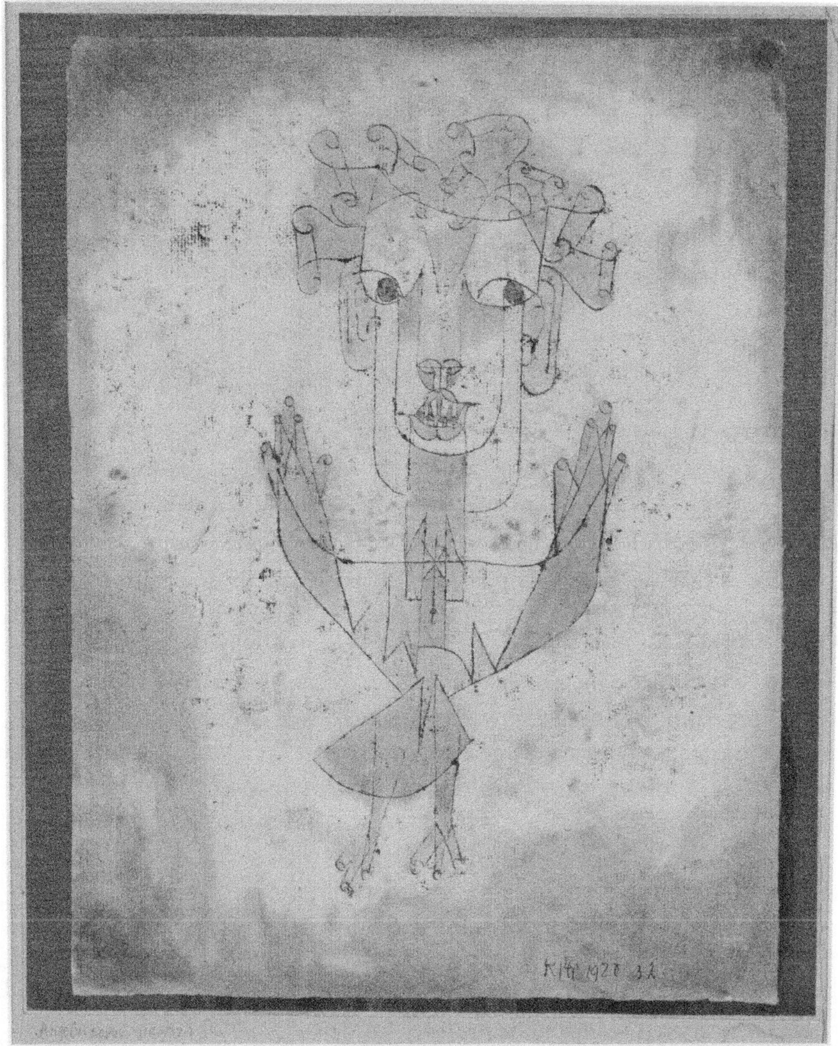

Figure 3.1
Paul Klee, Swiss, 1879–1940, *Angelus Novus*, 1920

Oil transfer and watercolor on paper, 318 × 242 mm

Collection The Israel Museum, Jerusalem

Gift of Fania and Gershom Scholem, Jerusalem, John Herring, Marlene and Paul Herring, Jo-Carole and Ronald Lauder, New York

B87.0994

Photo © The Israel Museum, Jerusalem by Elie Posner

his renowned theses 'On the Concept of History' (1940) is a kind of parable:

> There is a picture by Klee called *Angelus Novus*. It shows an angel who seems about to move away from something he stares at. His eyes are wide, his mouth is open, his wings are spread. This is how the angel of history must look. His face is turned towards the past. Where a chain of events appears before *us, he* sees one single catastrophe, which keeps piling wreckage upon wreckage and hurls it at his feet. The angel would like to stay, awaken the dead, and make whole what has been smashed. But a storm is blowing from Paradise and has got caught in his wings; it is so strong that the angel can no longer close them. This storm drives him irresistibly into the future, to which his back is turned, while the pile of debris before him grows towards the sky. What we call progress is *this* storm.[7]

In the aftermath of another war these words made the angel famous, as if catapulting him into the present. At the same time they became one of the most celebrated passages in Benjamin's celebrated œuvre. Here is a reminder that the historical fate of the Great War was to be turned into a sort of prequel. The Second World War presupposes a First. After Munich, after Auschwitz, it is almost impossible to see the Great War plain, *sui generis*, rather than through the prism of the later, greater catastrophe. For the British, as David Reynolds has lamented, the meaning of the Great War often tends to focus on one sacred day, the first day of the Somme, 'understood as a holocaust moment'.[8] Walter Benjamin himself committed suicide, in despair, not long after he wrote that passage on the angel of history. He was on the run; his angel was in hiding. He met his end in the holocaust moment – the true holocaust moment. His message, like the angel's, is ravelled in the unmasterable past: in poppy and memory, in Paul Celan's haunting encapsulation.[9]

His words are also a reminder that the provenance of a work of art is part of its fascination – its *aura*, to use a Benjaminian term – and part of the story it has to tell. At once object biography and intellectual history, provenance makes for a revealing study in international politics, much underrated in that context.[10] Klee's *Angelus Novus*, like Braque's *Guitar Player* (1914), bears witness to its blood-soaked century. It is a survivor. It passed through the hands of three of the foremost intellectuals of the age, Walter Benjamin, Theodor Adorno and Gershom Scholem, close friends, widely scattered by wars and rumours of wars. It was much coveted, but also endangered. It lived a peripatetic life, hugger-mugger, first in Germany, then in France, then in exile in the United States, before returning to Germany and eventually finding its way to the promised land. It now resides in the Israel Museum in Jerusalem.

Angelus Novus appeared immediately after the Great War. In the catalogue raisonné of Klee's work it is described as 'oil transfer and watercolour on paper and cardboard' – a kind of drawing in oil, to which he later applied watercolour.[11] It is small and delicate (roughly 32 by 24 centimetres): its size belies its strength. Early in his career Klee devised a personal '*œuvre catalogue*' of finished works, a comprehensive listing, almost a compulsion, maintained over thirty years. Every year, each work was allocated a number, in chronological order, entered in a book, and so designated on the work itself. *Angelus Novus* is designated 1920, 32, indicating the thirty-second work he made that year, or at any rate the thirty-second to attain the dignity of the *œuvre catalogue*.

In principle, therefore, it is possible to get an idea of what was preoccupying him at any given time. Early in 1920, not long before *Angelus Novus*, there is *Aerial Combat* (1920, 2) and *Memorial to the Kaiser* (1920, 3) – a caricature – which seems to lend credence to the idea that the angel is in some way entangled in the Great War. But there is also *They're Biting* (1920, 6), a marvellous little fable of some lugubrious fish, falling hook, line and sinker for two gormless anglers – which may or may not support the argument, unless the fable is an allegory. Plainly Klee worked on more than one thing at a time. Moreover, he was extremely reluctant to alter the number of a work in the *œuvre catalogue*, once allocated, even if he later reworked it, as he often did. The sequencing may be misleading, or downright perplexing. What looks like a preparatory drawing of the *Angelus Novus* (1920, 96) bears a later number than the painting.[12] It transpires that Klee was at once scrupulous and not so scrupulous about ordering and reordering, shaping and reshaping, fashioning and refashioning, especially when it came to self-fashioning, or self-presentation.

From 1898 to 1918, from the age of nineteen to thirty-nine, he also kept a diary, which was not so much a diary traditionally understood as an essay in autobiography (or mythography), serially revised, with an eye to posterity. Klee's diary is an important document – it contains major statements – but it is an essentially literary product, as heavily reworked as any item in the *œuvre catalogue*. His writings are for the most part authentic reconstructions. They speak eloquently of the art and the artist; they leave a lot unsaid. 'I cannot be grasped in the here and now. For I reside just as much with the dead as with the unborn. Somewhat closer to the heart of creation than usual. But not nearly close enough.'[13]

Perhaps it is only to be expected that there is an ungraspable element to his images and intentions. Klee was a formidable intellectual and a distinguished pedagogue – Master at the Bauhaus, Professor at the Kunstakademie Düsseldorf – but in this realm he was rarely explicit or programmatic. More scope for the magic. It is clear that he found angels highly conducive to his philosophy of life and means of expression. He produced around eighty in all, many of them in the last two years of his life, 1939–40, under siege from within and without. From *Angelus Descendens* (1918, 96) to *Angelus Militans* (1940, 333), they vary considerably in attitude and aspect. They are not all angelic. Some are demonic. Lucifer, after all, was a 'fallen' angel. It may be that they are beyond good and evil. (Klee knew his Nietzsche.) Whatever their moral valence, they are hard to read. A certain ambiguity – *Angelus Dubiosus* (1939, 930) – can harden into malevolence – *Child-Eater* (1939, 1027) – or veer off into cartoon – *A Genius Serves a Little Breakfast* (1920, 91), an angel reminiscent of the Roadrunner. Klee's angels have the lightness of thoughtfulness, as Italo Calvino put it, as well as the lightness of frivolity.[14] The artist himself offered no explanation or interpretation of his angelology in general or of *Angelus Novus* in particular. 'With the angels,' he observed gnomically, 'everything is the same as it is here, just angelic.'[15]

They are often hybrids, or crossbreeds. Klee's imagination outran the common cosmology; he trafficked in heart-fish, clock-plants and, it seems, human angels. An early etching, *The Hero with the Wing* (1905, 38), is man, not angel, yet almost angel. He stands, naked, awkwardly but resolutely, his wooden leg rooted in the earth. His left arm is strapped up. His right arm is missing; a short, stubby wing sprouts from the shoulder. In the bottom corner of the sheet the artist has written: 'Especially endowed by nature with one wing, he has therefore formed the idea of being destined to fly, whereby he perishes.' Klee enlarged on this in his diary: 'The man, born with only one wing, in contrast with divine creatures, makes incessant efforts to fly. In doing so, he breaks his arms and legs, but persists under the banner of his idea. The contrast between his statue-like, solemn attitude and his already ruined state needed especially to be captured, as an emblem of the tragicomic.'[16] The tragicomic strain recurs.

If the angels are human, all too human, it is plausible to speculate that they are intimately bound up with Klee's own history and identity as artist-creator, thus raising the possibility of self-portraiture. One authority has concluded that the *Angelus Novus* is indeed a self-portrait of Klee as an artist.[17] That self or self-image emerged out of his experience in the Great War. Flying was central to it. So was crashing to earth.

One of the most significant entries in Klee's diary is also one of the most reworked. It dates originally from early 1915. In the fair copy that he transcribed in 1920–1: 'I have had this war within me for a long time. Therefore it does not concern my innermost self. In order to work myself out of my ruins, I had to fly. And I did fly. In that shattered world I remain only in memory, as one thinks back sometimes. Thus I am "abstract with memories".'[18] These reflections, part of a longer series of reflections on art and war, evolved in a dialogue with his fellow artist Franz Marc, who rushed to the front in August 1914, and quickly published an article, 'In War's Purifying Fire'. Klee for his part was not so sure about the sense or sensibility of war; nor about the efficacy of the one in which the Reich was now engaged. Ambivalent at first, he progressively withdrew to a well-defended position of studied aloofness, distancing himself from any expressions of militaristic or nationalistic pride. His friend August Macke was killed in action almost immediately, in September 1914; the two artists had explored Tunisia together earlier in the year. How the loss affected him is difficult to assess. For the next eighteen months he was allowed to pursue his vocation, more or less undisturbed. He made few images of war, as such. *Death for the Idea*, a lithograph in which a dead body can also be discerned, made an appearance in December 1914, yet Klee recorded it in his *œuvre catalogue* as the first work of 1915, as if to synchronize it with the first entry in his diary: 'Within me, the heart that once beat for this world has been hit, as if mortally.'[19] Another lithograph, on a significant theme, *Destruction and Hope* (1916, 55), was one of his last direct references to the world at war.[20] Klee was by no means a war artist conventionally defined. 'Some will not recognise the truthfulness of my mirror,' he wrote, as early as 1901. 'Let them remember that I am not here to reflect the surface (this can be done with a photographic plate), but must penetrate inside. My mirror probes down to the heart. I write words on the forehead and the corners of the mouth. My human faces are truer than the real ones.'[21]

He received his call-up papers in March 1916, together with a telegram informing him of Marc's death in the mill of Verdun.

Klee's war was a cushy one. His status as an artist exempted him from being sent to the front. He was posted first to the recruits' depot at Landshut and then to the airfield at Schleissheim, near Munich, where he was part of the hangar crew responsible for maintaining and repairing Bavarian military airplanes. In January 1917 he was transferred to another flying school at Gersthofen, near Augsburg. Here he worked in the accounts office, but he also had to fill in for the photographer whose job it was to document any flying accidents. As he realized full well, his position was replete with irony. As an artist, he had to fly. As a reservist, he hugged the ground. By a curious twist of fate, crashes became his *métier*. Creation and destruction intertwined.[22] He practised droll detachment in his diary:

[27 October 1917]
It was a black day for the flying school; in the morning one cadet crashed and broke a number of bones; in the afternoon a lieutenant crashed to his death from a considerable height. *Guten Appetit* for tomorrow's Sunday flying. To be sure, I sit here safe and warm and feel no war within me. The battle of Isonzo, which is becoming a disaster for the Italians, is, moreover, only being fought there so we can return home a bit sooner.

[21 February 1918]
Yesterday the golden wedding anniversary of Their Majesties, we were on duty, with the usual crash. Tonight the entire camp is without light. Went to bed with the chickens. Nothing more consoling in sight.

This week we had three fatal casualties; one man was smashed by the propeller, the other two crashed from the air! Yesterday a fourth came ploughing with a loud bang into the workshop. Had been flying too low, caught on a telephone pole, bounced on the roof of the factory, turned a somersault, and collapsed upside down in a heap of wreckage. People came running from all sides; in a second the roof was black with mechanics in working clothes. Stretchers, ladders. The photographer. A human being pulled out of the debris and carried away unconscious. Loud cursing at the bystanders. First-rate movie effect. This is how a royal regiment celebrated the golden wedding. In addition, three smashed airplanes are lying about in the vicinity today. It was a fine show.[23]

Klee returned to civilian life over Christmas 1918. He had not been officially discharged, but in the midst of revolution, abdication and immiseration he made up his mind to resist. 'I am acting upon internal orders,' he informed his wife. 'I will bid farewell with grace, send my regards in writing, and quote a passage from the "Götz".'[24] The following year he joined the Action Committee of Revolutionary Artists established by the Munich Soviet Republic, with a will, but without disclosing any specific political orientation, revolutionary or otherwise. His commitment to political action remained untested. The Munich Soviet Republic was instantly suppressed. Klee wrote philosophically to Alfred Kubin: 'As ephemeral as this communist republic seemed from the very beginning, at least it provided an opportunity to assess the subject possibilities of living in such a community,' adding, characteristically, 'Although it was just an imaginary state, we are not yet ready for it.'[25] Soon enough he found a different community. In October 1920 he was invited to take up a position at the Bauhaus. Ensconced in that hothouse of modernism, he soared. 'Klee had the courage to walk this clean-swept platform of the twentieth century and not to continue in the shade of Renaissance standards,' wrote the painter Jankel Adler in an obituary notice. 'He made a survey of this place for others who will come.'[26]

Walter Benjamin bought *Angelus Novus* from Klee's dealer in Munich in 1921 for 1,000 marks ($14). It hung for a while in Gershom Scholem's apartment in that city, before occupying a place of honour in his own apartment, first in Berlin, and then in Paris. Charlotte Wolff was a regular visitor: 'Walter and I used to sit opposite each other at a long oak table, covered with his manuscripts. The walls of his room were made invisible through rows of books which reached from floor to ceiling. There was, however, one large space left on the back wall, to house a picture Walter loved – the *Angelus Novus* by Paul Klee. He had a personal relationship with this picture, as if it were part of his mind.'[27]

Benjamin was already an aficionado. He owned another Klee, *Introducing the Miracle* (1916, 54), a birthday present from his wife, Dora, the previous year. 'Are you familiar with Klee?' he asked Scholem. 'I really love him and this is one of the most beautiful of all his paintings I have seen. I hope you will get to see it here in September [1920].' Later, he paid Klee the supreme compliment of comparing him to Kafka, as one of a kind, 'whose work in painting is just as essentially *solitary* as Kafka's work is in literature'.[28] The *Angelus* was Benjamin's constant reference throughout the interwar period. An abortive idea for a journal carried the title *Angelus Novus* (1922). A compressed meditation on the journalist and writer Karl Kraus (1931) concluded with an allusion to Klee's *New Angel*, 'who preferred to free men by taking from them, rather than make them happy by giving to them'. As if to anticipate Klee's *Child-Eater*, the peroration invoked 'a creature sprung from the child and the cannibal . . . a monster, a new angel. Perhaps one of those who, according to the Talmud, are at each moment created anew in countless throngs, and who, once they have raised their voices before God, cease and pass into nothingness. Lamenting, chastising, or rejoicing? No matter – on this evanescent voice the ephemeral work of Kraus is modelled.' Two versions of a cryptic autobiographical text, 'Agesilaus Santander' (1933), speak of 'the name that binds together all the forces of life' (and the gift of appearing human). 'In the room I occupied in Berlin, even before that person had emerged fully armoured and accoutred from my name, he had fixed his image to the wall: New Angel.' Scholem speculated later that, if the *i* is set aside as an ornamental flourish, the name in the title is an anagram of *Der Engel Satanas*, 'Satan's Angel'.[29]

Benjamin's interpretation of *Angelus Novus* in the theses on the concept of history is now part of the culture. But it did not arrive fully armoured and accoutred; nor was it produced unaided. It was nearly twenty years in gestation, and profoundly influenced by his extended dialogue with Scholem, the co-conspirator, the fount of knowledge on angelology, who may be said to have inspired the authorized version. Scholem too was governed, or haunted, by an angel. As early as 1913 he noted in his journal: 'Lurking over me is the sneering face of the angel of insecurity, and it whips me through the silent valleys carved into the depths of my life. It's anyone's guess what my life would look like without this angel, who is for me both fate and doom, but also a severe master and stimulus.'[30] Benjamin's thesis on the angel of history has an epigraph which makes the inspiration clear:

My wing is ready for flight,
I would like to turn back.
If I stayed everliving time,
I'd still have little luck.[31]

The verse is credited to Gershom Scholem, 'Greetings from the Angelus'. It comes from a poem he composed for Benjamin's twenty-ninth birthday, 15 July 1921, a homage to friend and angel alike. The epigraph is not much remarked, perhaps because the complete poem only came to light much later, and because Scholem has been overshadowed by the stardust of Benjamin's posthumous acclaim – heavy with history and memory and guilt – acclaim which Scholem himself did so much to substantiate. It runs as follows (in a variant translation):

I hang nobly on the wall
Looking at nobody at all.
I have been from heaven sent,
A man of angelic descent.

The human within me is good
And does not interest me
I stand in care of the highest
And do not need a face.

From whence I come, that world
Is measured, deep, and clear.
What keeps me together in one piece
Is a wonder, it would appear.

In my heart stands the town
Whence God has sent me.
The angel who bears this seal
Does not fall under its spell.

My wing is ready to beat,
I am all for turning back.
For even staying in timeless time
Would not grant me much fortune.

My eye is darkest black and full,
My gaze is never blank.
I know what I am to announce
And many other things.

I am an unsymbolic thing.
My meaning is what I am.
You turn the magic ring in vain.
I have no sense.[32]

Benjamin had another co-conspirator: Theodor Adorno. It was Adorno who acted as a kind of guardian angel for Benjamin himself, who edited the first posthumous edition of Benjamin's works, who offered *Angelus Novus* sanctuary in New York, and who recognized it as his friend's 'chosen emblem'.[33] Adorno was intimately familiar with Benjamin's world; and he had views of his own about the identification of the angel:

During the First World War or shortly after, Klee drew cartoons of Kaiser Wilhelm as an inhuman iron eater. Later, in 1920, these became – the development can be shown quite clearly – the *Angelus Novus*, the machine angel, who, though he no longer bears any emblem of caricature or commitment, flies far beyond both. The machine angel's enigmatic eyes force the onlooker to try to decide whether he is announcing the culmination of disaster or salvation hidden within it. But, as Walter Benjamin, who owned the drawing, said, he is the angel who does not give but takes.[34]

Adorno was quite right about the cartoons or caricatures. *Memorial to the Kaiser* was closely followed by *The Great Kaiser Rides to War* (1920, 173) and *Kaiser Wilhelm Raging* (1920, 206) – a drawing that became a painting, succinctly entitled *The Ex-Kaiser* (1921, 14) – to say nothing of *King of the Barbarians* (1917, 131) and *The Commander* (1918, 178). Whether the *Angelus* is the Kaiser transmogrified, however, is another matter.

More recently, an even bolder identification has been made: that *Angelus Novus* is none other than Adolf Hitler. 'Remember, it was late 1919 and 1920 when Hitler had just turned into a fulltime political agitator and haranguer on the Munich beer hall fringes,' writes Carl Djerassi. 'Could Klee have not used *angelus* in the Hebrew sense of "messenger" and *novus* in the bitter fearful way of the new messenger of the Germany to come – the equivalent of the Roman *homo novus* – the parvenu?' This sounds far-fetched, but the case has been made with considerable authority, first by the scholar Johann Konrad Eberlein; and the polymathic Djerassi (who was a discriminating collector) also pointed to Hitler-like images in at least two other works by Klee from the same period, *Bird Comedy* (1918) and *Demonry* (1925).[35]

It seems that the angel carries on giving, after all. 'No image does more to capture the subtle and contradictory elements embedded in European cultural history in the period of the Great War,' as Jay Winter has underlined. Benjamin's angel haunts the hecatombs, just as it haunts the pages of his successors, from Giorgio Agamben to W. G. Sebald.[36] Sebald's doctoral thesis contains a passage that is almost patterned on Benjamin's ninth:

> There is a Dürer engraving which shows a dark Angel surrounded by allegorical instruments – a pair of scales, an hour-glass, a death knell and a plane, a knife and a goat; but there is something else in the picture, a piece of rock with crystalline surfaces. Thus although the inorganic goal is represented in the picture, regression is transcended by the unflinching calm with which the Angel stares death in the face. In this way both the Angel itself and the tools of destruction appear to have their activity suspended: under the protection of melancholy the prospective victim savours a final interlude of living peace.[37]

'The luckless angel' was taken up repeatedly by the radical East German playwright Heiner Müller – often dubbed the heir to Brecht – first in an anti-Stalinist text written in the wake of the Soviet suppression of the Hungarian uprising in 1956, later in a poignant meditation on the fall of the Berlin Wall in 1989.[38]

> Between city and city
> After the wall the sheer fall
> Wind at the shoulders the alien
> Hand on solitary flesh
> The angel I can still hear him
> But his face is no more than
> Yours that I don't know

At the same moment, the angel of history himself reappeared, this time in 3D, in an installation by the prodigious Anselm Kiefer, an artist steeped in the unmasterable past (see Chapter 6): as a bomber, made of lead, with lead books and dried poppies on its wings, a work entitled *The Angel of History: Poppy and Memory* (1989), the most powerful artistic re-imagining of the short twentieth century. Like *The Hero with the Wing*, Kiefer's leaden angel cannot fly; it is a vector of ideas. Characteristically, Kiefer is deeply interested in lead, materially and metaphysically. 'Standing for the first stage in the transformation of base metals into gold,' he muses, 'lead in a sense embodies development, evolution. Despite being very heavy, it is not rigid: as the Italians say, it is *morbido*, soft.' For Kiefer, it has magical properties. 'Lead is a substance that unaccountably contains in its depth a spark of light, a glimmer that seems to belong to some other world, one beyond our reach.' His train of thought or association embraces angels, apocalypse, and a marvellous ambiguity.

> The Gnostic Valentinus resorts to a strange metaphor to convey the end of the world: he speaks of a waterwheel catching sparks of light falling into matter, thereby distinguishing between two domains and hinting at the vision of the earth being transformed into a desert – a void. . . . For Valentinus, lead is dull and heavy, insofar as the sparks of light, the shower of human memories, are wrenched from the here and now and spin into the hereafter.
>
> It would be interesting to compare this image to the myth of the Fallen Angels and to observe how the two things point in different directions. We observe a downward movement when the rebel angels are cast from heaven, whereas Valentinus's sparks of light are constantly borne upwards. In either case we have an apocalypse. Now, the two movements are really only one and the same movement, as when Goethe's Faust cries

out as he goes down to see the mothers, 'steigend, steigend, sinke neider' ('rising, rising, I sink down').[39]

Paul Klee died in 1940. Walter Benjamin died in 1940. Kaiser Wilhelm died, improbably, in 1941. *Angelus Novus* lives on, melancholy perhaps, but still messianic. The wreckage piles up. The urge to make good remains. Protean and productive, this five-fingered talisman has been called an icon of the left and a hobo of thought.[40] The angel of history is also a vessel of hope.

> We cannot part with our friends. We cannot let our angels go. We do not see that they only go out that archangels may come in. We are idolaters of the old. We do not believe in the riches of the soul, in its proper eternity and omnipresence. We do not believe there is any force in today to rival or recreate that beautiful yesterday. We linger in the ruins of the old tent where once we had bread and shelter and organs, nor believe that the spirit can feed, cover, and nerve us again. We cannot find aught so dear, so sweet, so graceful. But we sit and weep in vain. The voice of the Almighty saith, 'Up and onward for evermore!' We cannot stay amid the ruins. Neither will we rely on the new; and so we walk ever with reverted eyes, like those monsters who look backwards.[41]

Notes

1. Anne Carson, 'Wildly Constant', *London Review of Books*, 30 April 2009.

2. See Laurence Binyon, 'For the Fallen', http://www.theguardian.com/world/2008/nov/14/for-the-fallen-laurence-binyon (last accessed 26 November 2013). First published in *The Times*, 21 September 1914, before Binyon himself went to war. The poetic tradition continues: see Carol Ann Duffy (ed.), *1914: Poetry Remembers* (London: Faber, 2013).

3. See, e.g., David Reynolds, *The Long Shadow* (London: Simon & Schuster, 2013). For an argument for poetry, broadly conceived, see Alex Danchev, *On Art and War and Terror* (Edinburgh: Edinburgh University Press, 2011), ch. 6; for a profound reflection on the war poetry of the Western Front in historical perspective, see Jon Stallworthy, *Survivors' Songs* (Cambridge: Cambridge University Press, 2008).

4. Brian Turner, 'The Martyrs Brigade', in *Here, Bullet* (Tarset: Bloodaxe, 2007), p. 38. Turner served as an Infantry Team Leader in Iraq in 2003–4. He is the author of 'The Hurt Locker', inspiration for Kathryn Bigelow's award-winning film about an Explosive Ordnance Disposal team in that war (2008).

5. Wilfred Owen, 'Anthem for Doomed Youth' (1917), in Jon Stallworthy (ed.), *The Poems of Wilfred Owen* (London: Chatto & Windus, 1990), p. 76. 'The pity of war' is from Owen's draft preface for a collection of war poems that he hoped to publish in 1919, had he lived. ('My subject is War, and the pity of War. The Poetry is in the pity.') 'Some desperate glory' is from the closing lines of 'Dulce et Decorum Est' (1917): 'My friend, you would not tell with such high zest/To children ardent for some desperate glory,/The old lie: Dulce et decorum est/Pro patria mori.' See pp. 117 and 192. 'The Charge of the Light Brigade' (1854) is Alfred, Lord Tennyson, on the Battle of Balaclava in the Crimean War.

6. See Jay Winter and Antoine Prost, *The Great War in History* (Cambridge: Cambridge University Press, 2005).

7. Walter Benjamin, trans. Harry Zohn, 'On the Concept of History' (1940), in Howard Eiland and Michael W. Jennings (eds), *Selected Writings* (Cambridge, MA: Harvard University Press, 1996–2003), vol. 4, p. 392. This passage may be more familiar to readers from 'Theses on the Philosophy of History', in *Illuminations* (London: Fontana, 1973), first published in English in 1968. In *Selected Writings* the translation has been revised.

8. Reynolds, *Long Shadow*, p. 360. Zara Steiner's recent work is dedicated to the proposition that 'the line from 1919 to 1939 was not a straight one'. See *The Lights that Failed* (Oxford: Clarendon Press, 2005).

9. Cf. Charles S. Maier, *The Unmasterable Past* (Cambridge, MA: Harvard University Press, 1998), complete with Klee image on the cover.

10. For a small demonstration of what a study of provenance can yield, see Danchev, *On Art and War and Terror*, ch. 3.

11. *Paul Klee Catalogue Raisonné* (Bern: Benteli, 1999), no. 2377 (hereafter CR). The provenance given in the CR is extremely scanty: Walter Benjamin (from 1921); Fania and Gershom Scholem (until 1987).

12. The provenance of the drawing is incomplete; it does not appear in the CR. It was shown at a retrospective in Berlin in 1923. It reappeared at an auction of modern art in Bern in 1975. It was sold to Raymond Bullack for 27,000 Swiss francs; the seller was Markus Kutter, from Basel. It is now in a private collection.

13. These words were first published in the house journal of the Galerie Golz, Munich, on the occasion of Klee's one-man show in 1920. Twenty years later they became the epitaph on his tomb.

14. Italo Calvino, trans. Patrick Creagh, *Six Memos for the next Millennium* (London: Vintage, 1996), p. 10.

15. Paul Klee, *The Angels* (Ostfildern: Hatje Cantz, 2012), p. 9. This book illustrates most of them.

16. Klee diary, 1905, in Felix Klee (ed.), *The Diaries of Paul Klee 1898–1918* (Berkeley: University of California Press, 1964), p. 162.

17. Perdita Rösch, *Die Hermeneutik des Boten* (Munich: Fink Wilhelm, 2009), p. 53. This perspective may have its origins in Otto Karl Werckmeister's view of it as 'an image of the artist's exaltation, by means of abstraction, into a spiritual counterworld'. *The Making of Paul Klee's Career 1914–1920* (Chicago: Chicago University Press, 1989), pp. 241–2. These speculations are adumbrated in Gregor Wedekind, 'With a View to Something Higher', in Klee, *Angels*, pp. 107–11.

18. Here I follow the translation and interpretation in Werckmeister, *The Making of Paul Klee's Career*, pp. 41ff. Cf. Klee, *Diaries*, pp. 313–15. On Klee's evolving attitude to the war, see also the exploration in Marcel Franciscono, *Paul Klee* (Chicago: University of Chicago Press, 1991), pp. 206ff.

19. Werckmeister, *The Making of Paul Klee's Career*, pp. 50–1.

20. Klee seems to have begun this lithograph (previously titled *Conquered Fort* and *Ruins and Hopes*) in late 1914 or early 1915. In a maze of signs, it depicts two caricatural figures; an allusion to Marc has been suggested. See Franciscono, *Klee*, pp. 208–9. Philippe Dagen has argued (wrongly, I think) that most artists were 'silent' on the war: *Le Silence des peintres* (Paris: Hazan, 2012).

21. Klee, *Diaries*, pp. 47–8.

22. Provokingly, Werckmeister suggests that *Angelus Novus* can be seen as a 'pendant' to *Airplane Crash* (1920, 209). *The Making of Paul Klee's Career*, p. 241.

23. Klee, *Diaries*, pp. 380, 387–8.

24. Klee to Lily Klee, 16 December 1918, in Eva Wiederkehr Sladeczek (ed.), *Paul Klee* (Ostfildern: Hatje Canz, 2012), p. 96. 'The Götz' is a reference to Goethe's historical drama, *Götz von Berlichingen* (1793), which gave rise to 'the Götz quote' or Schwabian salute: a line in the third act, when Götz, a free spirit, is besieged in his castle by the Imperial Army. Invited by the captain of the Army to surrender, he delivers his answer (freely translated): 'Tell your captain that for His Imperial Majesty I have, as always, due respect. But tell him that *he can kiss my arse.*'

25. Klee to Kubin, 12 May 1919, in Sladeczek, *Klee*, p. 96.

26. Jankel Adler, 'Memories of Paul Klee', in Matthew Gale (ed.), *Paul Klee* (London: Tate, 2013), p. 30.

27. Charlotte Wolff, *Hindsight* (London: Quartet, 1980), p. 67.

28. Benjamin to Scholem, 23 July 1920 and 12 June 1938, in Gershom Scholem and Theodor W. Adorno (eds), *The Correspondence of Walter Benjamin 1910–1940* (Chicago: University of Chicago Press, 1994), pp. 165, 224 (trans. Manfred R. Jacobson and Evelyn M. Jacobson). *Introducing the Miracle* is now in the Museum of Modern Art, New York.

29. 'Announcement of the journal *Angelus Novus*', 'Karl Kraus' and 'Agesilaus Santander', in Benjamin, *Selected Writings*, vol. 1, pp. 292–6; vol. 2, part II, pp. 456–7, 712–15. Cf. Gershom Scholem, trans. Werner Dannhauser, 'Walter Benjamin and His Angel' (1972), in Gary Smith (ed.), *On Walter Benjamin* (Cambridge, MA: MIT, 1988), pp. 51–89.

30. Quoted in George Steiner, *The Poetry of Thought* (New York: New Directions, 2011), p. 175.

31. Benjamin, *Selected Writings*, vol. 4, p. 392 (trans. Harry Zohn). In an earlier version, 'If I stayed timeless time,/I would have little luck.' Cf. *Illuminations*, p. 249.

32. *Correspondence of Walter Benjamin*, pp. 184–5 (trans. Gary Smith). 'All its wonderful beauty notwithstanding, the language of angels has the disadvantage of our being unable to respond to it,' replied Benjamin. 'And I have no choice but to ask you, instead of the Angelus, to accept my thanks.'

33. The angel's passage to New York remains something of a mystery. The accepted story is that Benjamin left it with his friend Georges Bataille when he fled Paris in 1940, and that Bataille hid it in the Bibliothèque Nationale, where he worked; it is then supposed to have found its way to Adorno in New York after the war, in 1947. More recently, however, it has emerged that it may well have reached Adorno as early as 1941, via a courier, at the behest of Benjamin's sister. The rather murky post-war provenance is recapitulated in Reto Sorg, 'The Angel of Angels', in Klee, *Angels*, pp. 126–9.

34. Theodor Adorno, 'Commitment' (1962), in *Aesthetics and Politics* (London: Verso, 2007), pp. 194–5.

35. Carl Djerassi, *Four Jews on Parnassus* (New York: Columbia University Press, 2008), p. 97. See also his letter to the *New York Review of Books*, 25 September 2014, protesting the 'glaring omission' of *Angelus Novus* and its interpretations in the recent 'critical life' of Benjamin by Howard Eiland and Michael W. Jennings. *Bird Comedy* (1918) is no. 2063 and *Demonry* (1925) no. 3885 in Klee's CR. Cf. Johann Konrad Eberlein, *Angelus Novus* (Freiburg: Rombach, 2006).

36. Jay Winter, *Sites of Memory, Sites of Mourning* (Cambridge: Canto, 1998), p. 223. See Giorgio Agamben, trans. Georgia Albert, 'The Melancholy Angel', in *The Man Without Content* (Stanford: Stanford University Press, 1999), p. 109; W. G. Sebald, trans. Anthea Bell, *On the Natural History of Destruction* (London: Hamilton, 2003), p. 68.

37. W. G. Sebald, 'The Revival of Myth: A Study of Döblin's Novels' (PhD thesis, University of East Anglia, 1973), pp. 180–1. Cf. Agamben, 'Melancholy Angel', p. 109. The engraving is *Melancholia I* (1514). On Sebald in this context, see Christopher Bigsby, *Remembering and*

Imagining the Holocaust (Cambridge: Cambridge University Press, 2006), pp. 86ff.

38. Heiner Müller, trans. Iain Bamforth, 'The Luckless Angel' (c.1958) and 'The Luckless Angel 2' (1991), *Grand Street* 69 (1999), pp. 233–4. Cf. Jeanette R. Malkin, 'Heiner Müller's Landscapes of Memory', in *Memory-Theatre and Postmodern Drama* (Ann Arbor: University of Michigan Press, 1999), ch. 3.

39. Anselm Kiefer, trans. Michael Taylor, *Art Will Survive its Ruins* (Paris: Regard, 2011), pp. 273–4.

40. See Otto Karl Werckmeister, 'Walter Benjamin's Angel of History, or the Transfiguration of the Revolutionary into the Historian', in *Icons of the Left* (Chicago: University of Chicago Press, 1999), pp. 9–34; Geoffrey Hartman, 'Benjamin in Hope', *Critical Inquiry* 25 (1999), p. 347, adapting Stanley Cavell's coinage of the philosopher as the hobo of thought.

41. Ralph Waldo Emerson, 'Self-Reliance', in *Essays: First Series* [1841], in *The Essential Writings* (New York: Modern Library, 2000), p. 170.

4

Infidels and Miscreants: Love and War in Afghanistan

It *wasn't* a war story. It was a *love* story.

Tim O'Brien[1]

For the best part of a year, in 2007–8, the writer and reporter Sebastian Junger and the photographer and filmmaker Tim Hetherington visited and revisited the Korengal Valley in eastern Afghanistan. They were 'embedded' with Second Platoon, Battle Company, 'The Rock' Battalion, 503rd Infantry Regiment, 173rd Airborne Brigade Combat Team, first of all in the forward operating base known as the Korengal Outpost (the KOP), and then in an outpost of the outpost, as far out on a limb as it is possible to get, witnessing the kind of war that would not have seemed completely foreign to Xenophon or Herodotus, give or take a whiff of grapeshot, or the smell of napalm in the morning.

Battle Company are real soldiers. 'Combat infantry carry the most, eat the worst, die the fastest, sleep the least, and have the most to fear,' reports Junger in his account of the experience. 'But they're the real soldiers, the only ones conducting what can be considered "war" in the most classical sense, and everyone knows it. I once asked someone in Second Platoon why frontline grunts aren't more admired.'

'Because everyone just thinks we're stupid,' the man said.
'But you do all the fighting.'
'Yeah,' he said. 'Exactly.'[2]

For these soldiers, the Korengal is a good approximation of hell on earth. In winter, bitter cold, so cold that they wear balaclavas under their helmets. In summer, a hundred degrees every day, crawling with tarantulas, infested with fleas. At night, the wolves begin to howl; mountain lions creep through the KOP looking for something

61

to eat. Colonies of monkeys invest the place, setting up a fearful screeching. There is a bird that sounds uncannily like an incoming rocket-propelled grenade; the men call it the RPG bird and flinch whenever they hear it. At the outpost there is no running water, no electricity, no hot food, no alcohol, no drugs, no communication with the outside world – no *life*, one of the soldiers explains, 'like being a monk in, like, Tibet'.

The enemy is everywhere, invisible. They can be overheard on the radio monitoring Battle Company's every move: 'The infidel are climbing the hill.' 'The infidel are at their base.' The infidel are us. Typically, the soldiers adopt the name with pride, and get it tattooed in heavy gothic script across their chests. The Taliban in their turn are called 'miscreants' by the battalion commander, Lieutenant-Colonel William Ostlund, a graduate of the Fletcher School of Law and Diplomacy, who wrote a thesis on the defeat of the Soviet military in Afghanistan and Chechnya. He also has the habit of speaking of them in the third-person singular – 'we cornered the enemy and destroyed him' – as if there were no hard feelings, Junger writes, 'and all this was just an extraordinarily violent lawn sport'.[3]

'Cornered' is an apt description. Who is cornered, however, is a moot point. If the mission is to drain the swamp, these men are in it up to the neck. The Korengal Valley is less a swamp than a fucking quagmire, as one of the platoon sergeants picturesquely says. 'Damn the Valley' becomes a kind of catchphrase, 'DTV' another tattoo. The Valley has a history. Nineteen American commandos perished there in a disastrous operation against the Taliban. Tactically and strategically, the miscreants have the upper hand.

Into the valley of death rode the 150 of Battle Company, who sometimes seem to bear the brunt of the whole war. According to Junger, they account for almost one-fifth of the combat engagements of NATO forces in Afghanistan. They get into as many as thirteen firefights in one day. Contact is inevitable yet unpredictable. They might be ankle-deep in spent cartridges; they might be left alone for weeks. There is no way of telling what will happen next: as like as not, it will be lethal. The intensity of such an experience is almost unimaginable. This is the task that Junger and Hetherington have set themselves: to convey to The World, as soldiers say – meaning the outside world, the civilian world, the terrifying normalcy of 'back home' – what it is like for men in war (for these men in this war) in the bubble of infidel and miscreant, small unit and sudden death.[4] 'Civilians balk at recognizing that one of the most traumatic things about combat is having to give it up,' Junger explains, with his customary lucidity. 'When men say they miss combat, it's not that they actually miss getting shot at – you'd have to be deranged – it's that they miss being in a world where everything is important and nothing is taken for granted. They miss being in a world where human relations are entirely governed by whether you can trust the other person with your life.'[5]

The locus of that investigation is Restrepo, 'a place where the unimaginable had to be considered in detail'. Restrepo is the outpost of the outpost, named after 'Doc' Restrepo, the much-loved company medic, who died soon after they arrived, shot in the face on patrol. His buddy O'Byrne had already written in his journal that Restrepo was too good a man for God to let him die – even though O'Byrne didn't believe in God – but Restrepo didn't make it to the field hospital. 'For a long time I hated God,' O'Byrne the unbeliever tells Junger. 'Second Platoon fought like animals after that.'

'I prayed only once in Afghanistan,' O'Byrne wrote to Junger after it was all over. 'It was when Restrepo got shot, and I prayed to God to let him live. But God, Allah, Jehovah, Zeus or whatever a person may call God wasn't in that valley. Combat is the devil's game. God wanted no part. That's why our prayers weren't answered: the only one listening was Satan.'[6]

Restrepo's death was not unusual. As Junger records:

Pretty much everyone who died in this valley died when they least expected it, usually shot in the head or throat, so it could make the men weird about the most mundane tasks. Only once did I know beforehand that we were going to get hit, otherwise I was: about to take a sip of coffee, talking to someone, walking about a hundred metres outside the wire, and taking a nap. The men just never know, which meant that anything they did was potentially the *last* thing they'd ever do. That gave rise to strange forms of magical thinking. One morning after four days of continuous fighting I said that things seemed 'quiet' and I might as well have rolled a live hand grenade through the outpost; every man there yelled at me to shut the fuck up. And then there were Charms: small fruit-flavoured candies that often came in the pre-packaged meals called MREs [Meals Ready to Eat]. The superstition was that eating Charms would bring on a firefight, so if you found a pack in your MRE, you were supposed to throw it off the back side of the ridge or burn it in the burn pit. One day Cortez got so bored that he ate a pack on purpose, hoping to bring on a firefight, but nothing happened. He never told the others what he'd done.[7]

This passage is characteristic Junger – acute, authentic, deeply serious, yet alive to irony, at once well-tuned and well-turned. As his previous work goes to show, Junger knows his business. His first book was *The Perfect Storm* (1997), 'a true story of man against the sea'. Embedding, it seems, is his *métier*, in one way of life or another. He is good at empathy; he has an ear for different voices; he is a master at simplifying and clarifying; he does his homework. He writes like a poet who has been to meteorology school, said Ruth Rendell of *The Perfect Storm*. His 'selected sources and references' on war would do credit to a doctoral thesis. He must have read much more, especially on the Vietnam war: not only Michael Herr's *Dispatches* (1977), a seminal text for a reporter, but surely also Tim O'Brien's *The Things They Carried* (1990). 'They carried all the emotional baggage of men who might die,' writes O'Brien in that signature story.

> Grief, terror, love, longing – these were intangibles, but the intangibles had their own mass and specific gravity, they had tangible weight. They carried shameful memories. They carried the common secret of cowardice barely restrained, the instinct to run or freeze or hide, and in many respects this was the heaviest burden of all, for it could never be put down, it required perfect balance and perfect posture. They carried their reputations. They carried the soldier's greatest fear, which was the fear of blushing. Men killed, and died, because they were embarrassed not to.[8]

'There are different kinds of strength,' reflects Junger, as if continuing the thought, 'and containing fear may be the most profound, the one without which armies couldn't function and wars couldn't be fought (God forbid).'

> There are big, tough guys in the Army who are cowards and small, feral-looking dudes, like Monroe, who will methodically take apart a SAW [Squad Automatic Weapon] while rounds are slapping the rocks all around them. The more literal forms of strength, like carrying 160 pounds up a mountain, depend more obviously on the size of your muscles, but muscles only do what you tell them, so it keeps coming back to the human spirit. Wars are fought with very heavy machinery that works best on top of the biggest hill in the area and used against men who are lower down. That, in a nutshell, is military tactics, and it means that an enormous amount of war-fighting simply consists of carrying heavy loads uphill.[9]

Somewhere near the heart of Junger's work is the question of how soldiers carry themselves. He follows Lord Moran's distinction between cowardice and fear. 'By cowardice I do not mean fear,' cautioned Moran in *The Anatomy of Courage* (1945). 'Fear is the response of the instinct of self-preservation to danger. It is only morbid, as Aristotle taught, when it is out of proportion to the degree of danger. In invincible fear – "fear stronger than I am" – the soldier has to struggle with a flood of emotion; he is made that way. But fear even when morbid is not cowardice. That is a label we reserve for something a man does. What passes through his mind is his own affair.'[10]

Fear is acceptable. Dereliction is not. 'Once they were clawing their way up Table Rock after a twenty-hour operation and a man in another squad started falling out. "He *can't* be smoked here," I heard O'Byrne seethe to Sergeant Mac in the dark, "he doesn't have the *right* to be."' 'Smoked' is slang for shattered or exhausted.[11] 'The idea that you're not allowed to experience something as human as exhaustion is outrageous anywhere but in combat,' as Junger explains. 'Good leaders know that exhaustion is partly a state of mind, though, and that the men who succumb to it have on some level decided to put themselves above everyone else. If you're not prepared to walk for someone you're certainly not prepared to die for them, and that goes to the heart of whether you should even be in the platoon.'[12] O'Byrne's response is telling, because it is not merely an expression of exasperation: it is an ethical proposition about soldierly reciprocity, or collective responsibility. Fighting and philosophizing are not mutually incompatible after all. In his own hard-drinking, blaspheming way, O'Bryne is something of a moralist (and afterwards, incongruously, an arborist); flawed as he may be, he becomes an almost ideal character, the platoon philosopher or mind reader, allowing Junger to tap into the subculture, perhaps even the subconscious. 'He was just one soldier out of thirty but seemed to have a knack for putting words to the things that no one else really wanted to talk about. I came to think of O'Byrne as a stand-in for the entire platoon, a way to understand a group of men who I don't think entirely understood themselves.' Lest this be thought an extravagant characterization, Second Platoon are not above extravagant characterizations of their own. Sergeant Buno is nicknamed Queequeg, after the tattooed, harpoon-toting cannibal, who turns out to be a very Christian cannibal, in Herman Melville's *Moby-Dick* (1851). Curiously enough, there is an Afghan connection of a kind, when Queequeg's shipmate Ishmael imagines the programme drawn up by Providence: 'Grand Contested Election for the Presidency of the United States. Whaling voyage by one Ishmael. Bloody battle in Afghanistan.'

The ethics of exhaustion are consonant with the Zen of not fucking up, as Junger puts it.

> Once I woke up in the middle of the night to grunts and shouting and went outside to find Staff Sergeant Alcantara smoking his entire squad. Whoever was on guard duty had let the batteries run down on a thermal sight called a PAS-13 that allowed them to scan the hillsides at night. On a dark night the PAS-13 was the only way they could see if the enemy was creeping close for a surprise attack, and dead batteries could literally put the base at risk of getting overrun. The best way to ensure that no one fucked up was to inflict collective punishment on the entire squad, because that meant everyone would be watching everyone else. Al had them out there in stress positions lifting sandbags and essentially eating dirt for so long that I finally just went back inside and went to sleep. The next morning I asked him if the punishment had wiped the slate clean – or was there some residual stigma that would take longer to erase?
>
> 'There are no hard feelings after everyone gets smoked,' he said. 'They're more pissed that they all let each other down. Once it's over it's over.'[13]

In other words, 'there was no such thing as *personal* safety out there; what happened to you happened to everyone.'

The ultimate test of these propositions is combat. Junger writes very well about combat, and in particular about small-unit combat effectiveness. His preferred metaphor is choreography. 'There is choreography for storming Omaha Beach, for taking out a pillbox bunker, and for surviving an L-shaped ambush at night on the Gatigal [spur above the Korengal]. The choreography always requires that each man make decisions based not on what's best for *him*, but on what's best for the group. If everyone does that, most of the group survives. If no one does, most of the group dies. That, in essence, is combat.'

Junger tells the story of the ambush. A dozen Taliban fighters with rockets and belt-fed machine guns suddenly open fire on First Platoon at a distance of fifteen or twenty feet. The Taliban are cunningly disposed and well concealed; First Platoon are sitting ducks in a shooting gallery. 'Within seconds, every man in the lead squad takes a bullet. Brennan goes down immediately, wounded in eight places. Eckrode takes rounds through his thigh and calf and falls back to lay down suppressive fire with his SAW. Gallardo takes a round in his helmet and falls down but gets back up. Doc Mendoza, farther down the line, takes a round through the femur and immediately starts bleeding out.' The Bravo team leader, Sal Giunta, had to work out what to do. Giunta joined the Army after hearing a radio commercial while working at a Subway sandwich shop in his home town in Iowa. He himself had taken rounds in his front armour plate and his assault pack, but he paid no attention, except to note that the fire seemed to be coming from straight ahead, close up, though he could also see sheets of tracer pouring in from his left. His first thought was that three of his friends had been hit, and that it would be very bad if the teams were separated. Within seconds, he proceeded to organize a counterattack. He assigned rates and sectors of fire to his team, ran to Gallardo's assistance, and threw three hand grenades while assaulting the enemy position. After emptying his magazine at the enemy who were dragging away the wounded Brennan, he pursued them down the hill. Audie Murphy had nothing on Sal Giunta. For this remarkable demonstration of grace under pressure, he was awarded the Medal of Honour.

'I did what I did because that's what I was trained to do,' he told Junger. 'There was a task that had to be done, and the part that I was gonna do was to link Alpha and Bravo teams. I didn't run through fire to save a buddy – I ran through fire to see what was going on with him and maybe we could hide behind the same rock and shoot together. I didn't run through fire to do anything heroic or brave. I did what I believe *anyone* would have done.'[14] And indeed every man in the platoon appears to have acted as purposefully and efficiently, if not quite as instantaneously and omnicompetently as Giunta.

How to explain choreography of this order? Training is necessary but not sufficient. 'Highly trained men in extraordinarily dangerous circumstances are less likely to break down than untrained men in little danger.' As Junger remarks, one of the most puzzling things about fear is that it is only loosely related to the level of danger. Training, however, will not do the trick. There is something else. 'Among men who are dependent on one another for their safety . . . there is often an unspoken agreement to stick together no matter what. The reassurance that you will never be abandoned seems to help men act in ways that serve the whole unit rather than just themselves.' *War* thus confirms two timeless observations about war, as H. R. McMaster has underlined in a laudatory assessment of the book.[15]

In combat, what happens to everyone becomes radically uncertain. As Clausewitz knew, war is the realm of chance and contingency and friction. Junger nods to that classic work but mines a somewhat later one, *The American Soldier: Combat and Its Aftermath* (1949), edited by the sociologist Samuel Stouffer and others, from which he quotes a Clausewitzian observation by the correspondent Jack Belden: 'Every action produces a counteraction on the enemy's part. The thousands of interlocking actions throw up millions of little frictions, accidents and chances, from which there emanates an all-embracing fog of uncertainty.' Out of this, Junger extracts the fundamental moral of his tale:

> Combat fog obscures your fate – obscures when and where you might die – and from that unknown is born a desperate bond between the men. That bond is the core experience of combat and the only thing that you can absolutely count on. The Army might screw you and your girlfriend might dump you and the enemy might kill you, but the shared commitment to safeguard one another's lives is unnegotiable and only deepens with time. The willingness to die for another person is a form of love that even religions fail to inspire, and the experience of it changes a person profoundly. What the Army sociologists . . . slowly came to understand was that courage *was* love. In war, neither could exist without the other, and in a sense they were just different ways of saying the same thing.[16]

Auden was right. 'We must love one another or die.'[17]

Curiously enough, love may be the richest part of Sebastian Junger's treatment of the subject. He is not the only reporter to have crafted a compelling work with a worm's-eye view. Perhaps embedding is conducive to that very stratagem. David Finkel's *The Good Soldiers* (2009) and Jim Frederick's *Black Hearts* (2010) immediately offer themselves for comparison. Finkel was embedded with the Second Battalion, 16th Infantry Regiment, in Baghdad in 2007–8; Frederick was embedded in Iraq in 2008, but made an intensive study of First Platoon, Bravo Company, 1st Battalion, 502nd Infantry Regiment, in the 'Triangle of Death', south of Baghdad, in 2005–6. The narrative frame and ethical freight of *The Good Soldiers* and *War* are somewhat similar, and the two books have certain other affinities, of stance and style and soldierly observation. Finkel, too, has an ear well tuned to the poetry of the private soldier.

> This place.
> The fucking dust.
> The fucking stink.
> The fucking all of it.
> This fucking place.

Finkel's account is less analytical than Junger's, but he poses the larger question of efficacy (or futility) more insistently, through the person of his battalion commander, Lieutenant-Colonel Ralph Kauzlarich, nicknamed 'Lost Kauz'. Where Ostlund has only a walk-on part in *War*, Kauzlarich is central to *The Good Soldiers*. He has comic potential, but he is ultimately a tragic figure. Like Ostlund, he is a student of history. Ominously, his study is Vietnam.

Vietnam is a kind of background hum in these books, *The Good Soldiers* in particular. Kauzlarich studies a celebrated account, *We Were Soldiers Once . . . and Young* (1992), by his predecessor Harold G. Moore; he has the book with him when he meets the author, and asks for his advice. Moore scribbles, 'Trust your instincts.' Finkel for his part sometimes sounds like Michael Herr. '"Truck went up. Smoke and fire," he said, shaking his head, neatly summing up a day.' This is the manner that Herr perfected in *Dispatches* – epic laconic: '"Patrol went up the mountain. One man came back. He died before he could tell us what happened, but it seemed not to be that kind of story.'[18]

Finkel and Junger are fortunate: they deal in good rather than bad apples. Frederick's *Black Hearts*, by contrast, is an altogether darker tale – a study in dereliction, dissolution and decay. It is in fact a textbook case of a body of men going bad; the Triangle of Death is a little like a latter-day version of *The Garden of Earthly Delights* by Hieronymus Bosch. By the end of their deployment fifty-one of around 135 soldiers in Bravo Company have been killed, wounded or moved to another unit, including all three platoon commanders, the first sergeant, a squad leader and a team leader. A malignant few are guilty of rape and murder. 'This was some vile carnage,' reflects one of the soldiers, 'but frankly, it was far from the worst he had ever seen in this Godforsaken country.'[19] God, love and discipline are in short supply.

All three books are exemplary works of long form reportage. Geoff Dyer has argued that the reportage trumps the fiction of the war on terror.[20] With such books as *The Assassins' Gate* (2005), by George Packer, and *The Looming Tower* (2007), by Lawrence Wright, it also trumps the history. In this select company the distinguishing feature of Junger's work is his sustained collaboration with Tim Hetherington. It is Hetherington who thickens their combined account with a kind of domesticity, even at times a tranquillity, amid the cacophony and the carnage; and it is perhaps the photographer who alerted the writer to the salience of shared commitment. In his introduction to Hetherington's photographs of this project, *Infidel*, Junger himself reflects that 'it was very easy to fall into the trap of thinking that without combat there was no story to tell'. He remembers 'one stifling June day in the middle of a real combat drought':

> It seemed to be the *definition* of a moment where there's no story to tell, and yet that wasn't quite true. Creeping through the outpost came Tim, camera in hand, grabbing photographs of the soldiers as they slept. 'You never see them like this,' he said to me later. 'They always look so tough, but when they're asleep they look like little boys. They look the way their mothers probably remember them.'
>
> He was absolutely right. I opened my notebook and wrote a description of what it was like to be at one of the most exposed outposts in the entire American sector with virtually every man asleep. The truth was that Tim saw things very differently from the way I did; he wasn't looking for dynamism so much as for beauty or strangeness or even ugliness.[21]

Hetherington died young, as war photographers do, during an assault on rebel forces in the Libyan city of Misrata in 2011. To all outward appearances he was a war photographer on the classic model of Robert Capa: the wild rover, debonair existentialist of the combat zone. Junger's documentary tribute to him plays tenderly on this persona, which had substance – *Which Way is the Front Line from Here?* (2013) is the question he asked his driver.[22] Yet Hetherington, like Capa, was surprisingly uninterested in carnage, or for that matter in battle, as Junger came to realize. What drove him was not atrocity but possibility – 'the lived knowledge of political possibility', as Susie Linfield puts it. Capa was a moralizer, one might say, as opposed to a demoralizer. 'His photographs record the twentieth century's moments of militant humanism,' resumes Linfield in a moving peroration; 'and they do this by how he, working at the time, made them and by what we, in the present, bring to them.'

> His images are anti-fascist because they document a flawed, deeply scarred humanity, and because they honour rather than scorn those flaws and those scars. Capa's photographs show us that human beings suffer, and make us want to know why; they show us that human beings endure, and make us want to know how. They show us that striving for a more-just world can sometimes succeed but more often fails, yet that to do so is never absurd or inconsequential.[23]

Hetherington shows us that soldiers are human beings too. His images are anti-fanaticist. The photographs in *Infidel* are shot through with love. There are some visceral images of combat – one with the eyes redacted, at the family's request – but for the most part the focus is on the soldiers at work and at play as they make a home

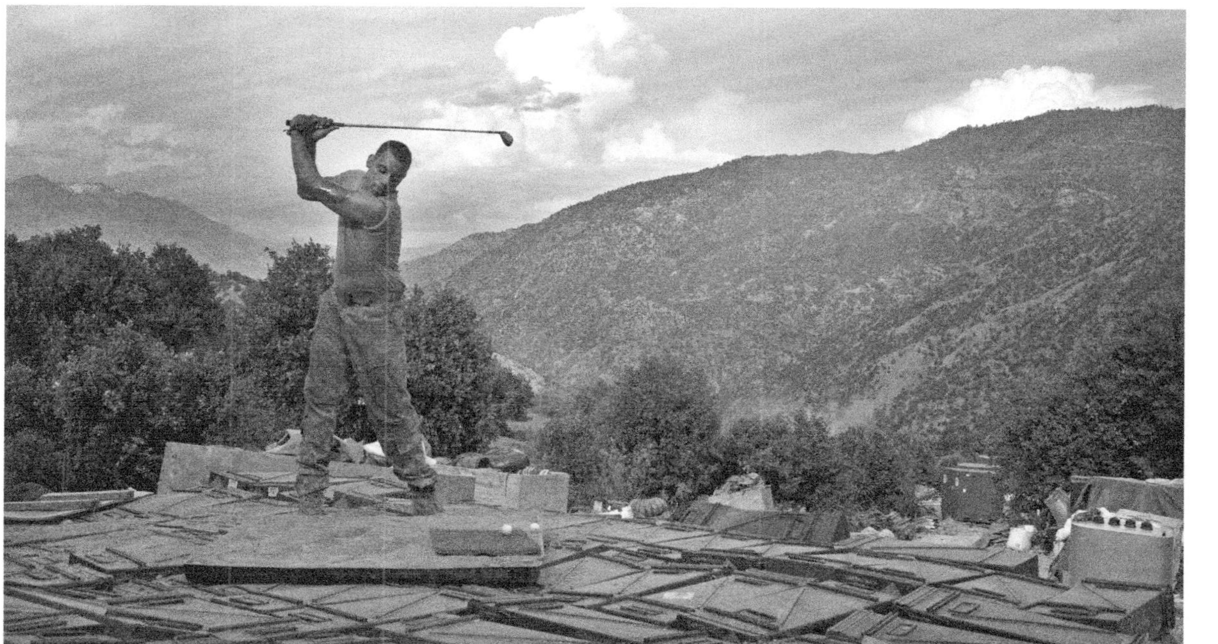

Figure 4.1
Tim Hetherington, *Restrepo*, 2008
AFGHANISTAN. Korengal Valley, Kunar Province. April 2008. Jones practices his golf swing while at the main KOP firebase in the valley. Soldiers spend about two weeks at the Restrepo outpost before coming back to the main KOP base where they can get a hot shower and call their family.

© Tim Hetherington / Magnum Photos

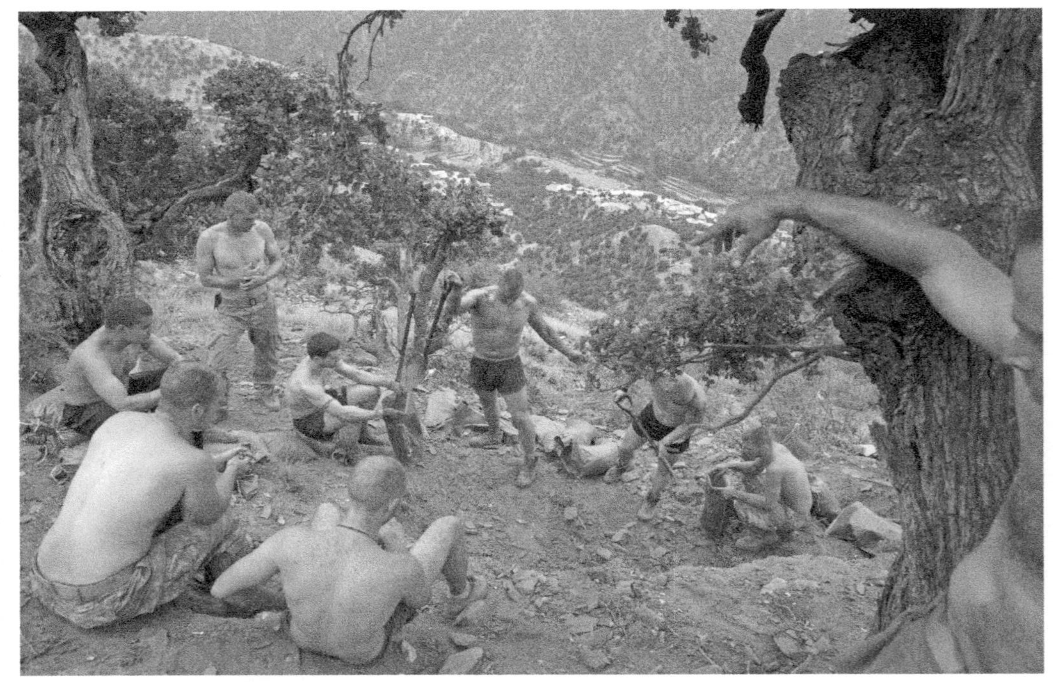

Figure 4.2
Tim Hetherington, *Restrepo*, 2008
AFGHANISTAN. Korengal Valley, Kunar Province. June 2008. Men from Second Platoon dig earth to use as sand bags to reinforce parts of the Restrepo bunker.
© Tim Hetherington / Magnum Photos

of Outpost Restrepo.[24] Strangeness and ordinariness commingle. One bizarrely beautiful image – reminiscent of *M.A.S.H.* (1970) – captures a soldier practising his golf swing, as if on a driving range, complete with mat and golf balls, perched on a small mountain of cartridge boxes, framed against a panorama of the Korengal. Golf, surely, is the triumph of the infidel.

Restrepo, the movie, is really an elegy to Restrepo, the man, and Restrepo, the mission. If the reportage trumps the fiction, then the documentary trumps the feature film, as the work of Laura Poitras serves to demonstrate (see Chapter 5). As Sue Halpern has observed, '*Restrepo* is everything *The Hurt Locker* is not: authentic, unsentimental, modest, nuanced.'[25] In documentary terms, it is fly-on-the-wall (or perhaps the helmet), filmed in close-up, often shakily, like a home movie or an amateur video. Wherever the men go, we go. We live it with them. This *cinéma vérité* is interspersed with interviews, after the fact, in which the soldiers reflect on what they have been through. The interviews, too, are filmed in close-up; the camera remains glued to their faces even when they fall silent. Indeed, it is the silent film that is often the most eloquent, as the muscles work, wordlessly, and the memories go off like depth charges under the skin. *Restrepo* is in every sense the face of battle.

As for the mission, the larger question remains. In one of his last acts before being fired, General Stanley McChrystal ordered all American forces out of the Korengal Valley in 2010. The Korengal was untenable and unwinnable.

So was Afghanistan.

Notes

1. Tim O'Brien, 'How to Tell a True War Story', in *The Things They Carried* (New York: Penguin, 1991), p. 90.
2. Sebastian Junger, *War* (London: Fourth Estate, 2010), p. 226.
3. Junger, *War*, p. 136.
4. 'I just can't hack it in The World,' a half-crazed, pill-popping Lurp (Long-Range Reconnaissance Patrolman) tells Michael Herr in *Dispatches* (London: Picador, 1978). Herr's work was hailed by John le Carré as 'the best book I have ever read on men and war in our time'.
5. Junger, *War*, pp. 233–4.
6. Junger, *War*, pp. 60, 235.
7. Junger, *War*, p. 57.
8. O'Brien, 'The Things They Carried', in *The Things They Carried*, pp. 20–1. The trope can be traced back to Graham Greene – 'she carried

her responsibilities carefully like crockery across the hot yard', a celebrated line from *The Power and the Glory* (1940) – and presumably further. *The Things They Carried* is avowedly 'a work of fiction', as it declares on the title page, but plainly one which gains from authentic experience. 'This book is lovingly dedicated to the men of Alpha Company, and in particular to Jimmy Cross, Norman Bowker, Rat Kiley, Mitchell Sanders, Henry Dobbins, and Kiowa.' In other words, O'Brien was there; he was one of them.

9. Junger, *War*, pp. 74–5.
10. Lord Moran, *The Anatomy of Courage* (London: Constable, 1945), p. 19. This passage, truncated, is used as an epigraph to Junger's book. It is also applied to himself. '"It's okay to be scared," Moreno said to me, loud enough for everyone else to hear, "you just don't want to *show* it . . .".' *War*, p. 74.
11. Often it has coercive or punitive connotations. In the war on terror, 'smoking' or softening up detainees was standard practice, prior to interrogation. As one soldier put it: '[The Military Intelligence officer] said he wanted the PUCs [Persons Under Control] so fatigued, so smoked, so demoralized that they want to cooperate.' See Alex Danchev, *On Art and War and Terror* (Edinburgh: Edinburgh University Press, 2011), p. 220.
12. Junger, *War*, pp. 76–7.
13. Junger, *War*, pp. 161–2.
14. Junger, *War*, p. 121.
15. McMaster's review is in *Survival* 52 (2010), pp. 210–12. See also Philip Caputo, 'Sebastian Junger's War', *Washington Post*, 9 May 2010.
16. Junger, *War*, p. 239.
17. The last line of 'September 1, 1939', in W. H. Auden, *Another Time* (New York: Random House, 1940), a poem he later repudiated.
18. David Finkel, *The Good Soldiers* (London: Atlantic, 2009), p. 115; Herr, *Dispatches*, p. 14.
19. Jim Frederick, *Black Hearts* (London: Macmillan, 2010), p. 7.
20. Geoff Dyer, 'The Moral Art of War', in *Working the Room* (London: Canongate, 2010), pp. 243–56.
21. Tim Hetherington, *Infidel* (London: Boot, 2010), pp. 15–16.
22. See Junger's interview with Andrew Pulver, 'I got out of war when Tim died', *Guardian*, 11 October 2013.
23. Susie Linfield, *The Cruel Radiance* (Chicago: Chicago University Press, 2010), p. 202.
24. See Hetherington, *Infidel*, pp. 180, 238.
25. Sue Halpern, 'Brotherhood', *New York Review of Books*, 19 August 2010. For a broader consideration of the cinema and the war on terror, see Danchev, *On Art and War and Terror*, ch. 9.

5

Trouble Makers:
Laura Poitras and the Problem of Dissent

Trouble in transit, got through the roadblock
We blended in with the crowd
We got computers, we're tapping phone lines
I know that ain't allowed

Talking Heads[1]

Most of us can say with some justice that we were good workmen. Is it equally true to say that we were good citizens?

Marc Bloch[2]

All change in history, all advance, comes from the nonconformists. If there had been no trouble makers, no dissenters, we should still be living in caves.

A. J. P. Taylor[3]

Laura Poitras is a trouble maker. She is also a filmmaker. She has the unusual distinction of achieving professional recognition in both fields. As the primary contact and conduit for the whistleblower Edward Snowden, the subject of her latest documentary, *Citizenfour* (2014), her status as trouble maker is inextricably intertwined with her status as filmmaker: her preoccupations or vocations have merged. For her recent work she has been garlanded with a MacArthur Fellowship, a George Polk Award for national security reporting, and a Pulitzer Prize for Public Service. In 2016 she has an exhibition at the Whitney Museum of American Art in New York; to be more precise, 'an installation of immersive environments using materials, footage and information that builds on themes she has been exploring in her film making, including NSA [National Security Agency] surveillance and post-9/11 America'.[4] Poitras has her finger on the pulse of post-9/11 America. The Academy Award was only a matter of time. The Academy was bold – she won for *Citizenfour*.

She had been nominated before, for *My Country, My Country*

75

(2006), the best documentary yet made about the Iraq War. As if to coincide with that nomination, she received another. She was placed on a terrorist watch list by the United States government. The central watch list is called the Terrorist Identities Datamart Environment (TIDE). It is kept by the National Counterterrorism Center; the NSA, the CIA, the FBI and other members of the intelligence community can all nominate individuals to be added to it. Evidently there are at least two subsidiary lists relating to air travel: a no-fly list, of those who are not allowed to fly into or out of the country, and a selectee list, of those who are earmarked for additional inspection and interrogation. As Poitras reveals in *Citizenfour*, there are said to be 1.2 million people on various stages of the watch list, a figure that shocked even Snowden.[5] She herself had the privilege of being a selectee. Federal agents would stop and question her as she was entering or leaving the United States. The same thing happened in other countries. In Vienna, she relates, 'I sort of befriended the security guy. I asked what was going on. He said: "You're flagged. You have a threat score that is off the Richter scale. You are at 400 out of 400." I said: "Is this a scoring system that works throughout all of Europe, or is this an American scoring system?" He said: "No, this is your government that has this and has told us to stop you."'[6]

In the US, the questioning was aggressive. Her notes and receipts were rifled, and sometimes copied; on one occasion her equipment was confiscated. Once, when she asserted her First Amendment right not to answer questions about her work, she was told, 'If you don't answer our questions, we'll find our answers on your electronics.'[7] She gave as good as she got, taking names and recording questions (until deprived of writing materials), protesting her treatment, writing to members of Congress, and submitting Freedom of Information requests. Over time, she went to ever greater lengths to protect herself and her data, leaving her notebooks overseas with friends or in safe deposit boxes, wiping her computers and mobile phones clean, taking elaborate precautions with her digital security. Her protestations and representations came to nothing. Altogether, she says, she was detained on at least forty occasions between 2006 and 2012, often at gun point, without explanation. Poitras is resilient – and not given to self-dramatization – but the endless stop and search felt like a violation. She let off steam to the investigative reporter Peter Maass. 'When did that universe begin, that people are put on a list and are never told and are stopped for six years?

I have no idea why they did it. It's the complete suspension of due process. I've been told nothing, I've been asked nothing, and I've done nothing. It's like Kafka. Nobody ever tells you what the accusation is.'[8] The arbitrary nature of the proceedings of *The Trial* (1925) corresponds eerily to the proceedings of the war on terror. 'Someone must have been telling lies about Joseph K., for without having done anything wrong he was arrested one fine morning.'[9]

With Laura P., it did not come to that. After six years, Poitras had had enough. She feared not so much for herself as for her material: her documents and her films. She took two drastic steps. She allowed her friend Glenn Greenwald to write about her case – which was a little like letting a highly trained attack dog off the leash – and she moved to Berlin. No sooner had Greenwald's article appeared in *Salon*, in 2012, than the airport interrogations stopped, as suddenly as they had begun.[10] In Berlin, Poitras came in from the cold – a nice historical reversal. She joined a community of dissident expatriates, including Jacob Appelbaum, a 'hacktivist' from WikiLeaks, who appears in *Citizenfour*; but she walked by herself. In Berlin, she regained her composure and her customary self-containment. 'Let's be honest,' she told George Packer of *The New Yorker*, an old ally. 'If I had darker skin, or was carrying a different passport, the cast of guilt, the shadow, would go a lot longer.'[11] Nevertheless, her life had changed. For Laura Poitras, security is a lived experience. Privacy is as much an instinct as a cause. She is a very private person, but she will never again be a truly private citizen. Politically and electronically, she is a marked woman, a target of the national surveillance state. Radicalization is something she understands from the inside.

Like Errol Morris (see Chapter 12), but in a different voice, she is also a public intellectual. She speaks of herself as a documentarian – a tribe of rootless cosmopolitans, strong on professional ethics and civic obligations – but she is prepared to embrace another identity. In 2014 an interviewer asked her what prompted her to become a dissenter. She replied:

It was a response to historical circumstances, particularly the build-up to the Iraq War and the prison at Guantánamo. I thought that there was a moral drift, that we'd look back on post-9/11 America as a dark chapter in US history. To have a prison where people are sent without charges, and then engaging in a pre-emptive war against a country that had nothing to do with 9/11 – that seemed like a frightening precedent, that we're going to attack a country because we think it might cause us harm in the future. I felt that these were dark times, that I felt compelled to say something about it, and that as a documentarian I had skills that would help me channel my impressions and thoughts.

At the very least, I would create a historical record. I don't know if my work changed anyone's opinion. The Iraq War continued for a long time. Guantánamo is still open. But I wanted to express something about a drift away from the rule of law and basic principles of democracy, to document what was happening. I thought I was choosing to make a film about the Iraq War or Guantánamo. When I finished *My Country, My Country*, the film on Iraq, I was shocked that Guantánamo was still open. It was 2005 when I knew I'd take a broader look at post-9/11 America, and that it would probably occupy me for a long time.[12]

The starting point for the film on Iraq was a coruscating article by George Packer on the American occupation of that country, 'War after the War', sub-titled 'What Washington doesn't see in Iraq'.[13] Packer's work is a mosaic of many tragedies, large and small, of which that experience is composed. What caught Poitras's eye was the tragedy of Captain John Prior, a rifle company commander on his first real-world deployment, as he calls it, who was put in charge of a patch of Baghdad: the rectangle of Zafaraniya, a largely Shiite slum in the south of the city, home to some 250,000 people. His mission was to improve the infrastructure of his patch, and at the same time to guarantee its security. He was also responsible for sewage disposal throughout the area occupied by his entire battalion, an area with a population of half a million people. Prior is a dedicated officer and a decent man. He hopes to make a career in the military. He wants to do something for his country and for the country he occupied: he wants to do good. He had mastered counter-insurgency. He had studied hearts and minds. He had read some history. He was a stranger to the real world. He was bewildered in Babylon. He was not trained in nation building, civil affairs, or sewage disposal.

Prior is well-intentioned. If he is not quite Pyle, the original Quiet American of Graham Greene's creation, there is a certain family resemblance.[14] His mission is beyond him, but he has an impregnable belief in the advertisement of American rectitude. Pyle talked self-righteously of 'clean hands'. In his own idiom Prior says much the same. He is nothing if not hard-working. By day, he chairs the local council and oversees reconstruction projects. By night, he raids homes and searches for suspected militiamen. The raids are fruitless; they succeed only in stoking resentment. One vexatious night, Prior's translator turns to Packer and says: 'Like Vietnam.' Fifty years on, Saigon spoke eloquently to Babylon.

Packer asked Prior whether his night work threatened to undo the good accomplished by his day work. 'He didn't think so: as the sewage started to flow and the schools got fixed up, Iraqis would view Americans the way the Americans see themselves – as people trying to help.' Packer continues:

But Prior was no soft-shelled humanitarian. He called himself a foreign-policy realist. Fixing the sewer system in Zafaraniya, he believed, was an essential part of the war on terror. Terrorists depended on millions of sympathizers who believed that America was evil and Americans only wanted Middle East oil. 'But we come here and we're honest, trustworthy, we're caring, we're compassionate,' Prior said. 'We're interested in them. We're interested in fixing their lives. Not because we have to, but because we can, because we can be benevolent, because we *are* benevolent.'

Poitras took leave to doubt it. Packer's question served to crystallize her own thinking. Prior's predicament exemplified the contradictions inherent in the American project as she saw it. It was those contradictions that she set out to film.

In June 2004 she went to Baghdad and embedded with a civil affairs unit responsible for helping Iraqi officials organize the country's first democratic elections. Courtesy of the military, she could move around relatively freely, but she was frustrated to find that the civil affairs unit was largely confined to the sanctuary of the Green Zone. Soon after she arrived, she went to film an inspection of the notorious Abu Ghraib prison. There she encountered an Iraqi doctor, Riyadh al-Adhadh, who was compiling complaints, medical and procedural, from the prisoners. Dr Riyadh, a Sunni from the Adhamiya district of Baghdad, turns out to be a voluble character and a public-spirited citizen. 'This is not Vietnam,' he admonishes his American military minders, on camera, apropos the flattening of Fallujah. 'This is a new century.' Dr Riyadh is a brave man. Adhamiya is a hotbed of anti-American sentiment and insurgent activities; in his community, participation in the political process is tantamount to collaboration. Nonetheless, he is determined to stand for election to the Baghdad Provincial Council. Already an active member of the local council, where nine of his colleagues have been killed, he is not enamoured of the existing order. 'We are an occupied country with a puppet government,' he observes succinctly.

Poitras had found her subject. For the next eight months she embedded instead with Dr Riyadh, who courageously invited her to stay at his house, and to visit his clinic. *My Country, My Country* is a chronicle of that experience. It is an intimate film amid the carnage, piercingly human and deeply poignant. It is also an essential document of the war (and the war after the war). Like all of her films, it is a self-effacing treatment. Poitras aims for a kind of inter-subjective understanding. The documentarian and the doctor are both trouble makers, in their fashion; both risk their lives for their principles – for their practice – and so too do the doctor's wife and his six daughters. All of them know this full well. The women of the house are no pushovers. 'Politics are not good for you,' Dr Riyadh's wife tells him briskly. 'You do more good as a doctor.'

Poitras is her own camerawoman. Her modus operandi is disarming. Typically, she holds the camera at waist height and looks down at the viewfinder, rather than hiding behind the lens. 'The camera doesn't have to be a barrier,' she believes. 'It's a witness.' Her films are eye-witness accounts: camera-eye witness accounts. She is intensely present, yet unobtrusive; even the filming is unobtrusive. The code (or the ethic) may owe something to the exemplary documentary filmmaker Frederick Wiseman, whose *métier* is the study of institutions and their inmates, and whose signature is a conscientious austerity and simplicity, as David Thomson puts it, eschewing interviews, jump-cuts, narrative or music.[15] The emphasis is on scenes, fades, naturalism and actuality: in Poitras's words, 'people, in real time, confronting life decisions'. Unlike Wiseman, she concentrates on the inmates, but her films are also investigations of institutions of various kinds, above all the state, the consequences of its coercive power, and its moral purpose.

The human predicament is minutely observed – she sticks close to her protagonists, as she says – but she manages to retain a space for reflection and disputation, an openness, at once ethical and intellectual. Poitras is as empathetic as she is *engagée*. She is willing to listen. There is a stillness to her camerawork whilst she does just that. She encourages us to do the same. The effort is worthwhile. Her films are full of unforced insights. In *My Country, My Country*, Dr Riyadh's oldest daughter shows Poitras the images of torture and abuse from Abu Ghraib on her personal computer.[16] She goes out to vote, in spite of all, and comes back singing the Iraqi national anthem. The title of the film is drawn from the opening words of that anthem. For Poitras, as perhaps for Dr Riyadh, *My Country, My Country* is inescapably double-edged.

Her next film was to be about Guantánamo. Poitras had the idea of documenting the reintegration of a former inmate who had been found innocent and returned to his home country. She went to Yemen, the home country of many inmates of Guantánamo. On her second day in the capital, Sanaa, she had another extraordinary encounter. She was introduced to a taxi-driver called Nasser al-Bahri, whose nom de guerre was Abu Jandal. Once upon a time, Abu Jandal had been Osama bin Laden's bodyguard, and his 'emir of hospitality', in Afghanistan (c.1997–2000). What is more, his brother-in-law was exactly what Poitras thought she was looking for. Salim Hamdan, Osama bin Laden's driver, had spent six years in Guantánamo, where he became both a test case and a *cause célèbre*, as the locus of a legal challenge to the power of the state in the matter of the military commissions (the case of *Hamdan* v. *Rumsfeld*), and the first person to be tried under the hastily assembled Military Tribunals Act (2006). Salim Hamdan was eventually convicted of providing military support to Al-Qaeda, but acquitted of terrorist conspiracy. He was transferred to Yemen in 2008 and reunited with his family the following year. In 2012 his conviction was overturned on appeal. Salim Hamdan was famous, and victorious, but also religious. He had maintained a dignified silence throughout; in fact he had remonstrated with his interfering brother-in-law for talking too much.

Salim Hamdan would be a difficult subject. Abu Jandal, on the other hand, was a gift. He was garrulous in the extreme. He was a plausible liar (as Poitras clearly shows). He was a charismatic ex-jihadi who had supped with Sheikh Osama, as he called him, and claimed to know personally all nineteen of the 9/11 hijackers. He had fought in Bosnia, Somalia, Afghanistan. He had grown tired of fighting. He had been troubled by Sheikh Osama's pledge of loyalty to Mullah Omar, the Taliban leader in Afghanistan. He had been incarcerated and interrogated. He had been through a government rehabilitation programme. He was counselling young Yemenis who might sympathize with Al-Qaeda. He was worried about his children, one of whom had a bone disease. He had not entirely given up hope of revolution against the evil empire, the American colossus. He was a kind of jack-in-the-box. He loved to perform; it was difficult to tell when he was performing and when he was not. He was a bad character, or at any rate an unreliable one. 'He was never who you thought he was,' as Poitras remarked. This was not at all the story she had been looking for; it was a story that made her nervous, but it was not a story she felt she could ignore. She decided to change tack. She rented an apartment in Sanaa and asked Abu Jandal to install a camera on the dashboard of his taxi, so that he could be filmed plying his trade, dissimulating with inquisitive passengers, and philosophizing, as was his wont. He readily agreed. Abu Jandal is the star of *The Oath* (2010). Salim Hamdan is the ghost.

The Oath is ambiguous and unsettling, as George Packer has observed. The chief protagonist has none of the conspicuous humanity of Dr Riyadh. Abu Jandal is very slippery, a grey zone all of his own. As a documentarian, Poitras is plotless. She is suspicious of the constraints of plot, its perfidious consolations. 'Plot is so relentless. It's totally unforgiving, and it can also be simplifying. It can provide resolution where there should be none. It can provide false catharsis.' For much of this film it seems that she has lost the plot, possibly by design. Towards the end, however, a moral unfolds, or perhaps a message. Immediately after 9/11, we learn, Abu Jandal was interrogated in Yemen by Ali Soufan, a Lebanese-American FBI special agent. At the time, Soufan was something of a rarity in the FBI – an Arabic speaker (one of eight), a student of International Relations, a subtle mind, and a sophisticated interrogator. (In the course of his interrogation of Abu Jandal, he noted that his adversary declined some pastries, because he was diabetic; the next night, he brought him some sugarless wafers, a courtesy acknowledged by Abu Jandal.) As chief investigator of the sinking of the USS *Cole* the previous year, Soufan knew as much as anyone about Al-Qaeda at that juncture. A detailed account of his interrogation of Abu Jandal was published by Lawrence Wright in 2006.[17] It demonstrated beyond doubt that Soufan got Abu Jandal to talk – and not merely to talk, but to divulge actionable intelligence, the interrogator's holy grail – without recourse to any 'enhanced interrogation techniques' or coercion of any kind, but rather by playing on weakness, flattery, cunning and moral suasion. In the film Soufan underlines the point: using lawful procedures he gained vital intelligence – the kind of intelligence that torture does not yield.[18] For Poitras, this was the key. 'Maintaining those kinds of principles, you can actually get results, if the end goal is de-escalation of violence or de-radicalization.' That is the message of *The Oath*.

The third in the trilogy of her investigations of American power and purpose after 9/11 was intended to bring it home, in more ways than one. Poitras was interested in domestic surveillance and the resistance to it. Surveillance and resistance are not easy subjects for the filmmaker to engage: there is no there there.[19] Various strategies have been proposed to make visible the invisible. Trevor Paglen, for example, takes ultra-long-distance photographs of national security sites, facilities invisible to the naked eye, or impenetrable to the democratic gaze; some of his images of the Intelligence Community Comprehensive National Cybersecurity Initiative Data Center, an expansionist development in Utah, are incorporated in *Citizenfour*. Poitras for her part focuses on the human. 'The historian is like the ogre of the fairy tale,' wrote Marc Bloch. 'Where he smells human flesh, there he finds his quarry.'[20] As with the historian, so with the documentarian. She began filming Julian Assange, in England; Glenn Greenwald, in Rio de Janeiro; Jacob Appelbaum, in Berlin; and a retired cryptanalyst and mathematician named William Binney, in Maryland, home of the National Security Agency.

Binney had worked for the NSA man and boy. In that community he was a legendary figure; he has been described as one of the best analysts in history. He resigned as Technical Leader for Intelligence in October 2001, soon after he had concluded that the NSA was heading in an unethical direction. Binney was outraged at the NSA's failure to foil the 9/11 plot. He believed that he and his team had developed a system called ThinThread that could solve the agency's basic problem – it was overwhelmed by the amount of digital data it was collecting. ThinThread was rejected in favour of a rival approach, unwisely christened Trailblazer, built by private contractors. In 2006, Trailblazer was abandoned as a $1.2 billion flop. Meanwhile, in the wake of 9/11, and under pressure from the White House, the directorate of the NSA sanctioned an extensive programme of warrantless domestic surveillance. The programme was developed in secret. Binney was not 'read in', but some of his people were; from the reports he received, he became convinced that it employed a bastardized version of his brainchild, stripped of privacy controls. Binney was all in favour of monitoring, code breaking, data mining and signals intelligence – he had spent a professional lifetime trying to perfect such techniques – but he was fundamentally opposed to what he saw as illegal, unconstitutional, unaccountable, unjustifiable and indiscriminate spying on American citizens, not to mention the corruption and malfeasance that he thought had led to this debacle.

So did a copper-bottomed patriot and doyen of the secret world turn whistleblower. William Binney is an unlikely trouble maker, but an unbeatable source. He is old enough to remember Watergate and 'Deep Throat' (later revealed to be Mark Felt), the source for Carl Bernstein and Bob Woodward, the investigative reporters of the

Washington Post. He alludes to this history in a cameo appearance in *Citizenfour.* The lineage of dissent is well-learned by the dissenters.

Poitras made an Op-Doc about him, *The Program* (2012), for the *New York Times.*[21] Op-Docs are shorts, the filmic equivalent of op-eds. Binney explains his position, with sweet reason, making light of the risks he is taking – he mentions in passing a raid on his house, by heavily armed FBI agents, one of whom pointed a rifle at his head as he emerged from the shower. It was left to Poitras to spell out the seriousness of his situation in an accompanying article: 'He is among a group of NSA whistleblowers, including Thomas A. Drake, who have risked everything – their freedom, livelihoods and personal relationships – to warn Americans about the dangers of NSA domestic spying.'[22]

The Program became a taster. One of its many online viewers was Edward Snowden, who was already familiar with Poitras's work and something of her personal history. In January 2013 he emailed her, anonymously, using the alias Citizenfour. 'I am a senior member of the intelligence community,' he told her, with pardonable exaggeration. 'This won't be a waste of your time.' He asked for her encryption key. She gave it to him. She was hooked. So was he.

They embarked on a kind of crypto-courtship. Each wanted to establish the bona fides of the other: to find a basis of trust. Poitras was afraid of entrapment. 'I don't know if you are legit, crazy or trying to entrap me,' she wrote. Snowden (still anonymous) was afraid of exposure and arrest, or worse, before he had even begun. He was also afraid of being ignored. 'I'm not going to ask you anything,' he replied. 'I'm just going to tell you things.'[23] He needed Poitras, in order to do what he had to do; he knew that he would have to convince her to take him seriously. He had already tried and failed with Greenwald, who had not troubled to install the necessary encryption software for them to communicate securely, despite repeated nudges from Snowden. Poitras was sound on security; tradecraft was meat and drink to her. Still she seemed suspicious. Ultimately, that was all to the good, as Snowden recalled:

We came to a point in the verification and vetting process when I discovered that Laura was more suspicious of me than I was of her, and I'm famously paranoid. The combination of her experience and her exacting focus on detail and process gave her a natural talent for security, and that's a refreshing trait to discover in someone who is likely to come under intense scrutiny in the future, as normally one would have to work very hard to get them to take the risks seriously. With that putting me at my ease, it became easier to open up without fearing the invested trust would be mishandled, and I think it's the only way she ever managed to get me on camera. I personally hate cameras and being recorded, but at some point in the working process, I realized I was unconsciously trusting her not to hang me even with my naturally unconsidered remarks. She's good.[24]

Poitras was in deep, and she knew it. 'It clearly pulled me in in every way – emotionally, psychologically. Unlike my previous films, this was somebody I had built a dialogue with, and wanted to meet. Because I cared.' Much to her surprise, after three months of emailing, Citizenfour informed her that he would not seek to remain anonymous once the story broke and his treasure-trove of documents were in the pipeline to the public domain. 'I'm not cleaning the metadata,' he wrote. 'I hope you will paint a target on my back and tell the world I did this on my own.' Her immediate response was that she wanted to meet and that she wanted to film. Citizenfour was horrified. 'It's too dangerous, and it's not about me – I don't want to be the story.' 'Like it or not,' she replied, 'you're going to be the story, so you might as well get your voice in.' That argument carried the day. 'After that,' she told Packer, 'I became a filmmaker.'

And yet it was not quite as simple as that, as Poitras herself clearly recognized. The Snowden case, or rather the Poitras case, is the paradigm case of the participant-observer. Like it or not, she had become an actor in her own drama. Indeed, she was in some sense the moving force – the director – without any idea of the identity or proclivity of her pseudonymous leading man. This gave rise to a number of urgent questions, practical and ethical. Unlike Michael Moore, for example, Poitras never films herself conducting interviews or interacting with others; that would violate the code of the documentarian. When she filmed Snowden she would have need of an accomplice. Happily, Snowden himself was of the same mind. He urged her to find a collaborator to publish the documents and explicate their meaning – not a simple task. His preferred choice for this key role was Greenwald, an inspired choice, as it turned out, despite the technical hiccoughs.

The rest of the story reads like le Carré crossed with Kafka, as the *New York Times* put it. Snowden transited from Hawaii to Hong Kong, with four laptops and little else, apart from nearly two million highly classified documents – a world record. Poitras recruited Greenwald. Greenwald enlisted the *Guardian*. (He was then a *Guardian* columnist, semi-detached.) Shadowed by Ewen MacAskill, the paper's respected Washington correspondent, they decamped to

Hong Kong. En route they browsed in the cache of documents that Citizenfour had entrusted to Poitras. Among them was an impassioned self-declaration, written specially for them. It concluded as follows:

> Many will malign me for failing to engage in national relativism, to look away from [my] society's problems toward distant, external evils for which we hold neither authority nor responsibility, but citizenship carries with it a duty to first police one's own government before seeking to correct others. Here, now, at home, we suffer a government that only grudgingly allows limited oversight, and refuses accountability when crimes are committed. . . . When officials at the highest levels of power, to specifically include the Vice President [Dick Cheney], are found on investigation to have personally directed such a criminal enterprise, what should happen? If you believe that investigation should be stopped, its results classified above-top-secret in a special 'Exceptionally Controlled Information' compartment called STLW (STELLARWIND), any future investigations ruled out on the principle that holding those who abuse power to account is against the national interest, that we must 'look forward, not backward' [as President Obama said], and rather than closing the illegal program you would expand it with even more authorities, you will be welcome in the halls of America's power, for that is what came to be, and I am releasing the documents that prove it.
>
> I understand that I will be made to suffer for my actions, and that the return of this information to the public marks my end. I will be satisfied if the federation of secret law, unequal pardon, and irresistible executive powers that rule the world that I love are revealed for even an instant. If you seek to help, join the open source community and fight to keep the spirit of the press alive and the internet free. I have been to the darkest corners of government, and what they fear is light.
>
> Edward Joseph Snowden[25]

Characteristically, Snowden gave them precise instructions for their rendezvous: a conference room on the third floor of the Mira Hotel, by a plastic alligator; he would be carrying a Rubik's Cube (unsolved). They were to have an exchange about the hotel food, and then to follow him. After a certain stutter – they were too early, he was too young – they arrived in his room. Without further ado, Poitras proceeded to set up her camera. In a matter of minutes she was ready. 'I'm going to begin filming now,' she announced quietly, and so it began.

She filmed for some twenty hours, over eight days. This is the core of *Citizenfour*: the encounter with Snowden in hiding; making and breaking the story in the same breathless moment. In short order

Greenwald produced a series of incendiary articles, and Poitras produced a trailer, *NSA Whistleblower Edward Snowden*, a video on the *Guardian* website.[26] It is this extraordinary set-up – people, in real time, confronting life decisions, with a vengeance – that makes the full-length film so compelling: at once thriller and fable; a chamber piece (a bedchamber piece) and a political event of tremendous significance; a model of *cinéma vérité*, and in its own peculiar way almost an ideal speech situation. *Citizenfour* is riveting. So is Edward Snowden. He sits on the bed, tense but collected. He speaks in sentences, sometimes in paragraphs. He is cogent, principled, realistic, modest. There are flashes of wit, self-knowledge, even self-irony. The modus operandi is as understated as ever. Poitras's empathy does not fail her: it matches Snowden's integrity.[27]

She was surely right to intuit that he was genuine, in every sense, notwithstanding persistent attempts to demonize, psychologize, or trivialize, fitting him for the standard repertoire of stock characters for which dissenters are always fitted: traitor, narcissist, 'useful idiot'.[28] Motivations are often tangled, as Dostoevsky observes in *Crime and Punishment*: 'Sometimes actions are performed very skilfully, most cleverly, but the aims of the actions and their origin, are confused, and depend on various morbid influences.'[29] That may be true of Snowden, as of others, but there is no sign of it. 'If there was a Zen prize for whistleblowers, Snowden would win without trying,' as Andrew O'Hagan has remarked: 'he checks and labels everything, he thinks out the moral, he cross-references and relates the material to possible future outcomes. Most of all: he let his name come out for the sake of veracity and to put a human face to the leaks, then he aimed to disappear and say little and profit nowhere, letting the story be bigger than him.'[30] Like Daniel Ellsberg, one of his exemplars, he depended on the *moral* proposition. 'Americans must look past options, briefings, pros and cons, to see what is being done in their name, and to refuse to be accomplices,' Ellsberg argued, Snowden-like, in 1971. 'They must recognize, and force the Congress and President to act upon, the *moral* proposition that the US must stop killing people in Indochina.'[31]

In truth, trouble makers like Laura Poitras and Edward Snowden have done the state some service. Dissenters are model citizens. As A. J. P. Taylor and J. M. Coetzee remind us, they are traduced at the time, and vindicated by posterity.[32] 'After all,' another great dissenter has written, 'we have gotten used to regarding as *valor* only valor in war (or the kind that's needed for flying in outer space), the kind that jingle-jangles with medals. We have forgotten another concept of valor – *civil valor*. And that's all our society needs, just that, just that, just that! That's all we need and that's exactly what we haven't got.'[33]

Notes

1. Talking Heads, 'Life During Wartime', on the album *Fear of Music* (1979).
2. Marc Bloch, *Strange Defeat* [1948], trans. Gerard Hopkins (New York: Norton, 1999), p. 173.
3. A. J. P. Taylor, *The Trouble Makers* (London: Hamilton, 1957), p. 14.
4. Whitney Museum of American Art, http://whitney.org/Exhibitions/ LauraPoitras (last accessed 10 January 2015).
5. Further information on the watch list has since been divulged by *The Intercept*, drawing on more leaked documents. Jeremy Scahill and Ryan Devereaux, 'Barack Obama's secret terrorist-tracking system, by the numbers', *The Intercept*, 8 May 2014, https://firstlook.org/ theintercept/2014/08/05/watch-commander (last accessed 20 January 2015). On the efficacy or otherwise of such procedures, see Mattathias Schwartz, 'The Whole Haystack', *The New Yorker*, 26 January 2015.
6. Peter Maass, 'How Laura Poitras helped Snowden spill his secrets', *New York Times*, 13 August 2013.
7. Laura Poitras, 'The program', *New York Times*, 22 August 2012.
8. Maass, 'Laura Poitras'. Maass speculates that her selectee status may relate to unfounded accusations about her prior knowledge of an attack on American soldiers while filming in Baghdad in 2004, or to money she sent to the subject of her film, suspected (groundlessly) of insurgent activities, when his family fled the civil war in 2006.
9. Franz Kafka, *The Trial* [1925], trans. Willa and Edwin Muir, in *The Collected Novels of Franz Kafka* (London: Penguin, 1988), p. 9, the celebrated opening sentence. See Alex Danchev, *On Art and War and Terror* (Edinburgh: Edinburgh University Press, 2011), ch. 8.
10. Glenn Greenwald, 'US filmmaker repeatedly detained at border', *Salon. com*, 8 April 2012.
11. George Packer, 'The Holder of Secrets', *The New Yorker*, 20 October 2014. Unless otherwise indicated, subsequent quotations from Poitras come from her conversation in this profile.
12. Conor Friedersdorf, 'What the war on terror actually looks like: Laura Poitras on *Citizenfour*', *The Atlantic* (October 2014), http://www. theatlantic.com/politics/archive/2014/10/what-the-war-on-terror-actually-looks-like-laura-poitras-on-em-citizenfour-em/381749 (last accessed 10 January 2015).

13. George Packer, 'War after the War', *The New Yorker*, 24 November 2003, subsequently woven into a profound study of America in Iraq, *The Assassins' Gate* (London: Faber, 2006), ch. 7.

14. Graham Greene, *The Quiet American* [1955] (London: Vintage, 2004). Packer weighs the parallel in *Assassins' Gate*, p. 89.

15. David Thomson, 'Frederick Wiseman', *A Biographical Dictionary of Film* (London: Deutsch, 1994), pp. 817–18, a scintillating and sceptical assessment. Wiseman's first and most controversial film was *Titicut Follies* (1967), on the Bridgewater State Hospital for the criminally insane. His latest is *National Gallery* (2014).

16. On the images and their currency, see Danchev, *On Art and War and Terror*, ch. 9.

17. Lawrence Wright, 'The Agent', *The New Yorker*, 10 July 2006, a slice of his celebrated study of Al-Qaeda and the road to 9/11, *The Looming Tower* (London: Penguin, 2007), ch. 20. Poitras makes reference to Wright's account in her interview with Friedersdorf, 'Poitras on *Citizenfour*'.

18. For more on this issue, see Danchev, *On Art and War and Terror*, ch. 8.

19. Cf. Frank Möller and Rune S. Andersen, 'Engaging the limits of visibility: photography, security and surveillance', *Security Dialogue* 44 (2013), pp. 203–21, focusing on Simon Norfolk and Trevor Paglen.

20. Marc Bloch, *Apologie pour l'histoire, ou métier d'historien* (Paris: Colin, 1949), p. 4.

21. Laura Poitras, *The Program* (2012), http://www.nytimes.com/video /2012/08/22/opinion/100000001733041/the-program.html (last accessed 16 January 2015).

22. Poitras, 'The program'. The group consists of Binney, Drake, J. Kirk Wiebe and Edward Loomis: 'the NSA four'. Jane Mayer, 'The Secret Sharer', *The New Yorker*, 23 May 2011, sub-titled 'Is Thomas Drake an enemy of the state?', is a penetrating analysis of his case, which sheds light on all of them, Binney included – and on the punitive response of the Obama administration to whistleblowers.

23. The story is told in the well-informed instant history by Luke Harding, *The Snowden Files* (London: Faber, 2014); and in the first person by Glenn Greenwald, *No Place to Hide: Edward Snowden, the NSA and the Surveillance State* (London: Penguin, 2014), chs 1 and 2. Greenwald has his faults, and his detractors, but his book is an invaluable account of the Snowden affair by one of the main actors. Supplemented by his website (glenngreenwald.net), it is also a source-book of documents. For judicious critiques of his sometimes simplistic position on the issues, see David Cole, '*No Place to Hide* by Glenn Greenwald, on the NSA's sweeping efforts to know it all', *Washington Post*, 12 May 2014; and George Packer, 'Intoxicating Conviction', *Prospect* (June 2014), pp. 48–52.

24. 'Q & A: Edward Snowden speaks to Peter Maass', *New York Times*, 13 August 2013.

25. Reproduced in Greenwald, *No Place to Hide*, pp. 31–2.

26. Laura Poitras, *NSA Whistleblower Edward Snowden*, 9 June 2013, http://www.theguardian.com/world/video/2013/jun/09/nsa-whistleblo wer-edward-snowden-interview-video (last accessed 15 January 2015). Greenwald's opening salvo focused on dragnet collection calculated to outrage the American public: 'NSA collecting phone records of millions of Verizon customers daily', *Guardian*, 6 June 2013. They were also concerned to make the point that GCHQ is in some respects even more invasive, as *Citizenfour* underlines. See, for example, Ewen MacAskill et al., 'Mastering the internet: how GCHQ set out to spy on the world wide web', *Guardian*, 21 June 2013.

27. David Bromwich suggests something similar in 'The Question of Edward Snowden', *New York Review of Books*, 4 December 2014.

28. See, for example, Jeffrey Toobin, 'Edward Snowden is no Hero', *The New Yorker*, 10 June 2013; Nigel Inkster, 'The Snowden Revelations: Myths and Misapprehensions', *Survival* 56 (2014), pp. 51–60; and Loch K. Johnson (ed.), 'An *INS* Special Forum: Implications of the Snowden Leaks', *Intelligence and National Security* 29 (2014), pp. 793–810, in particular the contribution of Rose McDermott (pp. 802–4).

29. Fyodor Dostoevsky, *Crime and Punishment* [1866], trans. Jessie Coulson (Oxford: World's Classics, 1998), p. 217. Snowden read this book in Moscow, his next way station after Hong Kong.

30. Andrew O'Hagan, 'Text-Inspectors', *London Review of Books*, 25 September 2014.

31. Daniel Ellsberg, 'Laos: what Nixon is up to' [1971], reprinted in his *Papers on the War* (New York: Simon & Schuster, 1972), and quoted in his memoir *Secrets* (New York: Penguin, 2003), p. 355, another book on Snowden's Moscow reading list. The admiration is mutual. See the conversation between them, 'Daniel Ellsberg: Snowden kept his oath better than anyone in the NSA', *The Atlantic* (July 2014), http://www. theatlantic.com/politics/archive/2014/07/daniel-ellsberg-snowden-kept-his-oath-better-than-anyone-in-the-nsa/375031 (last accessed 15 January 2015).

32. Taylor, *Trouble Makers*, p. 16; J. M. Coetzee to Chelsea Manning, 2 December 2014, printed in *Guardian*, 17 December 2014.

33. Alexander Solzhenitsyn, trans. Thomas P. Whitney, *The Gulag Archipelago* (London: Harvill, 1974), parts I–II, pp. 461–2.

6

The Silage of History:
Anselm Kiefer and the Kieferworld

An original painter or an original writer follows the path of the oculist. Their painting or their prose acts upon us like a course of treatment which is not always agreeable. When it is over, the practitioner says to us: 'Now look.' And at this point the world (which was not created once and for all, but as often as an original artist is born) appears utterly different from the one we knew, but perfectly clear. . . . Such is the new and perishable universe that has just been created. It will last until the next geological catastrophe unleashed by a new painter or writer with an original view of the world.

Marcel Proust[1]

That geological catastrophe has Anselm Kiefer's name on it. Like all great artists, his work is his own, an untracked continent as yet unclaimed. Contrary to popular belief, it is given to artists, not politicians, to create a new world order. The Kieferworld is rich and strange, boundless and immersive, elemental and metaphysical. This artist traffics in fundamental truths. 'Art is an attempt to get to the very centre of truth,' affirms Kiefer. 'It never can, but it can get quite close.'[2]

There is something cataclysmic about the Kieferworld – heaven and earth take their chances in the rag and bone shop of the heart that is the artist's studio.[3] Its most striking quality is the procedure. Kiefer sees artworks as actions, as he says, and not as consummate creations.[4] In this material world the artworks are in the process of perpetual transformation. They slip and slide, corrode and erode. They age, and shed, and flake. They are weathered and distressed. Climate change comes indoors. Violence may be done to them, with an arsenal of weapons. They may or may not be happy in their skin. The time comes for them to leave the studio, but they are never really finished. In the Kieferworld, 'finish' is a misnomer. The dates of the works testify to an epic struggle: *Ash Flower (Aschenblume)*

(1983–97), for example, a characteristic blend of oil, emulsion, acrylic paint, clay, ash, earth and dried sunflower on canvas – canvas of continental proportions (over seven metres long and nearly four metres high). An installation made specially for the Royal Academy in London in 2014 brings home the sense of action and transformation, and the sheer physical presence of these stupendous works. *Ages of the World* (*Die Erdzeitalter*), summarized rather coyly in the exhibition catalogue as mixed media, is a kind of recapitulation; it seems to speak of last things. The installation filled a whole gallery. It was described there as part totem, part funeral pyre. One might add part pyramid, part tomb; part sacrifice, part pile of the artist's signature stuff. Awed visitors circled it, a little warily. The material is infused with meaning; the stuff tells stories. The Kieferworld elicits wonderment.

There is a place for belief in the Kieferworld view, belief in something above and beyond the featherless biped, but not a 'salvator' or saviour. His outlook is more mineral than spiritual. Painting is the stuff of life, and the stuff of life is painting. This is a well-thought out position. Kiefer is a thinker-painter, or rather a philosopher-painter. Like Cézanne – another law student turned artist – he is a mighty reader. In an almost biblical sense, the book is central to his practice. Books and their authors are Kiefer's interlocutors. The call and response can produce surprising results. Invited to respond to *The Cathedrals of France* (1914), a book by the sculptor Auguste Rodin, Kiefer produced a book of his own with the same title, combining studies of cathedrals with erotic watercolours: another speciality of the celebrated sculptor. One shameless sheet shows a lascivious nude with an erect cathedral in her lap – Rodin meets Magritte.

Kiefer makes books of his own (books of lead and books of words); he ransacks the pages of the poets for their wisdom. 'I think in images,' he told the assembled company, accepting the Peace Prize of the German Book Trade, in 2008. 'Poems help me do this. They are like buoys in the sea. I swim to them, from one to the next; in between, without them, I am lost.'[5]

The most sustained engagement is with the poems of Paul Celan (1920–70), entwined with those of Ingeborg Bachmann (1926–73), his lover, considered by Kiefer the greatest poet of the second half of the twentieth century. Celan's 'Deathfugue' ('Todesfuge') is now canonical. For Kiefer it is a foundational text, and an imperishable act of witness. Celan was nothing if not a moral witness (see Chapter 2). He grew up in Czernowitz in Bukovina. His parents disappeared

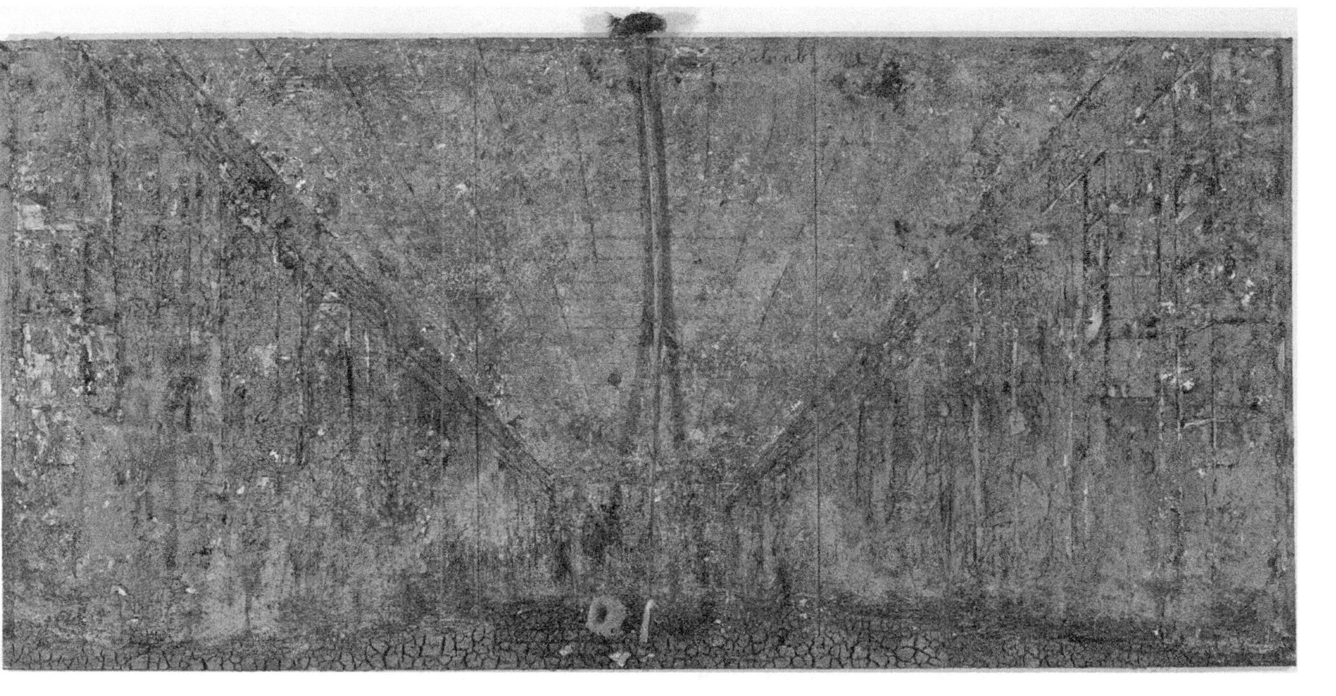

Figure 6.1
Anselm Kiefer, *Aschenblume (Ash Flower)*, 1983–1997
382.3 × 761.4 cm

Acrylic, emulsion, ash, earth, sunflower on canvas

© Anselm Kiefer
Collection Modern Art Museum of Fort Worth, Texas

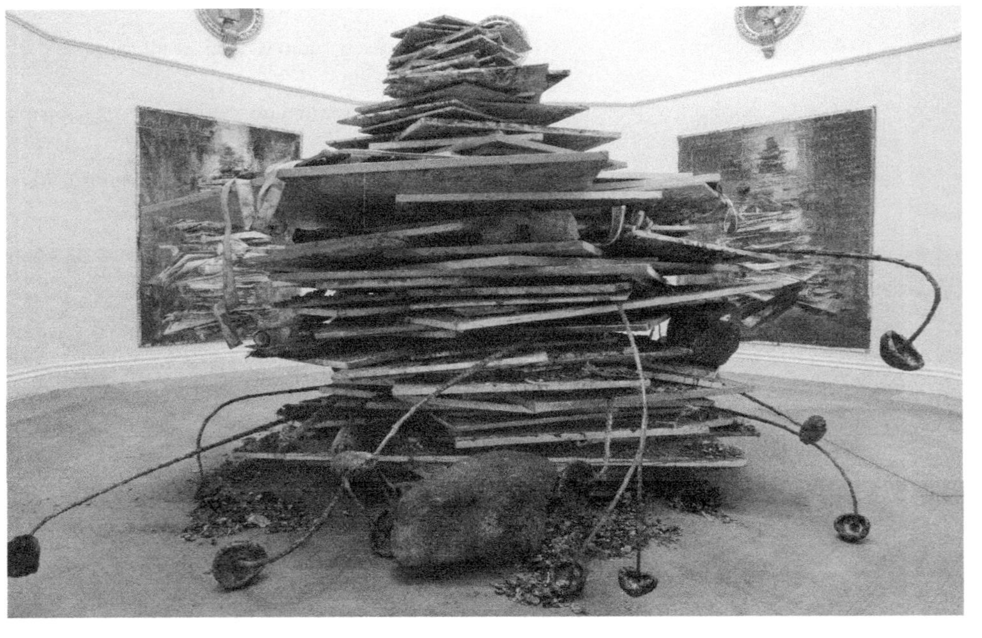

Figure 6.2
Anselm Kiefer, *Die Erdzietalter (Ages of the World)*, 2014

Installation with two gouache-painted photographs on canvas
and one sculpture (mixed media)
Dimensions variable

© Anselm Kiefer
Photo courtesy Royal Academy of Arts, London
Photography Howard Sooley

one night in 1942, in a round-up, when he was away; he never saw them again. He divulged very little of his own privations. Twenty years later he mentioned 'the war years, which off and on I "spent" in so-called labour camps in Romania'. He seems to have written 'Deathfugue' (originally 'Death Tango') in 1944, immediately after he emerged from the camps. It was first published in Germany in 1952 in the seminal collection *Poppy and Memory*, another title taken up by Kiefer (see Chapter 3). It became one of the critical poems of the twentieth century, the benchmark of poetry after Auschwitz – defying Adorno's supposed interdiction – and a kind of model for the process or programme of coming to terms with the past.[6] On the fiftieth anniversary of Kristallnacht, in 1988, an actress recited it in the Bundestag. One phrase in particular has passed into the language: 'we dig a grave in the air', words the poet himself insisted were 'neither borrowing nor metaphor'. In Jean Améry's luminous reflections on the shame of torture – the Nazis tortured, he writes, 'with the good conscience of depravity' – he describes the resurgence of German anti-Semitism in the 1970s as a 'playing with the fire that dug a grave in the air for so many'. In Primo Levi's *If Not Now, When?* (1982) the song of the partisans tells of their slaughtered brothers 'who have dug themselves a grave in the air'. 'I "stole" this image from Celan's "Todesfuge",' confessed Levi. 'But, as you know, in literature the borderline between stealth and homage is blurred.' The poem inhabited him: 'I carry it inside me like a graft.'[7] 'Deathfugue' is hypnotic, incantatory. Its opening stanzas run as follows:

Black milk of daybreak we drink it in the evening
we drink it at midday and morning we drink it at night
we drink and we drink
we shovel a grave in the air where you won't lie too cramped
A man lives in the house he plays with his vipers he writes
he writes when it grows dark to Deutschland your golden hair
  Margareta
he writes it and steps out of doors and the stars are all sparkling he
  whistles his hounds to stay close
he whistles his Jews into rows has them shovel a grave in the ground
he commands us play up for the dance
Black milk of daybreak we drink you at night
we drink you at morning and midday we drink you at evening
we drink and we drink
A man lives in the house he plays with his vipers he writes

he writes when it grows dark to Deutschland your golden hair
  Margareta
Your ashen hair Shulamith we shovel a grave in the air where you won't
  lie too cramped[8]

Bachmann's 'Darkness Spoken' is less well known, but no less vital. Her work was a touchstone for Celan himself.

> The string of silence
> taut on the pulse of blood,
> I grasped your beating heart.
> Your curls were transformed
> into the shadow hair of night,
> black flakes of darkness
> buried your face.[9]

Celan and Bachmann dealt in the same darkness, brokered the same black flakes. (And perhaps fell prey to the same demons. Celan drowned himself in the Seine. Bachmann died an accidental death, consumed by fire in her apartment, after falling asleep while smoking a cigarette in bed.) Kiefer pays tribute to the poems and the poets in his meditation on their plight. His exploration honours theirs: he probes the limits of language and the possibilities of art. 'No new world without a new language,' wrote Bachmann famously. 'With art,' said Celan, 'you go into your very selfmost straits. And set yourself free.'[10]

The Kieferworld is a free world, but a heavily burdened one, full of dead souls. Kiefer's art is among other things an inquest and a reckoning – a reckoning with history and memory – a reckoning with *Margarete* (1981) and *Shulamith* (1983). The golden-haired Margarete (from Goethe's *Faust*) is a guard in the camp. She is represented by straw on the canvas. 'An initially rigid substance, straw softens into *materia prima*,' explains Kiefer. 'Combined with animal excrement, its dazzling colour changes into a dark matter ready to be received by the earth.'[11] The ashen-haired Shulamith (from the Song of Solomon) is an inmate. Her hair has turned to ash in the ovens. She is represented by seven flames in her mausoleum – an allusion to the Menorah of the Temple of Jerusalem – modelled on the Funeral Hall for the Great German Soldiers in Berlin, transformed by the artist into a Holocaust memorial.

'To regain time does not mean remembering the past with nostalgia,' observed Kiefer in the lectures he delivered as Chair of Artistic Creation at the Collège de France in 2010–11; 'it means generating

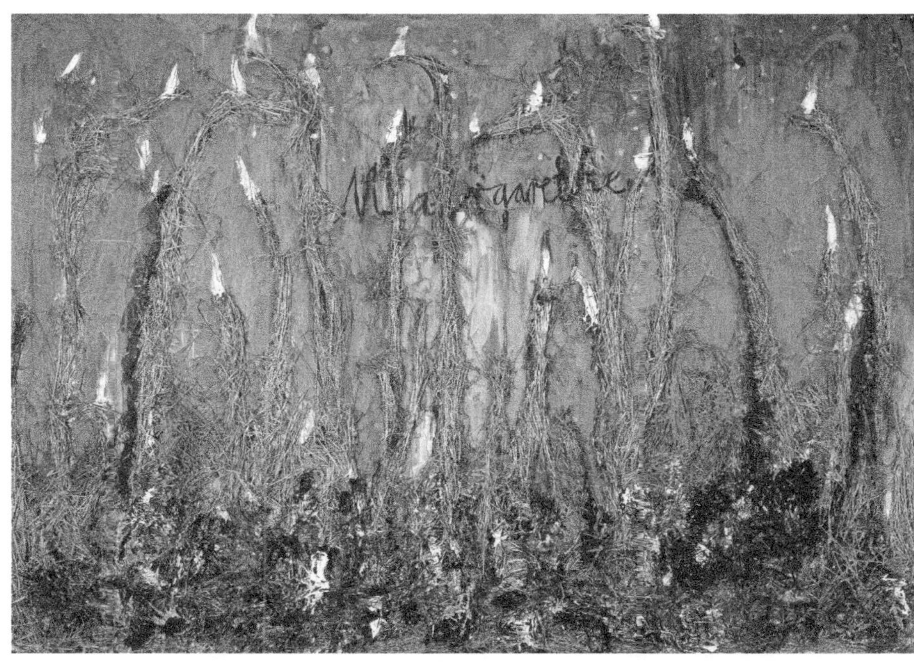

Figure 6.3
Anselm Kiefer, *Margarethe*, 1981

Oil, acrylic, emulsion and straw on canvas
292 × 401 cm

© Anselm Kiefer
Private collection

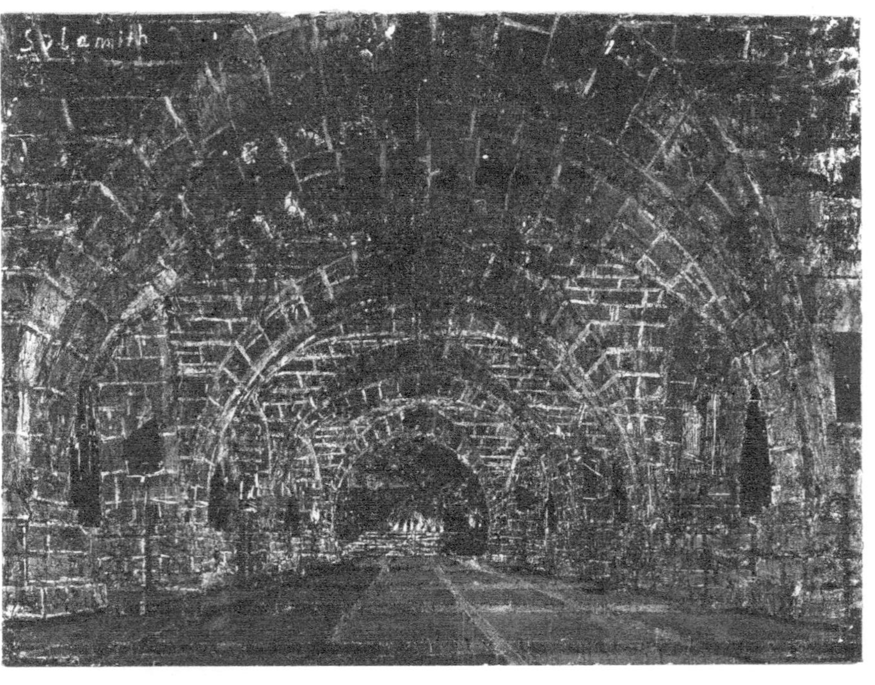

Figure 6.4
Anselm Kiefer, *Shulamith*, 1983

Oil, acrylic, woodcut, emulsion and straw on canvas
290 × 370 cm

© Anselm Kiefer
Private collection

"sparks" from the material at hand in order to go beyond both past and present.' Chair of Artistic Creation is an apt calling. Kiefer's lectures are compelling, erudite, individual. As a thinker, he is at once playful and profound. 'Some artists wait all their life for the word of God, and it never comes. This is the case with K., who waits in vain in Kafka's *The Castle*; and even more radically with Vladimir and Estragon in [Beckett's] *Waiting for Godot*, who merely play at waiting. Like spoken words, a painting may happen to contradict itself. It is by nature an aporia. It feeds on chance, signifies everything but ordains nothing.'

Kiefer waits for no man. Manifestly, inspiration is not in short supply. When it comes to explanation, there is a certain diffidence, but also an impressive lucidity:

> What is a work of art? I can only describe the process of how a work comes into existence.
>
> It begins in the dark after an intense experience, a shock. At first, it is an urge, a pounding. You don't know what it is, but it compels you to act. And, at first, it is very vague. It must be vague, otherwise it would just be a visualization of the shock experience.
>
> I am then in the matter, in the paint, in the sand, directly in the clay, in the darkness of the moment. Because the spirit is already contained in the material. . . . It is a strange, contemplative internal state, but also a form of suffering in its lack of clarity.[12]

The emphasis on *matter* is fundamental to his art and thought. 'It's not from the idea to the thing,' he insists, 'it's from the thing to the idea that's important.'[13] For Kiefer, this is nowhere better expressed than in the extraordinary phenomenology of the poet Francis Ponge, the Lucretius of our time, who was also an acute commentator on art and artists. Ponge's prose poem 'Earth' captures exactly Kiefer's feelings.

> Past, not as memory or idea, but as matter.
> Matter within reach of all, of the least baby; that you can seize in handfuls, shovelfuls.
> If speaking of earth like this makes me a miner poet, an earth tiller, that's what I want to be! I do not know a grander subject.
> As we were speaking of History, someone seized a handful of earth and said, 'Here is all we know of Universal History. But this we really know, we see it, we hold it, we have it well in hand.'
> What veneration in those words!
> Here also is our sustenance; where our sustenance is prepared for us. We camp on it as on the silage of history, where each clod contains the germ and roots of the future.[14]

If Ponge is a miner poet, as he quips, then surely Kiefer is a miner painter – mining the past for its elusive meaning, mining the ground on which we stand, mining and undermining our inflations and our intoxications, our certainties and our complacencies, our vanities and our vainglories. Kiefer subscribes to the absurdity of history, especially History with a capital H – the grand narrative, the intellectual construct, the received truth – 'ABSURD! And in each case, the absurdity has a different colour – so Albert Camus is different from Arthur Schopenhauer or from the Marquis de Sade and so on – but it's all about different colours of absurdity for me.'[15] Ambiguity and absurdity are two of his favourite words. Kiefer's kind of history is what he finds in Jules Michelet, one of his heroes, 'more than just a storyteller describing the past: the images he conjures up – I am thinking among other things of his description of the colour and consistency of the blood of queens – transform history into a material from which he extracts the essence of things and releases them from the confinement of time, releases them to the point where the future no longer seems to hold any threat'.[16] Put like that, Jules Michelet's project sounds very much like Anselm Kiefer's. Perhaps he is a history painter after all.

The idea of mining is not strange to him. 'Novalis speaks of miners as reverse astrologists,' he relates, 'and E. T. A. Hoffmann says that in the deepest depths, by the faint light of the pit lamp, the eye becomes clairvoyant and is able to see in the wonderful stones the reflection of what is hidden by the clouds.'[17] There may be a degree of identification here. According to Beckett in his disquisition on Proust, 'the only fertile research is excavatory, immersive'.[18] Kiefer himself is a notable excavator, tunnelling in his former domain of La Ribotte, a 200-acre site near Barjac, in the South of France, an enterprise glimpsed in Sophie Fiennes's documentary film, *Over Your Cities Grass Will Grow* (2010). 'As there was nothing to see on the surface . . ., I went underground', Kiefer reflected, adding revealingly, 'it wasn't an idea but a reflex'.[19] In Paris he has colonized an underground car park.

Heraclitus believed that 'you will not find out the limits of the human soul by going, even if you travel over every way'.[20] So it is with Kiefer. The voyage of discovery sails inwards. The process of creation is a mining of the self. Thus the Kieferworld is unconfined. Exploration of this order is encapsulated in his beloved Proust:

This labour of the artist, this attempt to see something different beneath the material, beneath experience, beneath words, is the exact inverse of what is accomplished in us from minute to minute, as we live our lives heedless of ourselves, by vanity, passion, intellect and habit, when they overlay our true impressions, so as to hide them from us completely, with the repertoire of words, and the practical aims, which we wrongly call life. . . . The work carried out by our vanity, our passion, our imitative faculties, our abstract intelligence, our habits, is the work that art undoes, making us follow a contrary path, in a return to the depths where whatever has really existed lies unrecognized within us.[21]

The miner need not be a prospector or traveller as traditionally conceived. Kiefer has done his travelling – he travelled for several months in China and India, in 1993, along the old Silk Route, photographing as he went. His reflections on the experience are at once material and civilizational:

The Silk Route crosses a region where kilns were erected roughly every dozen miles on Chairman Mao's orders to furnish bricks for road building. As the work for which they had been erected progressed the kilns were moved forward – a mode of production in which the production unit is made up of the material it produces. Once the bricks for a certain section of road had been baked, the site where they were produced was dismantled and the bricks from which it was made were loaded onto trucks. . . . These brickyards gave visibility to different aspects of temporality. . . . Some of the bricks have been stacked and form low walls resembling portions of dwellings waiting to be erected. They also remind me of archaeological digs, of cities unearthed, where only the foundations of walls have been left standing. The physical structure of the bricks directs us at once to the past and the future. These brickworks almost entirely buried in sand impressed me more than any other sight along the Silk Route.[22]

Kiefer's vision of a lost city appears before us in *For Ingeborg Bachmann: The Sand from the Urns (Für Ingeborg Bachmann: der Sand aus den Urnen)* (1998–2009), which takes its title from the first collection of Paul Celan's poems, published in 1948. For Kiefer, everything is connected. 'I border, like little else, on everything more and more,' as Bachmann wrote – a line he likes to quote.[23] Bricks are the building blocks of his ideas. 'I think we only see something if we have a reverberation,' as he puts it. 'It's for this reason I'm interested by little things – by a brick or a tiny plant – because it reverberates in me and leads me to an idea. In effect, each brick is an idea.' Bricks are also carriers of memory and mythology.

When I was a young boy, four or five years old, I played with bricks because there were ruins all around us; our house was a ruin and I had the most beautiful playground. That was the most basic reverberation.

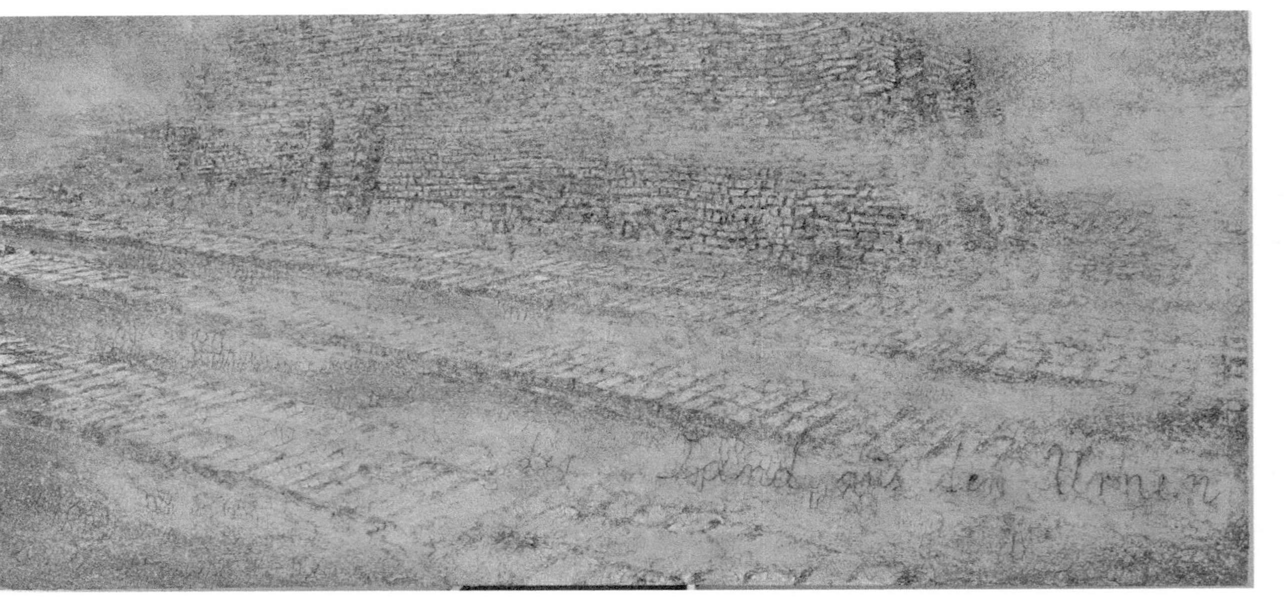

Figure 6.5
Anselm Kiefer, *Für Ingeborg Bachmann: der Sand aus den Urnen (For Ingeborg Bachmann: The Sand from the Urns)*, 1998–2009

Acrylic, oil, shellac and sand on canvas
110 1/4 × 220 1/2 in. (280 × 560 cm)

© Anselm Kiefer
Photo: Charles Duprat
Private collection

But then you see the bricks in the beginnings of the written word, in cuneiforms right up to the *Trümmerfrauen* – the women who cleared the bricks in the ruins after Germany was defeated in 1945. For me, that's the latest mythology about bricks.[24]

Increasingly, he immerses himself in a world of his own making. He even makes his own matter (and delights in so doing). In one area of the vast precincts of his studio in Croissy, on the outskirts of Paris, there is a machine that crushes stones. Otherwise he is surrounded by the archive of his actions: earlier work, work in progress, and the alchemical elements and constituent parts of future projects – Kiefers-to-come – everything from photography to ironmongery. Late Kiefer is more gatherer than hunter. Assemblage is critical to his modus operandi. Now it can be enacted on an epic scale, with the artist as a kind of time-traveller in his own work, performing variations on a theme or themes of his choosing. Assemblage, in fact, does not do justice to the whole. What he has assembled is an œuvre.

An integral part of that œuvre is a series of paintings called *Let a Thousand Flowers Bloom*. Kiefer has been making works with that title since at least 1998.[25] Curiously enough, Chairman Mao the road builder has become one of his familiars. He has painted more Maos than Andy Warhol. The master slogan or injunction derives from a celebrated episode in the history of Communist China, a deeply contested episode, known as the Hundred Flowers campaign. 'Let a hundred flowers bloom,' declared Mao. 'Let a hundred schools of thought contend.'[26] Allowing disparate voices to make themselves heard could resolve the contradictions in the country, remove the roadblocks of his enemies 'bureaucratism' and 'sectarianism', and reinvigorate the Chinese Communist Party (CCP). Later, this would be seen as a ruse to lure the snakes and 'poisonous weeds' of reaction into the open, in order to destroy them. Mao's post-facto rationalization, and the falsification of a key speech, only served to buttress that interpretation. But those actions were necessary to sustain the myth of his infallibility. At the time, it is quite possible that he believed what he was saying.

Gradually, over the next few months, people became emboldened and protest grew, not only among intellectuals and students, but also among the proletariat in whose name the CCP claimed to rule. Denunciations of the Party spoke of its 'malevolent tyranny' and 'Auschwitz fascist methods'. Mao was not exempt from criticism. The Chairman was the incarnation of the Party; their fate was indissolubly linked. The Party had to be preserved, and with it his supremacy. In 1957 he turned the whole initiative on its head. Critics were accused of trying to overthrow the CCP, restore bourgeois dictatorship, and 'resubjugate the Chinese people to the rule of imperialism and its running dogs'. The Hundred Flowers campaign was consigned to the dustbin of history. Mao dismissed it as a set of 'queer arguments', as if they had nothing to do with him.

Kiefer and Mao go back to the heady days of the 1960s. 'My brother was in the Communist Party, and was invited to spend time in China and was absolutely seduced,' recalls the artist. 'He is much more intelligent than me, but he came back saying "there are no more flies because it is so clean".'[27] Kiefer himself was a student during the Cultural Revolution, which began in 1966. He remembers the cult of the Great Helmsman, who had known the way ever since the Long March of 1934–5 – variations in his studio bear the legend 'This Way' – and in particular the *Little Red Book* (1964), with its all-encompassing belief system covering everything from 'Correcting Mistaken Ideas' to 'War and Peace' (a steal from Clausewitz). Here was a book that was supposed to cure illnesses and raise someone from the dead. Immune to Maoist propaganda but intrigued by the hysteria and the hubris, Kiefer was a fascinated spectator. Mao was a monster with super-human status; to his people he was at once mass-murderer and saviour. In the end, This Way was a cul-de-sac. Mao and his myrmidons were morally and economically bankrupt. The Cultural Revolution died with him in 1976. Ten years of 'the greatest revolutionary transformation of society, unprecedented in the history of mankind' ended at an economic cost estimated at the equivalent of \$34 billion and a human cost that is to all intents and purposes incalculable. The Helmsman once remarked that the First Emperor had buried 460 scholars alive, 'but we have buried 460,000' – a drop in the ocean of the bad elements and snake spirits who perished along the way.

This crop of paintings are appropriately ambiguous works. If they are flower pieces, they are also killing fields. Ambiguity is inscribed in their creation. They have their origins in a shock in the Auvergne: an explosion of colour – flower power – photographed, blown up, and painted over. Not simply painted, of course, but *mattered*, in the way of the Kieferworld: blackened and charred, caked and scored, splotched and splattered, and in at least one case pock-marked with red pellets, as if the landscape itself has been wounded, and the Great Helmsman holed. 'Have landscapes become repositories for history?' asks Kiefer suggestively. 'Are they destined to become subjects in their own right, reacting as such to the least provocation? Quivering and trembling subjects that seem indifferent to human cries?'[28]

There are connections to be made with some of Kiefer's other preoccupations. One of these paintings, *The Sleeper in the Valley*, a subject he has tackled before, takes its title from a favourite poem by Arthur Rimbaud. A young soldier sleeps peacefully in a pastoral idyll; or so it seems, until the overturning end:

> The perfumes do not make his nostrils quiver;
> He sleeps in the sun, his hand on his breast
> Peaceful. He has two red holes in his right side.[29]

The sleeper in the valley connects with a tutelary presence in the Kieferworld, Vincent Van Gogh. Van Gogh is an inspiration: a philosopher-painter of heartbreaking eloquence. 'I do not say that my work is good, but it's the least bad that I can do,' wrote Vincent to his brother Theo. 'All the rest, relations with people, is very secondary, because I have no talent for that. I can't help it.'[30] Kiefer has been brooding on his life and work for half a century. In 2010, after seeing an exhibition of Van Gogh's letters and paintings, side by side, he recorded in his notebook:

> I observed that it is possible to complete a lifetime's work in three years. In fact, nothing significant till then, just like Rimbaud. A touching lack of talent: i.e. the anatomy is there, hands and feet the hardest to render, but he nevertheless manages to make us forget the contingencies. Van Gogh aspires essentially to stop being the torn, stateless, friendless artist (Gauguin has left). Vincent is left behind, and for him there can be no peace. He doesn't linger on the result. The minute he finishes a painting he sends it off to Theo. Think only of what he did not succeed in accomplishing. An endless tension-filled wandering between the inability – due to lack of talent – to attain an inaccessible goal, one that was doubly inaccessible because his incapacity was both social and human, as well as professional and pictorial, not to mention the fact that his pictures were unsellable. Painting without ever reaching one's goal. And what does it matter if gold does not stream down on the corn fields, and that at night galaxies invade the earth while the fields that extend as far as one can see glow like garish green light panels. . . . It is in the tension between the finite and the infinite that the painter's body seems racked.[31]

The blood on the last letter Van Gogh stuffed in his pocket the day he shot himself reminds Kiefer of the red holes in the sleeper in the valley.

The silage of history is stained with blood.

Notes

1. Marcel Proust, trans. Mark Treharne, *The Guermantes Way* [1920–1] (London: Penguin, 2002), pp. 325–6.

2. Kiefer interview with Nicholas Wroe, 'A Life in Art', *Guardian*, 18 March 2011.

3. I am grateful to Anselm Kiefer for his hospitality during a visit to his studio in Croissy, near Paris, in 2012. Unless otherwise indicated, statements or views attributed to the artist derive from his conversation on that occasion. I thank also Tim Marlow, who took me along, and Honey Luard of White Cube for making this possible; and Waltraud Forelli of Studio Kiefer for generous provision of further information.

4. Anselm Kiefer, trans. Michael Taylor, *Art Will Survive its Ruins* (Paris: Regard, 2011), p. 303.

5. Anselm Kiefer, trans. The Hagedorn Group, *Friedenspreis des Deutschen Buchhandels* (Paris: Regard, 2008), p. 45.

6. Adorno's famous pronouncement, 'To write poetry after Auschwitz is barbaric,' was issued in the early 1950s and repeated for a decade. He later took back his words, grudgingly, as J. M. Coetzee remarked, perhaps as a concession to 'Deathfugue'. In a much-anthologised article he reiterated the original pronouncement, but added the crucial rider, 'literature must resist this verdict'. Theodor W. Adorno, trans. Samuel and Shierry Weber, 'Cultural Criticism and Society' [1951], in *Prisms* (Cambridge, MA: MIT, 1967), p. 34; trans. Francis McDonagh, 'Commitment' [1962], in Andrew Arato and Eike Gebhart (eds), *The Essential Frankfurt School Reader* (New York: Continuum, 1975), p. 312. See J. M. Coetzee, 'Paul Celan and his Translators' [2001], in *Inner Workings* (London: Harvill Secker, 2007), p. 120; and Jacques Rancière, trans. Julie Rose, *Figures of History* (Cambridge: Polity, 2014), pp. 49–50. George Steiner's influential reading is a misreading, or a partial reading, taking no account of the later modification: 'Silence and the Poet' [1966], in *Language and Silence* (London: Penguin, 1979), p. 75.

7. Celan to Erich Kahler and Walter Jens, 25 April 1962 and 19 May 1961, in John Felstiner, *Paul Celan* (New Haven: Yale University Press, 2001), pp. 15, 288; John Felstiner, 'Preface' to *Selected Poems and Prose of Paul Celan* (New York: Norton, 2001), p. xii. See Jean Améry, 'Preface' to *At the Mind's Limits* (Bloomington, IN: Indiana University Press, 1976), p. x; Primo Levi, trans. William Weaver, *If Not Now, When?* (London: Penguin, 2000), p. 168.

8. Paul Celan, trans. John Felstiner, 'Deathfugue', *Selected Poems and Prose*, p. 31.

9. Ingeborg Bachmann, trans. Peter Filkins, 'Darkness Spoken', in *Darkness Spoken* (Brookline, MA: Zephyr, 2006), p. 11. Celan is said

to have had a special regard for Bachmann's story 'Among Murderers and Madmen' (1961).

10. See Bachmann, *Darkness Spoken*, p. xxxi; Celan, 'The Meridian: speech on the occasion of the award of the Georg Büchner Prize' [1961], *Selected Poems and Prose*, p. 411.

11. Kiefer, *Art Will Survive*, p. 275.

12. Kiefer, *Friedenspreis*, p. 55, amending the translation of *der Materie* (*la matière*) from 'the material' to 'the matter'.

13. Kiefer in conversation with Tim Marlow, 'Spaces of Transition', in *Karfunkelfee and the Fertile Crescent* (London: White Cube, 2009), p. 45.

14. Francis Ponge, trans. John Montague, 'Earth', in *Selected Poems* (London: Faber, 1998), p. 159. For his equally remarkable writings on art see *Atelier contemporain* (Paris: Gallimard, 1977).

15. Kiefer, 'Spaces of Transition', p. 39.

16. Kiefer, *Art Will Survive*, p. 305.

17. Kiefer, *Friedenspreis*, p. 46. He continued: 'When we speak of descending into history, of descending into ourselves, into our innermost being . . .'.

18. Samuel Beckett, *Proust* [1931] (London: Calder, 1965), p. 65.

19. Kiefer, *Art Will Survive*, p. 330.

20. Charles H. Kahn, *The Art and Thought of Heraclitus* (Cambridge: Cambridge University Press, 1979), p. 126.

21. Marcel Proust, trans. Ian Patterson, *Finding Time Again* [1927] (London: Penguin, 2002), pp. 204–5.

22. Kiefer, *Art Will Survive*, p. 279.

23. Bachmann, 'Bohemia Lies By The Sea', in *Darkness Spoken*, p. 617. Cf. Kiefer, *Friedenspreis*, p. 54; *Art Will Survive*, p. 208.

24. Kiefer, 'Spaces of Transition', p. 41.

25. See *Let a Thousand Flowers Bloom* (London: Anthony d'Offay, 2000), and *Kiefer e Mao: che mille fiori fioriscano* (Milan: Skira, 2008).

26. 'Letting a hundred flowers bloom and a hundred schools of thought contend is the policy of promoting the progress of the arts and sciences and the flourishing socialist culture of our land.' *On the Correct Handling of Contradictions Among the People*, 27 February 1957.

27. Interview with Wroe, *Guardian*, 18 March 2011.

28. Kiefer, *Art Will Survive*, p. 300.

29. Arthur Rimbaud, 'Le Dormeur du val' [1870], in *Poésies* (Paris: Gallimard, 2011), p. 70. My translation.

30. Vincent to Theo and Jo Van Gogh, c.21 May 1890, at http://van goghletters.org/vg/letters/let874/letter.html (last accessed 9 February 2015).

31. Kiefer notebook, 20 June 2010, in *Art Will Survive*, p. 295.

7

Footfall:
The Moral Economy of Reinhard Mucha

I have laid out the burrow and it appears to be successful.

My prison cell – my fortress.

Franz Kafka[1]

What do we know about Reinhard Mucha? The official biography:

Born 1950 in Düsseldorf.
Lives and works in Düsseldorf.

This biography is surprisingly revealing.

We know that he has a profound sense of place, and placelessness. His place is Düsseldorf; more specifically, his studio, his burrow, the refuge of all things and all notions, a building with a history, where he has laid out a labyrinthine network of workspaces – workplaces – conducive to his modus operandi and means of production. This is his domain. Here he submits himself to the discipline of his vocation – he speaks feelingly and unaffectedly of the demands the work makes on him – creating and recreating, assembling and disassembling, constructing and deconstructing, collecting and reflecting, hoarding and restoring. 'Everything here is a Mucha,' he says, with a touch of pride, of the restoration work on the building; and indeed the whole project is a giant Mucha – less a studio than an ecosystem.[2] Like Kafka's burrow, it is a life's work. 'All the great artists have been great workers,' as Nietzsche knew, 'inexhaustible not only in invention, but also in rejecting, sifting, transforming, ordering.'[3] Mucha is nothing if not a great worker.

He is also a master craftsman – a woodworker, a metalworker. He was once a blacksmith. He so loved art that he joined the artillery, as Apollinaire liked to boast; doing his military service he became a trained geometer. Technical drawing is part of the discipline. His art is arduous: a perfectionist reconciliation of vision and precision.

108

He has practical wisdom – a nut and bolt sit in the top of his sugar shaker to stop the flies getting in – and a certain intellectual rigour. When the jury at the 1990 Venice Biennale gave him one of three special awards for 'the rigour and precision of his work', they may have chosen to ignore the historical and political dimensions of an installation called *The Germany Machine* or *The Germany Device* (1990/2002), but they were not altogether wrong.[4] His *métier* is meticulousness.

Place-markers are freighted with meaning for him. At the entrance to the studio is a commemorative plaque carved by a stonemason at Mucha's behest:

Built 1908
Düsseldorf Railway Equipment Corp.
Formerly Carl Weyer & Co.
Carriage Factory
1861–1939
Paul Kahle Pipeline Construction
1939–1980

It is not too much to imagine an additional line commemorating the next occupant – the one who saved the building from destruction or development, who wrestled with the municipal authorities for eight years before he was allowed to buy it, who planted vines at the rear, who preserved the safe and the transformers, who populated and revivified it. Mucha is the very last person to make an exhibition of himself, yet in his fastness he does just that. 'The exhibitions that are most important to me take place in my studio every day.' The studio is the prime site of the self-examined life by which the artist sets so much store, the Proustian proving ground. 'Excuses have absolutely no place in art,' announces Proust in *Finding Time Again*. 'Mere intentions do not count for anything, the artist has to listen to his instinct all the time, with the result that art is most real thing there is, the most austere school of life, and the true Last Judgement.'[5] For Mucha, Kafka is the true Last Judgement – 'The Burrow' has almost scriptural authority for him, inspiring a work of the same title – but it is tempting to think that he takes Proust to heart. Losing time is anathema to Mucha. Proverbially, however, he will not be rushed. The work demands nothing less. Invitations come and go; Muchas gestate at their own pace – 'Mucha pace'.

Other place-markers pullulate in the work. *Waiting Room* (1982) is a continuously evolving collection of the signs of German railway stations or former stations – Zingst, Minden, Tholey, Uelzen, Seelze, Hennef – hundreds of them, extracted from a 1930s directory, painted by the artist in imitation of the originals, and installed in stacks of drawers on wheels. All of the place names are six letters; apparently the selection is a matter of chance. Does Mucha's waiting room resonate with Ingeborg Bachmann's? The furnishings, mental and other, bear some resemblance.

> We no longer share a language.
> Together we are waiting.
> A chair,
> a bench,
> a window
> through which the light in our room
> falls
> on our hands,
> on our eyes,
> and otherwise
> on the floor.
>
> Heal our eyes
> so that we can again find the words,
> so multi-coloured, that I can say to you.[6]

The place names recur as titles for a series of wall-mounted sculptures, often a 'two-part work ensemble' with free-standing sculptures in vitrines. His recent exhibitions in New York and Berlin, for example, featured an ensemble called *Freedom for Berlin*, 2008/ *Minden*, 2013 (*Freiheit for Berlin/Minden*).[7] The free-standing sculpture *Freedom for Berlin* is more free-standing than most – it floats above the ground, like most of Mucha's vitrines. 'Free-standing, they no longer have any contact with the ground of facts,' as the artist puts it, 'and this makes them stand out even more.'[8] Barnett Newman said that 'the self, terrible and constant, is for me the subject matter of painting'. Mucha speaks in a different register: '"Where am I?" is the name of the game.'[9]

The sculpture is not so much a sculpture as an assemblage of the artist's signature materials. The components are always carefully specified: 'Solid wood, float glass *(display case)*; oil paint print on bituminized feltbase *(flooring, found material)* on blockboard *(pedestal)*; wood *(3 footstools, found objects)*; aluminum *(9 folding rulers)*; binding wire.' Oil paint print on bituminized feltbase ('the poor people's carpet') is one of Mucha's favourite materials, evoking

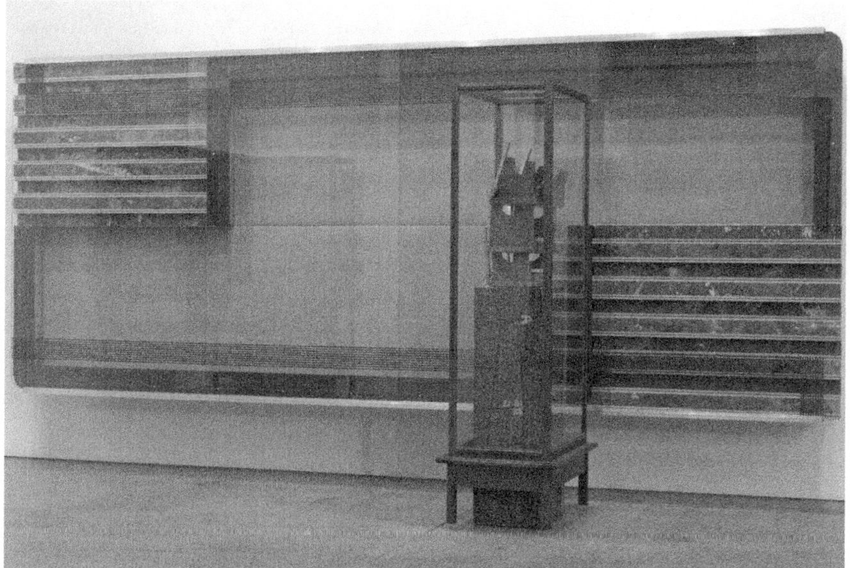

Figure 7.1
Reinhard Mucha, *Freiheit for Berlin (Freedom for Berlin)*, 2008 / *Minden*, 2013
Two-part work ensemble

Free-standing sculpture
Freiheit for Berlin
Solid wood, float glass *(display case)*; oil paint print on bituminized feltbase
(flooring, found material) on blockboard *(pedestal)*; wood *(3 footstools, found
objects)*; aluminum *(9 folding rulers)*; binding wire
71.89 × 30.31 × 20.47 inches

Wall-mounted sculpture
Minden
Aluminum, float glass, alkyd enamel painted on reverse of glass; rails with so-called
diamonds, billiard cloth, cushion rubber *(carom billiards table, split found object)*;
residue of various oil paints, resin and dispersion paints, plywood *(floorboard from
an artist's studio, split found object)*; canvas, felt, plywood, blockboard
66.85 × 166.14 × 19.61 inches
© Mucha

a whole era in flooring and painting. As he leafs through his samples,
he identifies certain styles – 'a Polke', 'a Richter'. Occasionally,
Mucha is mischievous.

The wall-mounted sculpture *Minden* is also a kind of vitrine; it
too is a window on the Muchaworld, or an inventory of his magpie
eye: 'Aluminum, float glass, alkyd enamel painted on reverse of glass;

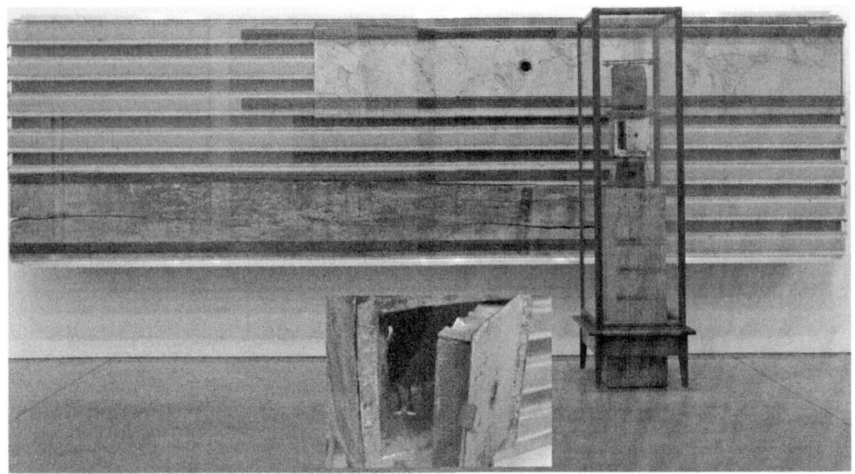

Figure 7.2
Reinhard Mucha, *Stunde Null (Zero Hour)*, 2006 / *Hennef*, 2009
Two-part work ensemble

Free-standing sculpture

Stunde Null
Solid wood, float glass *(display case)*; oil paint print on bituminized feltbase *(flooring, found material)* on blockboard *(pedestal)*; sheet steel *(6 parts of rails, model railway track 0)*; pear wood, steel wire *(gaffer mold, found object)*; stove enamel, steel, fire clay, cast iron *(kiln, found object)*
71.65 × 20.47 × 30.31 inches
182 × 52 × 77 cm

Wall-mounted sculpture

Hennef
Aluminum, float glass, alkyd enamel painted on reverse of glass; alkyd resin paint, wood *(wall panel, found object)*; wooden plank *(found object)*; canvas, industrial felt, blockboard
53.27 × 181.10 × 17.48 inches
35.3 × 460 × 44.4 cm
© Mucha

rails with so-called diamonds, billiard cloth, cushion rubber *(carom billiards table, split found object)*; residue of various oil paints, resin and dispersion paints, plywood *(floorboard from an artist's studio, split found object)*; canvas, felt, plywood, blockboard.'

The inspiration behind *Freedom for Berlin* is at once political and visual – or historical and material – a characteristic combination. It is signposted, clearly but mutely, in a complementary work: an untitled photographic collage in which the Berlin Airlift Monument at the former Tempelhof Airport is superimposed on shots of the sculpture. The monument was erected in 1951, to commemorate the airlift of 1948–9. It comprises three arcs pointing west to symbolize the three air corridors that were the city's lifeline during the blockade; Berliners called it the hunger claw or hunger rake. The three upturned footstools of the sculpture suggest an uncanny anatomy of the monument. The skyward ends of the arcs rhyme with the legs of the uppermost footstool – the hunger stool. Even the footstool can soar. *Per ardua ad astra in scabello*. And the billiard table, like the city, is divided.

In Mucha, there is much to unpack, even suitcases. Another ensemble, *The German Question* (2007)/*Dornap* (2007), is dedicated to Philip Nelson, his Paris dealer (who died the previous year). It was Nelson who pioneered the exhibition in France of the *wunderkinder* from the Kunstakademie Düsseldorf: Thomas Ruff, Thomas Schütte . . . Reinhard Mucha. 'The German Question' goes to the heart of modern European history – 'the most sombre, the most complicated, the most comprehensive problem of all recent history,' averred Constantin Frantz in 1866 – the question of how German unification was to be achieved. Its corollary is equally salient: how German power is to be exercised, or perhaps constrained. This question has preoccupied peoples and policy-makers ever since it was framed. In the wake of the Second World War the answer took the form of four occupation zones (American, British, French and Russian), consolidated as the Federal Republic of Germany in the West and the German Democratic Republic in the East. Petrified in the Cold War, that answer proved surprisingly durable. Yet it was ultimately unsustainable. After the fall of the Berlin Wall in 1989 and reunification the following year, the question of German power was posed afresh. The Germans have always been either too weak or too strong. That is their predicament. The struggle for mastery in Europe played out accordingly. For the Germans themselves the consequence was a post-war period shadowed by introspection, contrition, repression, coming to terms with the past, and keeping silent about it. There is an expression for coming to terms with the past, *Vergangenheitsbewältigung*. There is even a programme for it, in schools, making use of material as challenging as Paul Celan's 'Deathfugue' (see Chapter 6). In some quarters, nevertheless, the silence is loud.

In Mucha's lingua franca, *The German Question* finds expression in four cardboard suitcases (*found objects*) – one of them from his grandparents – to represent the four occupation zones, or the fate of the displaced, or the Four-Power Agreement of 1945 to try major war criminals before the newly created International Military Tribunal, thus paving the way for the Nuremberg Trials. (A variant, *The Four-Power Status of Berlin*, utilizes four radios.) If this suggests a broader reflection on the unmasterable past and the unspeakable things that went on there, then it is difficult to ignore *Stunde Null* (2006) / *Hennef* (2009). In German, *Stunde Null* (zero hour) is a highly charged term, an essentially contested concept. It derives from the end of the Second World War, and the moral and material devastation that had been wrought. It suggests a new beginning, as if from nothing or nowhere; an imperative for the Germans themselves to put that calamity behind them. 'The unspeakable passes, barely spoken, over the land,' as Bachmann wrote.[10] More dubiously, it carries the implication of a clean slate. It tends to absolve, or at any rate to lift any obligation to atone. It militates against the need to reflect with humility on the past, on ethical conduct and historical responsibility, not to mention the need to hold criminals to account for their crimes. It leapfrogs the past and expunges the memory. If the struggle of man against power is the struggle of memory against forgetting, in Milan Kundera's celebrated formulation, *Stunde Null* is on the side of forgetting.

Mucha is on the side of memory. 'It is not only about evoking, depicting, keeping, conserving and illustrating memories, pasts, "history",' as he puts it, 'but ... using the transitory vehicle of the vitrine to make clear – as clear as glass, as it were – the relevant Here and Now of a museum or other (art) context and bringing it to consciousness'.[11] His free-standing sculpture incorporates elements that are historically unforgettable: 'Solid wood, float glass (*display case*); oil paint print on bituminized feltbase (*flooring, found material*) on blockboard (*pedestal*); sheet steel (*6 parts of rails, model railway track 0*); pear wood, steel wire (*gaffer mold, found object*); stove enamel, steel, fire clay, cast iron (*kiln, found object*).' After the Holocaust, certain things have lost their innocence, railway tracks and ovens prominent among them. 'Nowadays,' Anselm Kiefer has remarked, 'any image of deserted tracks ... automatically brings Auschwitz to mind'.[12]

Mucha takes out the histrionics and leaves in the history, as Jerry Saltz once said. 'He doesn't put the disturbing facts of German history back in the closet so much as he cuts up that closet, reassembles it and combines it with other parts of the house in order to allude to rather than point directly at his subject. His sculpture has a reliquary, elegiac presence – the past fills his work with its absence.'[13] The work is heavy with history, though the focus is domestic rather than foreign. The history of the studio is indicative. Mucha's primary interest is in the largest sense ecological. His art is rooted in the cultural and industrial origins of the post-war German 'economic miracle', the *Wirtschaftswunder*, and in the peculiar ecology of the museum. 'Museums today are like railway stations,' he likes to say. 'In, out, both are places of placelessness.'[14] There is a hint of drollery here, and also an echo of Marx. 'All that is solid melts into air, all that is holy is profaned, and man is at last compelled to face with sober senses, his real conditions of life, and his relations with his kind.'[15] For Mucha, all that is solid remains solid – but recast. The self-confessed 68er might well assent to the rest of Marx's analysis of the bourgeois epoch. In his own idiosyncratic way he may be the foremost artist-anatomist of late capitalism in Europe. He makes machines – his *Germany Machine* takes its name from a hydraulic lift for railway coaches formerly manufactured by Dortmunder Machinenfabrik Deutschland AG – but he does not worship them. He is no Futurist. He is more akin to a Historicist. His works are embedded in place and space and time. They are site-specific (Here and Now) but more than site-specific: site-historic, organic. Mucha, it is safe to say, does not believe in miracles.

For all his fascination with railways, he is dedicated not to speed but to slowness, as a cardinal virtue. Except perhaps as a cyclist. If there is a cult of the bike, Mucha is a devotee. Two of the latest lightweight Italian racing bikes from Gios turn up in a recent work, or a work recently amended, complemented by two ancient French delivery bikes (*found objects*); and the artist has a high-gloss Gios of his own, personalized and customized in his studio workshop. Even on a bike, however, he hugs the earth. Ethically and otherwise, Mucha is grounded.

In the world of externalities, the artist is modest. He always installs his own exhibitions; otherwise, he travels but little. 'I am not a tourist.' As often as not, he walks. On the railways, he walks the line. After his exhibitions opened at the Kunsthalle Basel and the Kunsthalle Bern in 1987, under the auspices of Ulrich Loock and Jean-Christophe Ammann, he took the two museum directors for a walk along a mile-long section of abandoned railway line near Waldshut, a slice of the German Reich – history teaching by perambulation.[16] Thomas Grässlin, based in Sankt Georgen in the Black Forest, has the privilege of owning Mucha's totemic installation *The Burrow* (1980–4). He took Grässlin for a walk along the railway line that runs along the Swiss border, through a tunnel, deep into the mountain. The collector likes to tell how they had to duck into recesses whenever a train rushed in.

There is a certain simplicity to him. He is deeply attached to the lowliest objects. If Klee's signature device is an angel (see Chapter 3), Mucha's is a footstool. The provenance, according to the artist:

> Footstool. At first sight subordinate, the psychology of its unmistakable model-character oscillates, as we know, between self-abnegation and delusions of grandeur. Some spontaneous associations: *support – subservience – ordinariness – proportionality; unobtrusiveness – inconspicuousness – social work – office-holder – placeholder – proxy – joker – salon rebel.* The artist as *rabble rouser – illuminator – visionary – revolutionary – missionary? As artist – jester – trickster – fool? Disturbing, destroying, eternal child?*[17]

'So much on the subject of footstools. Lowest step. Try stepping on one . . .! You'll be astonished how far you can see from there, so much closer to Heaven.'[18] Mucha is in every way a serious artist – almost obsessively serious – but he does not lack wit. In his hands the footstool is capable of anything. He has also called it 'a metaphor illustrating the burden of being an artist' – a joke at his own expense – though he stockpiles images of footstools in art, and suggestive formal connections and juxtapositions, such as an upside-down castle whose turrets resemble the legs of a footstool. Mucha is a tireless hunter-gatherer of images for his archive, like Kafka's creature for its larder.

According to Nietzsche, 'one is an artist at the cost of regarding that which all non-artists call "form" as content, as "the matter itself"'.[19] Much of Mucha is his profound experience of form. In the matter of the footstool, form and content seem to pool their possibilities, metamorphic and metaphoric. The footstool, too, has a history. It bears weight and carries memories. It also has a lightness of being. The artist himself remembers playing with footstools as a boy; he would turn them upside-down and imagine them as some kind of vehicle or vessel (a sledge, perhaps, to anticipate a later motif). He is still playing with them as an adult; *Mucha's Tea-Tray, or the Sense and Use of Certain Reversals* is an upside-down footstool with a mug of tea on it. Footstools are fun. At the same time they are

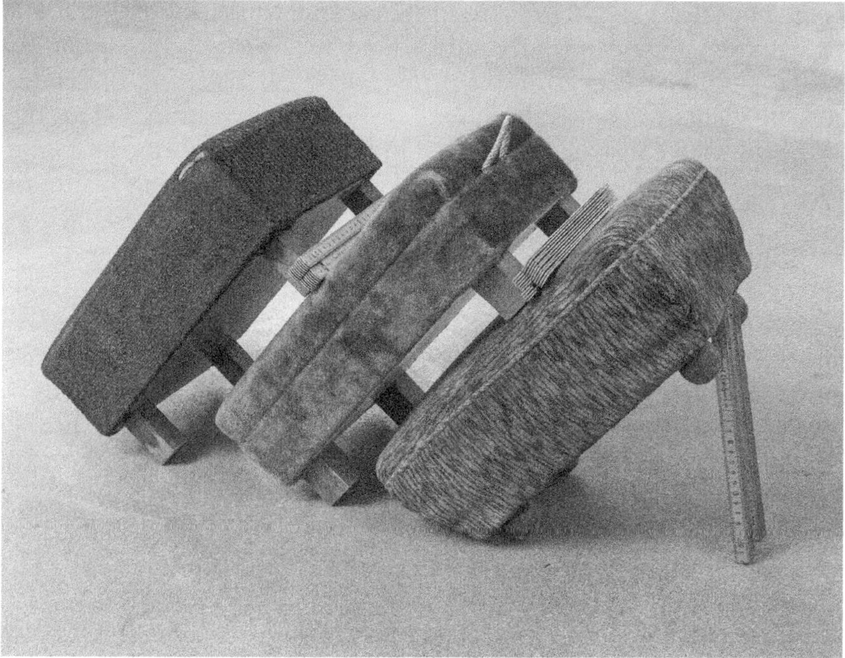

Figure 7.3
Reinhard Mucha, *Altbau gegen Neubau (Old Construction versus New Construction)*, 2014
3 footstools wood, various upholstery fabrics *(found objects)*, *6 folding rulers* aluminum
14.17 × 29.53 × 9.84 inches
36 × 75 × 25 cm
© Mucha

inexpressibly poignant. The economic miracle has passed them by, or rendered them obsolescent. Once ubiquitous, they are now almost extinct. *Old Construction versus New Construction (Altbau gegen Neubau)* (2014) is a study in senescence: '*3 footstools* wood, various upholstery fabrics *(found objects)*, *6 folding rulers* aluminum.' This trio have seen better days. They lean on each other, using rulers like crutches, as if blind and lame. They look curiously creaturely. In the post-miraculous age Mucha sources them on the internet.

'We must laugh and philosophize at the same time.' The wisdom of Epicurus, apt for Mucha, is gathered in a rare artist's book: *fifty postcards* (1997).[20] The fruit of a stint in Corsica in 1987, the postcards are mostly watercolours. Mucha is an accomplished watercolourist, it transpires, and an impish collagist. He is also a scintillating street photographer, especially in black and white, not to mention his activities as video diarist and sound recordist (found sound as well as found objects go into the mix). In New York for an exhibition, he wants to record the sound of the Brooklyn Bridge – not the traffic, but the construction work. On the way, he records the sound on the subway, and films from the front of the moving train. At Brooklyn Bridge station he photographs a wooden bench chained to the ground in an unsavoury hallway. 'This for my bench collection.' The bridge itself is stubbornly quiet. Mucha attends to the ker-thunk of cars on the patched-up surface, but this is not what he is after. There is no construction work. He is frustrated. 'They've taken my sound.' He will return another day. On the way back, he walks over Manhattan Bridge, recording the sound of the trains, and reflecting on the influence of the train on music. Walking through Chinatown, he passes near where he stayed in a loft on his first visit, in 1977. The young Mucha had to come. Whatever he thought about coca-colonization, there were things about the culture that he liked. He liked Raymond Chandler – his first exhibition, that same year, took its inspiration from the metaphors of colour in *The Long Goodbye*. He liked Robert Altman. Best of all, he liked Robert Mitchum as a world-weary Philip Marlowe in *Farewell My Lovely*. There is a photograph of Mitchum in his studio to this day.

And he was contending with Minimalism, as he has continued to do throughout his career:

> I have always countered the Minimal statement, 'What you see is what you see,' by saying 'You don't see what I see.' There are no neutral materials. My cupboards are covered with linoleum. Linoleum goes back to my childhood, to the tax office and public housing. But you do see exactly what you see! I reveal every single detail of what I'm doing and that's how I make a work. Linoleum as a natural product has a lot in common with artists' materials. It is a mixture of cork dust and linseed oil on canvas backing. In Carl André's case, the result is images, too, but done as if they were independent of context, etc. [Donald] Judd's works have always struck me as furniture and they changed depending on whether they were placed on the floor or on carpets. I would have made furniture to begin with . . . .[21]

Part scavenger, part fabulist, Mucha the furniture-maker manqué refuses the traditional oppositions and separations: for him there is no life and work, no early and late, no child and man. There is, instead, the total commitment required of the true artist. Mucha is monkish, unsparing – unsparing of himself. As he surveys his struggle, what he sees is an œuvre: a body of work that has grown organically, if haphazardly, like a giant jigsaw puzzle in progress. Aided perhaps by his artisanal bent, he found his voice early. At the Kunstakademie Düsseldorf, he already seemed to know what he was about. Gerhard Richter wanted him as a student, but he went instead to Klaus Rinke, an influential mentor. For Joseph Beuys, the presiding genius of German art in that period, he had unstinting admiration. Beuys remains a touchstone, an example of how an artist can be. Mucha's magnum opus *Frankfurter Block* (2012) pays characteristic tribute to Beuys and Rinke. For Anselm Kiefer, by contrast, he reserves a special disdain (see Chapter 6). Kiefer is a performer, in Mucha's book; grandiosity repels him.

These are ethical judgements first and foremost. Mucha the moralist cuts an unlikely figure, but it is perhaps the witness to his own time that will out when it comes to an assessment of his stature as an artist. Such an assessment is overdue. Mucha has burrowed deep into contemporary consciousness, but he has not yet found his place. In fact his place is under threat, almost as if Kafka's worst nightmare had come to pass. When the director of K21 in Düsseldorf announced her intention to remove *The Germany Machine* from the museum, the artist wrote to protest. His protest is at once principled and impassioned. It offers a kind of credo:

> The museum in change, the museum in transformation, art in movement, rotation, change of scene, change of sides – in my early works of the 1980s I anticipated and in my own way attempted to depict all of these things, created pictures of fairground carousels and space stations, images of placelessness, mobility and weightlessness, images that had outgrown the museum, as it were.

> *The Germany Machine* has the opposite thrust. Around the world there are only a very small number of museum works of contemporary art that are conceived to last and resist incessant change, transgenerational 'landmarks' in the museum landscape, so to speak. The Kunstsammlung NRW [Nordrhein-Westfalen] also contains works of this type, and *The Germany Machine* is one of them. Art lovers around the world see it this way, and this is exactly the way it was intended.[22]

Mucha's art is made to last. His work may fill a room or a gallery space. It is the very opposite of grandiose.

Central to his achievement is what might be called a moral economy of scale. Mucha himself quotes Siegfried Kracauer on the methodology of Walter Benjamin: 'He has always been at particular pains to show that great is small and small great. The divining rod of his intuition reacts in the realms of all things inconspicuous, generally devalued, ignored by history, and finds precisely here the highest significances.'[23]

Notes

1. Franz Kafka, trans. Malcolm Pasley, 'The Burrow' (the opening sentence) and diary, 19 February 1920, in *The Great Wall of China and Other Short Works* (London: Penguin, 1991), pp. 111, 185.
2. I am grateful to Reinhard Mucha for his hospitality and his patience in answering my questions in the course of two lengthy conversations, in Düsseldorf and New York, in 2013 and 2014. Unless otherwise indicated, all of the statements and views attributed to the artist derive from these encounters. I thank also Craig Burnett for the inspiration, and for moral support throughout; Judith Plodeck of Sprüth Magers in Berlin and Lauren Wittels of Luhring Augustine in New York for their assistance; and Paul Stoop for a close reading of an earlier version.
3. Freidrich Nietzsche, trans. R. J. Hollingdale, *Human, All Too Human* [1886] (Cambridge: Cambridge University Press, 1996), p. 83.
4. To add to the categorical confusion, Mucha shared the German Pavilion with Bernd and Hilla Becher, who received the international sculpture prize for their photographs. On *The Germany Machine*, see Patrick Javault, 'Toutes mémoires confondues', *Les Cahiers du MNAM* 71 (Printemps 2000), pp. 33–45.
5. Marcel Proust, trans. Ian Patterson, *Finding Time Again* [1927] (London: Penguin, 2002), p. 188.
6. Ingeborg Bachmann, trans. Peter Filkins, 'Waiting Room' [1962–3], in *Darkness Spoken* (Brookline, MA: Zephyr, 2006), p. 353.
7. 'Hidden Tracks' at Luhring Augustine in New York (2013) and 'Frankfurter Block' at Sprüth Magers in Berlin (2014).
8. Mucha to ****, October 2009, trans. J. W. Gabriel and Fiona Elliott. Courtesy of the artist.
9. Newman quoted in Alex Danchev (ed.), *100 Artists' Manifestos* (London: Penguin, 2011), p. 322; Mucha to ****.
10. Bachmann, 'Early Noon', in *Darkness Spoken*, p. 37.
11. Mucha to ****.
12. Anselm Kiefer, trans. Michael Taylor, *Art Will Survive its Ruins* (Paris: Regard, 2011), p. 245.
13. Jerry Saltz, 'History's Train', *Art in America* 82 (January 1994), p. 79.
14. See, for example, Grit Weber, trans. Nicholas Grindell, 'Reinhard Mucha, Galerie Bärbel Grässlin, Frankfurt', *Frieze* 5 (Summer 2012), p. 134.

15. Karl Marx and Freidrich Engels, trans. Samuel Moore, *The Communist Manifesto* [1848] (London: Penguin, 2002), p. 223.

16. Both men have written sympathetically about Mucha: see Ulrich Loock, 'Can a Contemporary Art Museum Support the Anachronism of a Work Which Fundamentally Challenges the Museum's Historic Mission?', *Cura* 3 (January–February 2010), pp. 58–62; Jean-Christophe Ammann, 'Vom Lob des Materials und seiner Verwendung', *Nordausgang: Kasse beim Fahrer* (exhibition brochure, 1987), and 'My favourite artists: Reinhard Mucha', at http://home.netvigator.com /~jasperl/rm.htm (last accessed 3 June 2015).

17. Mucha to ****.

18. Mucha to ****.

19. Freidrich Nietzsche, trans. Walter Kaufmann and R. J. Hollingdale, *The Will to Power* [1901] (New York: Vintage, 1968), p. 433.

20. Reinhard Mucha, *fifty postcards* (Köln: König, 1997), a limited edition of 1,000, in German, French and English, incorporating a section of 'found texts' assembled by Hannes Böhringer, under the general heading of 'Detachment' – also apt for Mucha.

21. Quoted in Patrick Frey, trans. Catherine Schelbert, 'Reinhard Mucha – Connections', *Parkett* 2 (1987), p. 119 (translation modified).

22. Mucha to Marion Ackermann, 14 July 2009, trans. John W. Gabriel. Courtesy of the artist. Ulrich Loock addresses himself to this controversy (see above). At the time of writing the installation remains in place, though there are signs of dereliction (one or two of the televisions have ceased to work).

23. Quoted from an article in the *Frankfurter Zeitung* (1926) in Mucha to ****.

8

Tony Blair's Vietnam:
The Iraq War and the Special Relationship

Utility is an impermanent thing: it changes according to circumstances. So with the disappearance of the ground for friendship, the friendship also breaks up, because that was what kept it alive. Friendships of this kind seem to occur most frequently between the elderly . . . and those in middle or early life who are pursuing their own advantage. Such persons do not spend much time together, because they sometimes do not even like one another, and therefore feel no need of such an association unless they are mutually useful. For they take pleasure in each other's company only in so far as they have hopes of advantage from it. Friendships with foreigners are generally included in this class.

Aristotle[1]

There are three kinds of friendship, Aristotle tells us, friendship based on utility, friendship based on pleasure, and friendship based on goodness. Of these three, only the last is perfect, as he says, for 'it is those who desire the good of their friends for the friends' sake that are most truly friends, because each loves the other for what he is, and not for any incidental quality'. In other words the friendship is essential rather than circumstantial, dedicated rather than calculated, persistent rather than evanescent. It does not wait on time and tide, terror and tyranny, suicide attack or simmering stockpile. It rests on character, and specifically on goodness, a scarce commodity. Friendships of this kind are rare, adds Aristotle, because men of this kind are few.

And in addition they need time and intimacy; for as the saying goes, you cannot get to know each other until you have eaten the proverbial quantity of salt together. Nor can one man accept another, or the two become friends, until each has proved to the other that he is worthy of love, and so won his trust. Those who are quick to make friendly advances to each other have the desire to be friends, but they are not unless they are worthy of love and know it.

122

To demonstrate worthiness of this sort is no easy task, individually or internationally. To maintain the conviction is even harder. 'The wish for friendship develops rapidly,' Aristotle concludes appositely, 'but friendship does not.'[2]

The 'special relationship' between Britain and America is a subtle case of friendship between foreigners posited on perfection. International relations in general are not known for their goodness, nor even their disinterestedness, as Aristotle himself underlined; yet the claims made for this particular relationship are founded on virtue. The special relationship is a 'thick' concept, as the philosophers say, or it is nothing. It is not merely an alliance of convenience. It is neither exploitative nor rapacious. It stands for something more than narrow self-interest. It is outward-looking; it has ethical substance and purpose; it speaks the language of 'good' and 'right' and 'ought'; it concerns itself with what should and should not be done, out there, in the world; its purview is global. The very idea of a special relationship suggests thick ties between the partners. Specialness implies rootedness. Hence the much-advertised 'values'.

Anglo-American apologetics echo Aristotelian ethics. The special relationship is an unusually self-conscious one. It creates its own myths and propagates its own legends. What is special about it is its capacity to do this – to invent and reinvent itself, to exploit its mythical potential – which may be as close as we get to its occult essence. The special relationship is a shimmering illusion lost in never-never land, marooned somewhere between a monumentalized past and a mythical fiction, to borrow Nietzsche's terms; and it continues to cast its spell.[3] More conventionally, it is a community of belief, whose celebrants dwell in high places. The stories they tell each other to sustain that belief are of consuming interest.

One such story was told by Tony Blair to Bill Clinton, his first best friend, at a White House dinner in February 1998. It was framed by Blair as a story of 'those great days of America and Britain standing together' in the Second World War. It turns on a fact-finding visit to Britain by Harry Hopkins, FDR's eyes and ears, in January 1941. The outcome of this visit would be critical in determining the President's assessment of Britain's chances of survival and the attitude he would take towards its buccaneer Prime Minister, as Winston Churchill well understood. The climax is reached at a farewell dinner – taking salt together is a rich seam of the tradition. As Blair recounted it:

> On the last evening before he left to take home a message to America he gave a speech to the dinner and sitting next to Churchill he said: 'I suppose you wish to know what I am going to say to President Roosevelt on my return.' And then Harry Hopkins said he would be quoting a verse from the Bible: 'Whither thou goest, I will go, and whither thou lodgest, I will lodge. Thy people shall be my people and thy God my God.' And Hopkins paused and then he said: 'Even to the end.' And Churchill wept.[4]

And Clinton in his turn wept, as Blair surely intended. (The tear-jerker is also part of the tradition. Milking emotion is one of the prerequisites of the special relationship.) Their weepings were incommensurable – if Churchill had nothing to offer but blood, toil, tears and sweat, Clinton had merely the Monica Lewinsky scandal – but the point was made. For the British, standing together is a kind of shibboleth. It is a proof of loyalty, and of dependability. Fifty years ago Oliver Franks observed wisely: 'In the Anglo-American relationship British policy has to pass the test: can the British deliver?'[5] The obligations of alliance are acutely felt by the weak.

In the beginning was the anti-fascist annunciation. The tale of Harry Hopkins is a moral tale. It tells of a good war, a war of indubitable legitimacy, that is the fount and origin of Anglo-American self-regard and raison d'être. It is told, and retold, for a purpose. Rigorous analysis of the grounds for a special relationship has always been too difficult. Adepts have opted instead to testify, like evangelicals. Ever since 1941 the relationship has led a double life: on the one hand, a hole-and-corner affair, secret and taboo, regularly disavowed; on the other, back-slapping bonhomie, brazen self-promotion, razzamatazz, showtime! In brief, private observance and public performance. For prime ministers and presidents, public performance would not be complete without the evangelical set-piece – the speech – a cocktail of primitive faith and popular history, emotionally charged, full of solemn incantation, shameless glorification, and ritual invocation of the household god Winston.

'There is a union of mind and purpose between our peoples which is remarkable and which makes our relationship truly a special one. I am often asked if it is special, and why, and I say: "It is special. It just is and that is that!"' Thus Margaret Thatcher, in characteristic vein, addressing the rubicund Ronald Reagan at the British Embassy in Washington in 1985. In all this testifying, a sort of rhetorical equiprobability has been smuggled in. Specialness is goodness. Goodness is specialness. Good men (and good women) make good wars. Being good is doing good, together. 'As Winston once said,' Thatcher went on, proprietorially, as if they were personally acquainted, '"The experience of a long life and the promptings of my blood have wrought in me the conviction that there is nothing more important for the future of the world than the fraternal association of our two peoples in righteous work, both in war and peace!" No one could put it better than that.'[6]

Tony Blair is a devil for righteous work. 'We are the ally of the US not because they are powerful, but because we share their values,' he admonished a gathering of British ambassadors in January 2003. 'I am not surprised by anti-Americanism,' he continued snappishly, 'but it is a foolish indulgence. For all their faults, and all nations have them, the US are a force for good; they have liberal and democratic traditions of which any nation can be proud.' On this argument, utility is subsumed in goodness. 'Quite apart from that, it is massively in our self-interest to remain close allies.' Pleasure is off, apparently, unless it is a certain uppishness. 'Bluntly there are not many countries who wouldn't wish for the same relationship as we have with the US, and that includes most of the ones critical of it in public.'[7] Stephen Potter, the original satirist of Hands-Across-The-Seamanship, should be living at this hour. 'It is not our policy continuously to try to be one-up, as a nation, on other nations; but it is our aim to rub in the fact that we are not trying to do this, otherwise what is the point of not trying to do this?'[8]

No European leader of his generation speaks so unblushingly of good and evil. *A force for good* was quintessential Blair, and something of a Blairite mantra. If the United States is a force for good, Washington is worthy of love. For the Prime Minister, this meant making a conquest of the tenant of the White House, whoever that may be. Britain too is a force for good, naturally, and also the British Army.[9] This is goodness militant. Tony was a true believer in the mission of the moment. Blazing sincerity was integral to his self-image, or self-construction. Like his folksy friend George (his next best friend), with whom he often looked so uncomfortable, he advertised himself as 'a pretty straight sort of guy'. He spoke with seeming frankness: *frank-seeming* is his *métier*, as Alan Bennett remarked. 'That Tony Blair ... will often say "I honestly believe" rather than just "I believe" says all that needs to be said.' *Time* magazine's correspondent at the Hutton Inquiry made a similar observation: 'In two and a half hours of apparently frank testimony – always thoughtful and reasoned, passionate when passion was called for – Blair gave a masterful performance.'[10]

Articulacy he could do – 'his brilliantly articulate impersonation of earnest inarticulacy'. Authenticity is another matter.[11] A dash of missionary zeal was all part of the service. 'I feel a most urgent sense of mission about today's world,' he told Congress in July 2003. 'September 11th was not an isolated event, but a tragic prologue. Iraq, another act; and many further struggles will be set upon this stage before it's over.'[12]

Doing good in the world was for Blair an ethical imperative and a practical necessity. One of his deepest concerns was said to be untutored unilateralism, to coin a phrase, and its baleful consequences. He told the journalist Peter Stothard, who shadowed his every move for the fateful month of March 2003, that if he was not there side-by-side with the President he feared America would rush in, topple Saddam, and rush out again, careless of the stability of the country it left behind. The same theme is threaded through his speeches. 'Prevention is better than cure,' he argued, beforehand. 'The reason it would be crazy for us to clear out of Afghanistan once we had finished militarily is that if it drifts back into instability, the same old problems will re-emerge. Stick at it and we can show, eventually, as in the Balkans, the unstable starts to become stable.' In sub-Churchillian mode, after the fact: 'Finishing the fighting is not finishing the job.' Most succinctly, six months on: 'We who started the war must finish the peace.'[13]

But there would be no more loose talk of regime change, not from this quarter. That was ruled out of order by the Attorney-General (Lord Goldsmith). The infamous Downing Street memorandum of a meeting of the Prime Minister's inner circle in July 2002 reveals among other things the Attorney-General's pithy advice, 'that the desire for regime change was not a legal basis for military action'.[14] Oratorically, the Prime Minister fell into line. Clandestinely, he continued on his chosen course. Iraq, too, was sold as a good war, but it was precisely the selling, or the misselling, that gave it a bad name. It was in fact a war of the worst kind, a war of false pretences; manufactured, as one might say, and of doubtful legality. Tony Blair was a party to the intrigue that brought it about. This was a war made in Washington, to be sure, and yet to all intents and purposes it was an Anglo-American intrigue – a sniff of the old exclusivity. Blair fulfilled the role of accomplice-in-chief (see Chapter 9).

In essence, he connived at a deception. The issue of the Prime Minister's deceptiveness, and the deliberateness of the deceptiveness, is an essentially contested question, prey to the prejudiced and the parti pris, and clouded further by an element of wishfulness or self-deception on Blair's part.[15] The documentary evidence is still thin (as thin as the credible intelligence). But the nature of the deception emerges with chilling clarity in the Downing Street memorandum, ironically, in a contribution from 'C', the Chief of the Secret Intelligence Service (Sir Richard Dearlove), recently returned from talks with the cousins: 'Military action was now seen as inevitable. Bush wanted to remove Saddam, through military action, justified by the conjunction of terrorism and WMD. But *the intelligence and facts were being fixed around the policy.*'[16] This last formulation (a neat one) was subsequently corroborated by the President himself in another leaked memorandum, of a tête-à-tête at the White House in January 2003, when he coolly informed the Prime Minister that 'the diplomatic strategy had to be arranged around the military planning'.[17]

At both of these meetings, the internal British one in July 2002 and the Anglo-American one in January 2003, the explicit assumption was that the United Kingdom would take part in any military action. British spear carriers were not strictly necessary, as the US Secretary of Defense made unpalatably plain at the time ('there are workarounds'), but Washington needed a fig-leaf of legitimacy for this fight.[18] London supplied it. That was its function. Churchill once said that all he expected was compliance with his wishes after reasonable discussion. Much the same is true of Washington and the special relationship. Compliance is expected; enthusiasm is super-erogatory. The British Prime Minister, 'that simpering little whore' in the immortal words of Hunter S. Thompson, is not exactly a harlot; British troops are not exactly mercenaries.[19] But the Hessian option was more nearly a reality in Iraq than in Vietnam. Whether or not the British Army is a force for good, it is a stake in the game. The stake bought a say, of a sort. It bought access – 'face time' – and kudos, at least in some circles. These are the traditional marks of favour in the relationship. Latterly they are in short supply. Twice blessed, Tony Blair strutted on the world stage in the role of cheerleader and whipper-in. The memorandum of the second meeting records his fealty: he declared himself 'solidly with the President and ready to do whatever it took to disarm Saddam'.[20]

When it came to military action, Blair had form. He was proud of that, as his speechifying indicated. He had also learned some lessons – he thought – on how to manage Anglo-American relations, in particular, the delicate business of being best friend. Tony Blair is now firmly ensconced in the public mind as the President's poodle. (In the British public mind, that is, and more weakly in the international one; in the American mind he has not yet lost his sheen. In this as in other respects, there is a parallel with Margaret Thatcher.) He himself has been conscious of 'the poodle factor' from the outset. 'If [terrorism] is the threat of the 21st century, Britain should be in there helping to confront it,' ran one apologia, 'not because we are America's poodle, but because dealing with it will make Britain safer.' He put a somewhat more sophisticated argument to the assemblage of ambassadors:

> The price of British influence is not, as some would have it, that we have, obediently, to do what the US asks. I would never commit British troops to a war I thought was wrong or unnecessary. Where we disagree, as over Kyoto, we disagree. But the price of influence is that we do not leave the US to face the tricky issues alone. By tricky, I mean the ones which people wish weren't there, don't want to deal with, and, if I can put it pejoratively, know the US should confront, but want the luxury of criticizing them for it. So if the US act alone, they are unilateralist; but if they want allies, people shuffle to the back.[21]

Disobedience, however, was not his forte. ('We keep waiting for his *Love Actually* moment,' bemoaned one of his ministerial colleagues, 'and it never comes.'[22]) Even before 9/11, perceptive observers noted his chronic lack of leverage, together with his promiscuous warmth, his serial devotion, his eager demeanour, his reluctance to challenge, even in private, and drew the inevitable conclusion about a relationship less special than spaniel. 'In Washington today,' wrote the distinguished commentator Hugo Young in February 2001, 'Tony Blair will do what history tells him. It isn't possible to imagine him doing anything else. He will shake George Bush by the hand, and set about getting as close to him as a weekend in Camp David permits.' 'Some day soon,' he added, a year later, 'Washington will eat him for breakfast, along with the morality it then spits out.' By September 2003, in his last, coruscating column, he was measuring the tragedy of Tony Blair – trust evaporated, credibility vanished – and pondering bleakly 'our country and what becomes of it in abject thrall to Bush and his gang'.[23] Others, equally perceptive, and if anything even more vituperative on the subject of Bush and his gang, conceived of Blair as a minstrel for the American cause, in John le Carré's sardonic phrase: not so much a poodle, more a seeing-eye dog. 'Your little Prime Minister is not the American President's *poodle*, he is his *blind dog*, I hear,' jeers one of the characters in le Carré's tract for the times,

Absolute Friends.[24] Lap dog or guide dog, the canine analogy may be more complex than at first appears, but the power relationship it proposes is as apt as it is unambiguous.

The dog barked in 1999. Blair boldly went to the Economic Club of Chicago, the citadel of isolationism, to deliver a speech entitled 'Doctrine of the International Community'. It was an important speech on an important subject. At the heart of it was the conundrum of humanitarian intervention. 'The most pressing foreign policy problem we face is to identify the circumstances in which we should get actively involved in other people's conflicts.' He offered five considerations:

First, are we sure of our case? War is an imperfect instrument for righting humanitarian distress; but armed force is sometimes the only means of dealing with dictators.

Second, have we exhausted all diplomatic options? We should always give peace every chance, as we have in the case of Kosovo.

Third, on the basis of a practical assessment of the situation, are there military operations we can sensibly and prudently undertake?

Fourth, are we prepared for the long term? In the past we talked too much of exit strategies. But having made a commitment we cannot simply walk away once the fight is over; better to stay with moderate numbers of troops than return for a repeat performance with large numbers.

And finally, do we have national interests involved? The mass expulsions of ethnic Albanians from Kosovo demanded the notice of the rest of the world. But it does make a difference that this is taking place in such a combustible part of Europe.[25]

The bones of Blair's argument had been provided on request by Professor Lawrence Freedman, one of a small coterie invited to covert coffee mornings on international affairs to help Blair prepare for government.[26] Pressed for time, Freedman turned for inspiration to a previous effort to codify the conditions under which the use of military force might be warranted: the so-called Weinberger Doctrine (1984), precipitated by a disastrous American peacekeeping mission in the Lebanon, a bloody failure capped by a humiliating retreat. More fundamentally, the Weinberger Doctrine embodied the consolidated lessons of the Vietnam War. As a template for decision-makers, it was designed to avert either fate – débâcle or quagmire. The sub-text of the Weinberger Doctrine was Never Again.

Given the course of events in Iraq since 2003, it is richly ironic that Tony Blair's guidance on the good intervention owed something to American determination on no more Vietnams. Not the least of the ironies concerns the vexed question of exit strategy. Blair's public pronouncements tended to give the impression that he considered talk of exit strategy so much hot air – prevarication or (worse) pusillanimity on Washington's part. Another portion of the Chicago speech, addressed specifically to Anglo-American resolve over Kosovo, contained the grandiloquent sound bite: 'Success is the only exit strategy I am prepared to consider.' This might possibly find an echo in Bushite absolutism on winning the war on terror, but Clinton and his people were not amused. Official Washington is impatient with exhortation. An undercurrent of mockery crept in. The President's henchmen began to refer to Blair as 'Winston'. The Deputy Secretary of State (Strobe Talbott) was heard to say privately that Winston was 'ready to fight to the last American'.[27]

Blair told one intimate that Kosovo could be his Suez. The ghost of Suez (1956) haunts British decision-makers, even those too young to remember it.[28] (Tony Blair was three.) Suez was traumatic: the special relationship was unhallowed, the Prime Minister (Anthony Eden) undone, the job unfinished. The lesson drawn by military men savoured of the inquest on Vietnam. 'What Suez lacked was coherent ministerial resolve,' reflected the Chief of the Defence Staff at the time of the Falklands War (1982). 'There were too many changes of mind, and changes of course, whereas I think the background to success of the Falklands was that we set our objective, and we stuck to it, absolutely, throughout.'[29] As for the politicians, the lesson drawn by Margaret Thatcher is a representative one. 'We should never again find ourselves on the opposite side to the United States in a major international crisis affecting Britain's interests.'[30] In plain language, never go to war without the Americans, an injunction very nearly flouted by Thatcher herself over the Falklands. In that little war the US Secretary of State (Alexander Haig) tried rather desperately to mediate; but even as he shuttled vainly between London and Buenos Aires he was clear that, whatever attitude the Americans took towards British belligerence, they would not repeat Suez, as they put it. 'By which they meant they would not pillory us, even if they did not agree with us,' Sir Nicholas Henderson has explained. 'They would not put us in the dock, as they had done in 1956 over Suez, and bring us to our knees.' In other words, they would not let their ally down. They might be equivocal, but they could not be impartial. They would do their bit. Notwithstanding the nay-sayers, they did.[31] The obligations of alliance are occasionally felt by the strong.

Blair came of age, politically, in the Falklands War. He was first selected as a candidate in a Parliamentary by-election in 1982, at the very moment of decision. He supported the dispatch of the Task Force, with reservations. 'At the same time I want a negotiated settlement and I believe that given the starkness of the military option we need to compromise on certain things. I don't think that ultimately the wishes of the Falkland Islanders must determine our position.'[32] For all the idealism, the moralism and the evangelism, there has always been a strong dose of pragmatism in Tony Blair. As Prime Minister he often seemed to combine a Gladstonian impulse with a Palmerstonian itch – saviour of a fallen world, with a gunboat. Ideologically, he travelled light. What matters is what works, he was fond of saying. *What works* is another Blairite mantra. On the Falklands, he was by no means alone in fearing that the military option might not work. On Iraq, twenty years later, a similar consideration applied. At the Downing Street meeting in July 2002, with his trusted advisors around him, he was most insistent. 'If the political context were right, people would support regime change. The two keys issues were whether the military plan worked and whether we had the political strategy to give the military plan the space to work.'[33]

The special relationship is also a political project, a feature of pragmatism for the twenty-first century. Utility rears its ugly head. The ardent pursuit of specialness had a party-political rationale. For Tony Blair, the messiah of New Labour, tightness with a Republican President and a Republican Administration would effectively neutralize the Conservative opposition. Labour, adept and ambidextrous, could work with Democrats and Republicans alike; even the Neo-Cons had no need of the Cons. The nub of the work was national security. New Labour, unlike old Labour, could be trusted with the defence of the realm. Another plank of the opposition platform had collapsed. The Conservatives supported the Iraq War – they could find no way to oppose it – but their support was redundant. In fact their redundancy was all but complete. They had been outflanked, or blindsided, and they knew it. They were reduced to internecine impotence. The project of specialness through adhesiveness had done its worst. As formulated by the Prime Minister's Foreign Policy Advisor, David Manning, 'At the best of times, Britain's influence on the US is limited. But the only way we exercise that influence is by attaching ourselves firmly to them and avoiding public criticism wherever possible.'[34] At home, the limpet strategy was a calculating powerplay.[35] In electoral terms it was a consummate success. Blair or Bliar, new or shop-soiled, Labour won three straight general election victories, in 1997, 2001 and 2005, an unprecedented feat.

Home and abroad are intertwined. In Anglo-American relations a friend in need is a friend in political difficulty. Asking for help in these circumstances is allowed and understood. So is an element of gamesmanship. Playing on domestic political difficulties is part of the repertoire. According to the well-informed Bob Woodward, Blair asked Bush for help during their tête-à-tête in January 2003. The pitch was that a second UN resolution was for him an absolute political necessity. 'Blair said he needed the favor. Please.' Bush heard, in his fashion. He called it 'the famous second resolution meeting'.[36] He tried, up to a point. It did not happen. Politically, however, *extra-specially*, as one might say, it was perhaps the conspicuous effort that was needed, as much as the resolution itself.

For it is also a question of pragmatism in the world. Blair recapped for the documentary filmmaker Michael Cockerell: 'The reason why we are with America in so many of these issues is because it is in our interests. We do think the same, we do feel the same, and we have the same – I think – sense of belief that if there is a problem you've got to act on it.'[37] Anglo-America is the sphere of clarity and action; Europe, turgidity and vexation. The White House has the capacity and the will – and latterly the faith. 'We're history's actors,' one of Bush's senior advisors memorably said to the journalist Ron Suskind, 'and you, all of you, will be left just to study what we do.'[38] But not Tony Blair. Blair the renegade from the reality-based community, Blair the interloper with the patter and the air-portable brigades, Blair the biddable best friend, would be in on the act. Tony was 'our guy'. He talked the talk and walked the walk. He had *cojones*, the President announced; he was someone 'who does not need a focus group to convince him of the difference between right and wrong'.[39] The others – Jacques, Gerhard, even Vladimir – they had their own issues to deal with. Tiger shooting was not their cup of tea.

Blair was committed. Commitment, he argues, is the crux of the matter. Michael Cockerell asked him if the special relationship depends in part on whether the British are prepared to send troops, 'to commit themselves, to pay the blood price'. He replied, unhesitatingly, 'Yes. What is important though is that at moments of crisis they [the Americans] don't need to know simply that you are giving general expressions of support and sympathy. That is easy, frankly. They need to know, are you prepared to commit, to be there when the shooting starts?'[40] On this analysis the special relationship is a sanguinary affair. The price of influence must be paid in blood. Blair is not alone in advancing such an argument; indeed, he may well have been reinforced in it by influential voices in the Army high command and the intelligence community. Not the least of its weaknesses is that it is apt to be circular, if not self-fulfilling. In 2009, for example, after six years of commitment in Iraq, the Chief of the General Staff could be found arguing publicly that 'credibility with the US is earned by being an ally that can be relied upon to state clearly what it will do and then do it effectively'.

> Credibility is also linked to the vital currency of reputation and in this respect there is a recognition that our national and military reputation and credibility, unfairly or not, have been called into question at several levels in the eyes of our most important ally as a result of some aspects of the Iraq campaign. Taking steps to restore this credibility will be pivotal – and Afghanistan provides an opportunity.[41]

Others are more sceptical. 'There comes a point where, if you hug too close, it becomes an end in itself,' as the Ambassador in Washington in the run-up to the Iraq War, Christopher Meyer, shrewdly remarked.[42] Meyer had put his finger on something fundamental. For the British, the special relationship tends to become an end in itself. Such a posture speaks of imprudence or impotence. Not only does it invite disappointment – as in Iraq, as in Afghanistan – it is ultimately self-defeating, for it puts in jeopardy the crucial element, the touchstone of specialness in a tarnished world: reciprocity. Without reciprocity, the special relationship is a thing of rags and tatters, a facsimile of its former self; a performance, increasingly hollow. Cue the practised appeal to past glories.

The quest for credibility goes back to the very beginnings of the relationship. The case for commitment was pressed on Tony Blair's Labour predecessor Clement Attlee (his polar opposite in stance and style) by the magisterial Oliver Franks, British Ambassador in Washington, on the outbreak of the Korean War in 1950. The question arose of a British military contribution, in particular, a token ground force. Franks took it upon himself to write a personal letter to the Prime Minister. The burden of his argument was twofold. First, 'the initial British reaction to any major question is the most important from the American point of view'. If the initial reaction appeared negative, or merely consultative, 'then we are "against it" no matter what happens afterwards. The reverse applies.' Secondly, 'the Americans will to some extent . . . test the quality of the partnership by our attitude to the notion of a token ground force'. This token, therefore, was a token of commitment, and also a token of friendship. Franks disclaimed any attempt to suggest what the outcome should be: the implication was clear enough. That course of action did not commend itself to London. But Attlee himself was convinced. He put it to his colleagues that they could not expect to maintain a special relationship purely on the strength of wise counsel. Disinterested advice was inappropriate. Sympathy was not enough. The Chiefs of Staff swallowed their scruples and decided to send a brigade group of British troops to fight alongside the Americans. Nothing less would do. The Cabinet endorsed the decision as 'a valuable contribution to Anglo-American solidarity'. The argument advanced by Oliver Franks carried the day.[43]

This seemed to be a lesson learned.[44] And yet the next Labour Prime Minister appeared quite deliberately to unlearn it. Throughout the Vietnam War, Harold Wilson steadfastly or serpentinely refused to make any contribution of that sort, resisting all blandishment and intimidation – resisting even the formidable, almost physical, persuasive power of President Lyndon Johnson. Wilson was not short of suggestions for a token ground force. When he offered to fly to Washington for talks in 1965, fearing further escalation, Johnson told him to mind his own business. 'I won't tell you how to run Malaysia and you don't tell us how to run Vietnam', adding that Britain should 'send us some folks to deal with these guerrillas'. When Wilson brought up Attlee's talks with Truman on Korea (in 1950), Johnson pointed out that Britain had troops in Korea but not in Vietnam.[45] 'A platoon of bagpipers would be sufficient,' the President informed him when they met the following year, 'it was the British flag that was needed'. As the Secretary of State (Dean Rusk) put it to the British journalist Louis Heren, in 1968, 'All we needed was one regiment. The Black Watch would have done. Just one regiment, but you wouldn't. Well, don't expect us to save you again. They [the Russians] can invade Sussex, and we wouldn't do a damned thing about it.'[46]

Johnson did not like to be denied. He was resentful. Wilson started low in his estimation and sank lower. The US Ambassador to London (David Bruce) confided to his diary the President's 'antipathy' for the Prime Minister.[47] Barely concealed contempt might be nearer the mark. There was something of the weasel about Wilson, he thought, weasel words, weasel gestures. On another occasion when London asked for a meeting, the President's response was well-nigh unprintable. 'We got enough pollution around here already without Harold coming over with his fly open and his pecker hanging out, peeing all over me.' When they talked, the obligations of alliance hung heavy between them. Without soldiers in the field, Britain was 'willing to share advice but not responsibility', Johnson reminded him, as if to anticipate Tony Blair.[48] Nevertheless, LBJ forbore from trying to take advantage of the chronic weakness of sterling to strong-arm Wilson into a deal – dollars for troops – less crudely, loans to support the pound in exchange for a token ground force, a move advocated by his National Security Advisor (McGeorge Bundy), who considered that 'it makes no sense for us to rescue the pound in a situation in which there is no British flag in Vietnam', and advised the President to indicate directly that 'a British brigade in Vietnam would be worth a billion dollars at the moment of truth for sterling'.[49]

Johnson's patience was sorely tried. Wilson had the irritating habit of presenting himself as a restraining influence on the US, another traditional Anglo-aspiration. In June 1966 the British Government publicly dissociated itself from the bombing of petrol, oil and lubricant installations in Hanoi and Haiphong. Tricked out in Parliamentary language, 'dissociation' looked uncommonly like posturing (and propitiating the Labour left wing). To Washington this was nothing other than a craven case of shuffling to the back. It rankled. McGeorge Bundy's successor, Walt Rostow, inveighed against 'an attitude of mind which, in effect, prefers that we take losses in the free world rather than the risks of sharp confrontation'.[50]

The Prime Minister almost had to beg for an audience with the President, but he was permitted to indulge his penchant for peacemaking. Over the winter of 1966–7 he was given a long enough leash to involve himself in a series of diplomatic initiatives with Moscow, in the person of the Soviet Premier Alexei Kosygin, only to find the rug pulled from under him by a combination of inattention, exasperation and suspicion on the part of the White House. Harold Wilson was apt to claim a privileged position and a special insight into both superpowers – the dream of Britain as moderator exercises a continuing fascination – but one of the many difficulties of his situation was that, if anything, the claim had more justification with Moscow than with Washington. When he floated the idea of a mission to Hanoi, an idea that emerged during his talks with Kosygin, it was time to call a halt to Harold's incontinent freelancing. The draft reply prepared for the Secretary of State ran as follows: 'Thank you, we are grateful for your steadfastness, persistence, skills, etc., etc., in talks thus far. Believe, in light of our various private ongoing efforts such a trip would be counter-productive at this time. Will keep in close touch. Thanks again, etc., blah blah blah.'[51]

On the face of it there is a stark contrast between the limpet strategy adopted by Tony Blair and the jellyfish strategy adopted by Harold Wilson. In November 1967 the Foreign Secretary (George Brown) recommended to Cabinet the continuation of 'our present policy of committed detachment'. He concluded: 'Uncritical alignment behind the Americans would be an act of folly.'[52] Under the Blair regime such a sentiment would have been unthinkable, or at any rate unspeakable, for any holder of high office. 'Committed detachment' was for Blair and his cohorts not merely oxymoronic but obviously moronic. Cabinet ministers were powerless to object. Cabinet as a collectivity was supine. In March 2002 the Prime Minister gave them their instructions: 'I tell you that we must steer close to America. If we don't we will lose our influence to shape what they do.'[53]

Wilson certainly demonstrated the impossibility of a relationship at the same time close and arms-length. His only commitment was detachment. Exactly when and how Blair committed himself to Bush is unknown, and perhaps unknowable in terms of time and date and precise wording, but the most striking thing about his modus operandi is the care he took to reassure the President of his good intentions. The dominant motif of his most private protestations in the long lead-in to the Iraq War is the reiterated pledge 'I'm with you.' He so averred in a personal letter to the President in July 2002; at 'the *cojones* meeting' in September 2002; and, repeatedly, during a decisive telephone conversation in March 2003, in which Bush gave him a chance to opt out – if that would avert the fall of his government – and Blair declined, with a little touch of Harry in the night. 'Thank you. I appreciate that. It's good of you to say that. But I'm there to the very end.'[54] Wilson offered Johnson no such reassurance. The reverse applies, as Oliver Franks might have said. Johnson must have felt that he could well do without him. But he would surely have appreciated that brigade group.

Beyond the protestations of faithfulness, however, there is a curious affinity of fate. Both Blair and Wilson ran their own show. Both focused their attention on the President. The relationship between Prime Minister and President is a combustible one. It is as high-maintenance as it is high-risk. Closed doors and personal diplomacy are prone to arouse suspicion. George Brown suspected Wilson of doing a deal with Johnson behind his back. Did Tony Blair's senior colleagues feel similarly? They have been careful to cover their tracks, but among the Defence Secretary's contributions to the Downing Street cabal of July 2002 is the remark that, 'if the Prime Minister wanted UK military involvement [in Iraq], he would need to decide this early'. The decision was Blair's, certainly, but they were all in it together. In the circumstances, one might have expected a more plural construction (we rather than he), and even a degree of encouragement. Was there perhaps an element of distancing here?[55]

Covering his tracks never held much appeal for George Brown. Barbara Castle recorded his tirade in her diary:

> 'God knows what he has said to him. Back in 1964 he stopped me going to Washington. He went himself. What did he pledge? I don't know: that we wouldn't devalue, and full support in the Far East. Both those have got to go. We've got to turn down their money and pull out the troops: all of them. I don't want them out of Germany. I want them out of East of Suez. This is the decision we have got to make: break the commitment to America. You are left-wing and I am supposed to be right-wing, but I've been sickened by what we have had to do to defend America – what I've had to say at the dispatch box.' 'Vietnam?' 'Yes, Vietnam, too. And I know what he'll say this time: let's get over this again, then he'll go to Washington and cook up some screwy little deal.'[56]

Wilson did no deal, yet he was deeply compromised by Vietnam. He acquired a reputation for deviousness unparalleled in British politics. He stood accused of an unsavoury mix of duplicity, complicity and mendacity. He had been cast as an apologist for a calamitous American war; he appeared now to have become an apologist for himself. There was a strong sense of hopes betrayed. Disenchantment set in, and even a certain distaste.[57] So much had been expected of Harold Wilson. It was a shame, according to some. Others felt differently. From their perspective it was worse than a shame. It was a disgrace.

If such an accounting exaggerates the wickedness of Harold Wilson, it describes no political career so well as that of Tony Blair. In an almost poetic sense, Iraq is Blair's Vietnam. Scheherazade-like, the folly continues to unfold. For Iraq the end is not yet in sight. For Tony Blair it has already arrived.

Notes

1. Aristotle, trans. J. A. K. Thomson, *Ethics* (London: Penguin, 1976), p. 262 [1156a16–b2].
2. *Ethics*, pp. 263–4 [1156b2–1157a9].
3. On Nietzsche and the storied past, see Alex Danchev, *On Specialness* (London: Macmillan, 1998).
4. Toast at the White House, 5 February 1998. The story was originally recorded by Churchill's doctor, who was there. Moran diary, January 1941, in Lord Moran, *Churchill: The Struggle for Survival* (London: Constable, 1966), p. 6. Blair came across it, he said, in Martin Gilbert's authorized biography. For Clinton's reaction, and the scandal-soaked atmosphere in Washington, see John Kampfner, *Blair's Wars* (London: Free Press, 2004), p. 89; Anthony Seldon, *Blair* (London: Free Press, 2005), pp. 372–3.
5. Oliver Franks, *Britain and the Tide of World Affairs* (Oxford: Oxford University Press, 1955), p. 35.
6. Speech at British Residence, Washington, 20 February 1985, http://www.margaretthatcher.org (last accessed 10 February 2015). There is a telling imbalance. Such speeches are more often delivered by prime ministers than presidents. Compare the irrepressible Bill Clinton, reminded of his obligation to mention the special relationship on the occasion of his first meeting with John Major, in 1993. 'Oh yes,' said Clinton. 'How could I forget. The "special relationship"!' And he threw back his head and laughed. Raymond Seitz, *Over Here* (London: Weidenfeld & Nicolson, 1998), p. 322. On the other hand, that was in private. In public, many gave as good as they got. See, for example, Ronald Reagan's response to Thatcher, above.
7. Speech at Foreign Office Conference, London, 7 January 2003.
8. Stephen Potter, 'Hands-Across-The-Seamanship', in *One-Upmanship* (1952), reprinted in *The Complete Upmanship* (London: Hart-Davis, 1970), p. 263.
9. See the Defence White Paper, *Delivering Security in a Changing World* (London: TSO, 2003). 'The Defence Vision' in this document is a three-pronged affair: 'defending the UK and its interests; strengthening international peace and security; a force for good in the world'.
10. Bennett diary, 29 May 2003, in Alan Bennett, *Untold Stories* (London: Faber, 2005), p. 331; Jeff Chu, 'Winning the battle, losing the war', *Time*, 8 September 2003.
11. John Lanchester, 'Unbelievable Blair', *London Review of Books*, 10 July 2003. On the authenticity project see Alex Danchev, *On Art and War and Terror* (Edinburgh: Edinburgh University Press, 2011), ch. 3.
12. Speech to Congress, 18 July 2003.
13. Speech at Bush Presidential Library, 7 April 2002; speech to Congress,

18 July 2003; speech to Labour Party Conference, 30 September 2003. See Seldon, *Blair*, p. 616, drawing on an interview with Sir Peter Stothard, 2 April 2004. Stothard's fly-on-the-wall diary is *30 Days* (London: HarperCollins, 2003). He records as axiomatic in Blair's circle by September 2002 that 'it would be more damaging to long-term peace and security if the Americans alone defeated Saddam Hussein than if they had international support to do so' (p. 87).

14. 'Iraq: Prime Minister's Meeting', 23 July 2002, in Mark Danner, *The Secret Way to War* (New York: NYRB, 2006), p. 91. At the meeting the AG listed three possible legal grounds for military action: self-defence, humanitarian intervention, and UNSC authorization. He discounted the first two, and considered the third 'difficult' on the basis of pre-existing resolutions. Blair's subsequent public pronouncements take their cue from this. 'Regime change alone could not be and was not our justification for war. Our primary purpose was to enforce UN resolutions over Iraq and WMD.' Speech in Sedgefield Constituency, 5 March 2004.

15. Cf. Danner, *Secret Way*; Andrew O'Hagan, 'King Tony', *New York Review of Books*, 16 November 2006; David Runciman, 'Liars, Hypocrites and Crybabies', *London Review of Books*, 2 November 2006.

16. Meeting of 23 July 2002, in Danner, *Secret Way*, p. 89 (emphasis added).

17. This memorandum, of a meeting on 31 January 2003, was disclosed in Philippe Sands, *Lawless World* (London: Penguin, 2006).

18. Donald Rumsfeld was asked at a press conference on 11 March 2003 whether the US would go to war without Britain. His answer is printed and discussed in Kampfner, *Blair's Wars*, pp. 290–1.

19. Hunter S. Thompson interviewed by Robert Chalmers, *Independent on Sunday*, 31 October 2004. 'I almost felt sorry for Bush, until I heard someone call him "Mr President", and then I felt ashamed. Every nation in the world despises us, except for a handful of corrupt Brits, like that simpering little whore, Tony Blair.'

20. Meeting of 31 January 2003. At this meeting Blair was still talking about a second UN resolution, though in purely instrumental (and somewhat debased) terms: as an 'insurance policy', providing 'international cover', in case anything went wrong with the military campaign, or Saddam raised the stakes (burning oil wells, killing children). Whether these were the terms he thought best calculated to appeal to the President is a matter for speculation, but they do not sit well with the public presentation of 'offering Saddam the prospect of voluntary disarmament through the UN'.

21. Bob Woodward, *Bush at War* (London: Pocket, 2003), p. 107, quoting an unnamed British official, apropos Blair's visit to Washington in

September 2001; speech to Labour Party Conference, 30 September 2003; speech at Foreign Office Conference, 7 January 2003.

22. James Naughtie, *The Accidental American* (London: Pan, 2005), quoting an unnamed British minister. In the 2003 film, the make-believe Prime Minister (the winsome Hugh Grant) finally repudiates the terms of the relationship. 'A friend who bullies us is no longer a friend.'

23. 'Blair might be a poodle, but at least he should bark', 'Blair the intervener', and 'Under Blair, Britain has ceased to be a sovereign state', *Guardian*, 22 February 2001, 30 April 2002 and 16 September 2003. The latter two are collected in Hugo Young, *Supping with the Devils* (London: Atlantic, 2004), pp. 141–4, 319–22. Young died a few days after the final column appeared. Blair paid him fulsome tribute.

24. John le Carré, *Absolute Friends* (London: Hodder, 2003), p. 257 (emphases in original). See also the interview with le Carré in Naughtie, *Accidental American*, p. 122.

25. Speech at the Economic Club, Chicago, 24 April 1999. The speech identified two dictators directly: 'Many of our problems have been caused by two dangerous and ruthless men – Saddam Hussein and Slobodan Milosevic.'

26. Kampfner, *Blair's Wars*, pp. 50–3; Seldon, *Blair*, p. 398. See Lawrence Freedman, 'Chicago Speech: Some Suggestions', 16 April 1999, and Freedman to Chilcot, 18 January 2010, both at http://www.iraq inquiry.org.uk/news/100118-freedman.aspx (last accessed 3 June 2015). The invitees included the former diplomats Sir Rodric Braithwaite, Sir Michael Butler, Sir David Hannay, Sir Nicholas Henderson, Sir Robin Renwick and Raymond Seitz, a transplanted American; together with Timothy Garton Ash and Freedman.

27. Kampfner, *Blair's Wars*, p. 48. Did Blair's advisors also come across Gideon Rose, 'The Exit Strategy Delusion', *Foreign Affairs* 77 (1998), conveniently available on the internet?

28. Kampfner, *Blair's Wars*, p. 49; Seldon, *Blair*, p. 395. See, for example, the interview with Jack Straw in *The Times*, 1 January 2002, quoted in Peter Riddell, *Hug Them Close* (London: Politico's, 2004), p. 141.

29. Admiral Lord Lewin interviewed in Michael Charlton, *The Little Platoon* (Oxford: Blackwell, 1989), p. 203.

30. See Margaret Thatcher, *The Path to Power* (London: HarperCollins, 1995), pp. 87–91.

31. Nicholas Henderson interviewed in Charlton, *Little Platoon*, p. 195; *Mandarin: The Diaries of Nicholas Henderson* (London: Weidenfeld & Nicolson, 1994), p. 444. Henderson was British Ambassador in Washington at the time. *The Official History of the Falklands Campaign* (London: Routledge, 2005) reveals an interesting strain of calculation and lack of whole-heartedness in Washington, mirrored by irritation and sense of grievance in London.

32. Kampfner, *Blair's Wars*, p. 6.

33. Meeting of 23 July 2002. Typically, this was an informal gathering, not a calendared meeting of the Cabinet or a Cabinet committee. Those present were the Defence Secretary (Geoff Hoon), the Foreign Secretary (Jack Straw), the Attorney-General (Lord Goldsmith), the Cabinet Secretary (Sir Richard Wilson), the Chairman of the Joint Intelligence Committee (John Scarlett), the Director of GCHQ (Francis Richards), the Chief of the Secret Intelligence Service (Sir Richard Dearlove), the Chief of the Defence Staff (Admiral Sir Michael Boyce), the Prime Minister's Chief of Staff (Jonathan Powell) and Foreign Policy Advisor (David Manning), the Director of Policy and Government Relations (Sally Morgan), the Director of Government Communications and Strategy (Alastair Campbell), and an aide to David Manning (Matthew Rycroft). These last were truly the Prime Minister's people.

34. Kampfner, *Blair's Wars*, p. 117.

35. See Robin Cook, *The Point of Departure* (London: Pocket, 2004), p. 104; Kampfner, *Blair's Wars*, p. 161.

36. Woodward, *Plan of Attack*, p. 297, apparently on the evidence of Bush himself.

37. Blair interviewed by Michael Cockerell in *Hotline to the President*, BBC2, 8 September 2002. The interview was conducted on 31 July 2002. Parts of it are in Naughtie, *Accidental American*, pp. 135–6.

38. Ron Suskind, 'Without a Doubt', *New York Times*, 17 October 2004.

39. Woodward, *Plan of Attack*, p. 178; Riddell, *Hug Them Close*, p. 199.

40. Cockerell, *Hotline*, extracted in BBC News, 'Britain will pay "blood price" – Blair', 6 September 2002.

41. General Sir Richard Dannatt, speech at Chatham House, 'A Perspective on the Nature of Future Conflict', reported in *Guardian*, 15 May 2009.

42. Christopher Meyer, *DC Confidential* (London: Phoenix, 2006), p. 248. Cf. James Meek, 'Worse than a Defeat', *London Review of Books*, 18 December 2014.

43. See Alex Danchev, *Oliver Franks* (Oxford: Clarendon, 1993), pp. 124ff.

44. By Margaret Thatcher and John Major during the Gulf Conflict of 1990–1, for example, as Tony Blair must have known.

45. Wilson-Johnson telephone conversation, 11 February 1965, PREM 13/692, National Archives (UK); Harold Wilson, *The Labour Government* (London: Weidenfeld & Nicolson, 1971), pp. 80, 116.

46. Wilson, *Labour Government*, p. 264; Louis Heren, *No Hail, No Farewell* (London: Harper & Row, 1970), p. 231.

47. Bruce diary, 22 March 1965, quoted in John Dumbrell and Sylvia Ellis, 'British Involvement in Vietnam Peace Initiatives, 1966–67', *Diplomatic History* 27 (2003), p. 117.

48. Jonathan Coleman, 'Harold Wilson, Lyndon Johnson and the Vietnam

War, 1964–68', *American Studies Today Online*, at http://www.ameri
cansc.org.uk/Online/Wilsonjohnson.htm (last accessed 15 June 2015);
Wilson-Johnson telephone conversation, loc. cit.

49. Bundy to Johnson, 28 July 1965, in Coleman, 'Harold Wilson', p. 3.

50. Coleman, 'Harold Wilson', p. 4.

51. Bruce and Cooper to Rusk, 11 February 1967, in Dumbrell and Ellis, 'Peace Initiatives', p. 140.

52. Cabinet meeting of 15 November 1967, in John Dumbrell, *A Special Relationship* (London: Macmillan, 2001), p. 150.

53. Cabinet meeting of 7 March 2002, in Cook, *Point of Departure*, p. 116.

54. Seldon, *Blair*, p. 76; Woodward, *Plan of Attack*, pp. 178, 338.

55. Meeting of 23 July 2002, in Danner, *Secret Way*, p. 92. The Foreign Secretary for his part had ample cause for suspicion: he was removed from his post in May 2006. Allegedly the White House had conveyed its displeasure over his expressed views on 'the military option' in the case of Iran.

56. Castle diary, 18 July 1966, in Barbara Castle, *The Castle Diaries* (London: Weidenfeld & Nicolson, 1974), p. 148.

57. Noted and contested by Blair himself, in an obituary appreciation, 'Lessons of the Wilson years', *Independent*, 25 May 1995. Cf. R. W. Johnson, 'So much was expected', *London Review of Books*, 3 December 1992; Hugo Young, 'Architect of Labour's ruined inheritance', *Guardian*, 25 May 1995.

9

Accomplicity:
Britain, Torture and Terror

Another guard from [Washington] DC asked me once where I was from. When I told her I was from England, she thought for a moment then asked, 'Y'all got lions, elephants, and shit there?'
'Only in zoos.'

Moazzam Begg[1]

I forgot to ask you first what sort of acquittal you want. There are three possibilities, that is, definite acquittal, ostensible acquittal, and indefinite postponement.

Franz Kafka[2]

grasp
this, there is no law, you are not open to

prosecution, look all you'd like, it will squirm for you, there, in this rising light, protected
from consequence, making you a
ghost, without a cry, without a cry the
evening turning to night, words it seemed were everything and then
the legal team will declare them exempt,
exemptions for the lakewater drying, for the murder of the seas, for the slaves in their
waters, not of our species, exemption named
go forth, mix blood, fill your register, take of flesh, set fire, posit equator, conceal
origin, say you are all forgiven, say these are only
counter-resistant coercive interrogation techniques, as in give me your
name, give it, I will take it, I will re-
classify it, I will withhold you from you, just like that, for a little while, it won't hurt
much

Jorie Graham[3]

They came for Moazzam Begg in Islamabad, Pakistan, on 31 January 2002. Begg was from Birmingham, where he had an Islamic book-shop. His family were from Pakistan. He was peaceable, thoughtful, and unfulfilled. He had gone regularly to Bosnia with a 'Convoy of Mercy'; he had visited Afghanistan; he had made a futile attempt to get to Chechnya. Like Tony Blair, he wanted to do good, but he did

143

not know how. His conventional loyalties were confused. When it came to cricket, he supported Pakistan in England, and England in Pakistan. He was for the underdog. To the warders and whippers of the war on terror, his intentions and his connections were axiomatically suspect. He was taken from his home at the dead of night and shipped to Kandahar. Moazzam Begg became Detainee 558. Bare life had begun.

Detainee 558 was given a full tour of the American penal colony. After Kandahar came Bagram; after Bagram, Guantánamo. He was tortured and abused wherever he went. He was held, often in chains, sometimes in solitary confinement. He was interrogated, ineffectually, as an 'enemy combatant'. The inevitable first question: 'When was the last time you saw Usama bin Laden or Mullah Omar?' In a bizarre twist, he was asked to identify the perpetrators and appear as a witness for the prosecution in an internal investigation of the death of a detainee – a homicide investigation. He himself was never charged, or never told. Three forlorn years later he was informed that 'any charges that we had pending have been dropped', and released without explanation or apology. In conversation he refers to 'the incarceration period' of his life.

Moazzam Begg was already on speaking terms with the Security Service before anyone thought of incarceration. He was haunted by MI5. Contact was first made in 1998, by a man who introduced himself as Andrew. Andrew wanted some information about an acquaintance of his: Begg supplied it. From then on Andrew kept an avuncular eye on his movements. Naturally, Andrew was not alone. Shortly after his abduction in Islamabad he had a visit from Ian, who asked him some questions about his travels to Muslim hotspots, advised him to co-operate with the Americans, and took his leave. At Kandahar, Andrew and Matt (known to the US Military Police as 'the pansies') came to ask him some more of the same. At Bagram, Andrew popped up again, eager to establish his liberal credentials. They had an imitation conversation. 'If we were sitting in a café,' said Andrew to his shackled companion, 'discussing political viewpoints, you'd be quite surprised at some of mine.' Begg told him what had been done to him during the interrogations, emphasizing that the Americans had intended to send him to Egypt to be tortured: 'I asked how he, and the British government, felt about what their top allies had done and were threatening to do. . . . He said that MI5 would never deign to be involved in things like that. I said that surely any information gathered by the Americans via abuse and torture had been shared with the British. He didn't answer that. He just reiterated that Britain would never take part in rendition and torture.'[4]

Evidently something of that 'never deign' attitude communicated itself to the American interrogators at Bagram. 'It sometimes seemed to me,' one of them recalled, 'even among the tough, stout Royal Marines [based there], that most of them regarded the American war mentality – our ferocious desire to defeat the enemy – as a little sophomoric, as if jingoism were beneath them.'[5] Quite so.

At Guantánamo, Begg had a visit from Lucy and a colleague, who brought him a book called *English Passengers* – their little joke, perhaps, or a reflexive account of the subject – and some photographs to identify. Several months later Matt arrived with another book, *The English*.[6] A pattern or a peace offering? Matt had turned solicitous. 'How are you holding out, Moazzam? Is your faith strong, or do you think you're weaker?' Begg took the opportunity to make the familiar complaints: no Muslim chaplain, no regular mail, no lawyers, no progress . . . . 'But why are you here?' 'We're concerned about you,' Matt replied, 'and wanted to let you know that MI5 are not that bad.' With that, MI5 disappeared from view.

After his release, Begg was returned to Britain. He resumed his life in Birmingham. Two or three days after the London bombings of July 2005, he had a long-awaited telephone call. It was Lucy. 'I don't know if you remember me?' Of course he did; in his world there was no Lucy. They wanted to talk to him about the bombings. Rather, they wanted him to talk to them about the bombings. They wanted his help. He met them, talked to them, and when he was talked out, he asked them about Bisher Al-Rawi, a fellow passenger, who had followed the same route from Bagram to Guantánamo, and who was reported to have acted as a conduit for MI5. He asked them if they were not ashamed to be complicit in abduction, and detention, and the extraction of information by torture. He asked them, finally, if they were recording this conversation. He did not believe the answer they gave.

Moazzam Begg is a reflective man. He appreciates irony, in the English way. His memoir of this period is entitled *Enemy Combatant*. Its closing thought is an epitaph on a spoiled relationship. 'MI5 were no different in Birmingham in 2005 than they had been all those other times we had met. They wanted something from me, but they didn't know what it was. I had nothing to give them.'[7]

Together with fifteen others, he set about suing the British government for complicity in rendition and torture. Following a court order to the government to disgorge classified documents relevant to the case, an out-of-court settlement was eventually reached in 2010, involving no concession of liability and no withdrawal of allegations. Clothed in high-minded declarations – 'Torture is illegal and abhorrent under any circumstances, and we have nothing whatsoever to do with it,' ventured the head of MI6 in his first public utterance in 2010 – this is standard operating procedure: deny responsibility; assert operational secrecy; cite obligations to allies (the so-called control principle of intelligence sharing); avoid disclosure at all costs. In Begg's case, the costs have not been disclosed, but the settlement is thought to be substantial, running to several million pounds.

They were not done with Moazzam Begg. On 25 February 2014 he was arrested on suspicion of attending a terrorist training camp and facilitating terrorism overseas. A few days later he was charged with providing terrorist training and funding terrorism overseas, and incarcerated once more, in the high security unit of Her Majesty's Prison Belmarsh. These charges related to Syria. Begg had indeed been visiting Syria – and Egypt, Tunisia and Libya – in his capacity as Outreach Director of the campaigning group Cage (formerly Cage Prisoners), 'to investigate leads into cases of British and American complicity in the rendition of terrorism suspects to the regime of Bashar al-Assad'.[8] These were not clandestine visits; he had written about them copiously, perhaps excessively, on the group's website. He had also written about continued harassment by the state. MI5 must have read all about it. On 1 October 2014, before the case came to trial, all charges were dropped. He was released, all over again.

It is easy to forget that Moazzam Begg is a British citizen. It was easily forgotten. Little or nothing was done on his behalf. His dealings with MI5 did not avail him. The kinder, gentler, book-loving, faith-healing MI5 did not stretch to intercession on his behalf. 'It's all in the hands of the Americans,' Andrew told him carelessly. 'They're calling the shots.' He was disappointed, but he was not surprised. He knew something of the case he brought up with Lucy, the case of Bisher Al-Rawi and his good friend Jamil El-Banna. They were neighbours at Bagram and swapped stories. Begg and El-Banna had met once before, at his bookshop in Birmingham. Meeting Al-Rawi for the first time, as they sorted meal packets, he was horrified by what he heard. Bisher Al-Rawi had learned a hard lesson.

They came for Bisher Al-Rawi in Banjul, Gambia, on 8 November 2002. He had been working for MI5 for about a year. In the wake of 9/11 he was contacted by two agents, Alex and the much-travelled

Matt, recruiting in the Muslim community in London. They asked him some questions and then asked if he would agree to speak to them again. He did. Soon the relationship was put on a more regular footing. Al-Rawi was a willing servant of the secret world, keen enough to do the state some service. He refused payment but accepted a mobile phone at the agents' insistence. In effect he acted as an informant and an intermediary. He was well-qualified for this work. Born in Iraq, he had lived in Britain since 1985; he was educated, fluent in English, and well-connected in the community – so well-connected as to be friendly with Abu Qatada, the radical Muslim cleric whose extremist rhetoric, available on video, had made him an object of interest to terrorists and counter-terrorists alike. Wilder speculation about his being 'Usama Bin Laden's right-hand man in Europe', or 'spiritual advisor to Al-Qaeda', appears to be baseless; but it seems Abu Qatada did have a relationship of some sort with MI5. The go-between was Bisher Al-Rawi.

Abu Qatada was taken into custody in October 2002. It was by all accounts a smooth operation, facilitated by Al-Rawi, assisted by El-Banna. The troublesome priest was freed on bail in August 2005, subject to a control order, but taken back into custody four months later. The Home Secretary wished to deport him to Jordan, arguing that his presence in the United Kingdom was 'not conducive to the public good for reasons of national security'. Abu Qatada for his part wished to remain, contending that 'the national security case against him is based on material obtained as a result of torture'.[9] This was an allusion to the torture of Al-Rawi and El-Banna, at American hands. The association between the various parties had been severed.

Someone must have been telling lies about Bisher Al-Rawi and Jamil El-Banna, for without having done anything wrong they were arrested one fine morning. The two men had gone to the Gambia to help Bisher's brother Wahab set up a mobile peanut-processing plant. This sounds so much like a cover story that it must be true.[10] In fact it was verified by MI5, who took the trouble to visit El-Banna at his London home, a few days before he was due to depart, to tell him so. Not only did they give him an explicit all-clear, they also offered him 'a new life' in an Islamic country if he would co-operate with them. He declined, though he had helped Al-Rawi to help the British authorities in the past. He too was well acquainted with Abu Qatada: they shared the same Jordanian-Palestinian origins. El-Banna had lived in Britain since 1994; he was granted refugee status in 2000. Like Al-Rawi, he was not a citizen but a resident. British residents, they would discover, were of scant concern to government ministers.

Al-Rawi and El-Banna were rendered by the British to the Americans – a most extraordinary rendition. In the officialese of the Joint Committee on Human Rights, 'the High Court recently found that certain intelligence information about two British residents detained in Guantánamo, who were arrested in the Gambia and allege that they were tortured while in American custody in Kabul and Bagram Air Base, was communicated to the authorities of another country by the British security and intelligence services, and that either directly or indirectly this came into the hands of the US authorities'.[11] In plain language, they were apprehended at the instigation of MI5, who gave advance warning of their arrival in a series of telegrams by turns ludicrous and mendacious, clearly designed to implicate the two men in terrorist activities. In a metamorphosis worthy of Kafka himself, the very reason they were cultivated by MI5 in the first place became a farrago of guilt by association and insinuation.

> Bishr [sic] AL-RAWI is an Iraqi Islamist extremist who is a member of ABU Qatada's close circle of associates. He has previously come to our attention for his financial activities in connection with Abu ANAS [the name used by El-Banna, according to MI5]. Bishr's enthusiasm for extreme sports has often brought him to the attention of the police. For example, he was seen driving away from the M4 flyover at Brentford in March 2001, which he and two other individuals had been seen climbing. He is also a qualified diver, a keen dinghy sailor and parachutist.[12]

Not content with that, MI5 alerted the Americans that 'some form of home-made electronic device' had been found in their baggage. 'Preliminary inquiries suggest that it may be a timing device or could possibly be used as some part of a car-based Improvised Explosive Device [IED].'[13] The improvised explosive device was a modified battery charger from Argos – but the damage was done. US Department of Defense records indicate that the pair were arrested in the Gambia while trying to return to Britain with electronic equipment. Both were classified as enemy combatants and members of Al-Qaeda. They were suspected of knowing terrorists and sponsoring terrorism, plotting to establish a training camp of their own in the Gambia, with the quick-hardening rubber cement, small shovel, solder and soldering iron, circuit board and rechargeable batteries in Al-Rawi's rucksack. The rest followed.

The two men were thrown to the lions. When El-Banna vented his anger at the American interrogators, they would say to him: 'Why are you angry at America? It is your government, Britain and the MI5, who called the CIA and told them that you and Bisher were in Gambia and to come and get you. Britain gave everything to us. Britain sold you out to the CIA.'[14]

From the Gambia, Al-Rawi and El-Banna were rendered to the notorious 'Dark Prison' in Kabul for a short period of softening up, and then to Bagram, where they were subject to two months of beatings, starvation, sleep deprivation and interrogation. The interrogators focused relentlessly on Abu Qatada. Repeated attempts were made to suborn testimony from both men, linking Abu Qatada to Al-Qaeda, and more specifically to a bombing in Jordan. El-Banna was offered $5 million to say such things, and given two days to think it over.

Then they came back and told me I could be a 'secret witness', and told me what they wanted me to say about Abu Qatada. This time they offered me $10 million and a US passport, and said that if I did not co-operate, not only would I continue to be held, but my wife would never get a British passport either. They gave me another two days to think about it. Before they even left that time though, I said, if you give me $100 million, I will not bear false witness against Abu Qatada or anyone else.

Then the interrogator came back with two others, and said: 'I am going to London. You know why? I am going to FUCK your wife! Your wife is going to be my BITCH! Maybe you'll never see your children again.' I was very upset by this. . . . I am afraid I spat at him. I was very angry. He slapped me. So I spat at him. He slapped me some more. He was a big guy. There was blood running down my mouth. By this time I was so angry, there were tears of anger running down my face.

After about five minutes of this beating, the interrogator told me that I would have two weeks to think about being a witness, and then he would come back. If not, I would get the Dark Prison again, perhaps for a year. Then I would get five or ten years in Cuba. 'In ten years you will have no family. Your wife will be a bitch, your children will be into drugs.' But actually two weeks later they took me to Cuba.[15]

Al-Rawi went too. In a letter to his mother he did his best to keep up appearances. 'I am writing to you from the seaside resort at Guantánamo Bay. After winning first prize in a competition, I was whisked to this nice resort with all expenses paid. . . . Everybody is very nice, the neighbours are very well-mannered, the food is first-class, plenty of sun and pebbles (no sand, I'm afraid).'[16] The visitors were the usual suspects: Alex, Matt and Martin, all of them familiar to Al-Rawi from encounters in London. They engaged in a little light interrogation, proposed that he return to work with MI5 on his release – he agreed – and told him that it would take between one and six months to get him home.

Three years later, nothing had changed. In 2004 both men appeared before a Combatant Status Review Tribunal (CSRT). Al-Rawi testified under oath to his relationship with MI5, and requested that evidence be sought from the agents involved to corroborate his story. In such unusual circumstances, the tribunal president instructed the military prosecutor to contact the British government. The British government were not forthcoming. They were unwilling to provide the information; they would neither confirm nor deny the relationship. The tribunal had only Al-Rawi's word for it. That would not suffice. In 2006 the High Court ruled that Britain had no obligation to intervene on Al-Rawi and El-Banna's behalf. Lord Justice Latham and Mr Justice Tugendhat were not unsympathetic, but they judged that a formal request regarding the men's case 'would be an interference in the relationship between sovereign states which could only be justified if a clear duty in domestic or international law had been identified'. For all the recent emphasis on humanitarian intervention and the responsibility to protect, national sovereignty still rules in individual cases. There was a sliver of hope. After considering Al-Rawi's 'specific representations', the Foreign Office agreed in his case to make a 'security-related request' to the United States. Following a year of discussions between the Foreign Office and the American authorities, he was released without charge on 30 March 2007. Some months later, on 19 December 2007, El-Banna duly followed.

Less fantastic but more infamous is the case of another British resident, Binyam Mohamed, at once the best-documented and the most revealing to date.

They came for Binyam Mohamed in Karachi Airport on 10 April 2002. He spent three months in the care of the Pakistani authorities. He later told his lawyer (Clive Stafford Smith) that he was interrogated there by British officials: 'One of them did tell me that I was going to get tortured by the [Arabs].'[17] In July 2002 he was rendered by the Americans to Morocco, where that prediction came true. Moroccan officials assured him that they worked closely with MI5; they asked him questions about his past life that he believed could only have come from British sources. In January 2004 he was rendered to Kabul, and in September 2004 to Guantánamo, where he remained for the next four years. On 23 February 2009 he was repatriated to the UK, and released after questioning.

Responding to an inquiry by the Intelligence and Security Committee (ISC), MI5 conceded that a member of the Service had indeed 'interviewed' Mohamed in Karachi, once, for a period of approximately three hours. 'The interview was conducted by an experienced officer,' reported the ISC, 'and was in line with the Service's guidance to staff on contact with detainees. The Security Service denies that the officer told [Mohamed] that he would be tortured, as he alleges. Furthermore, the officer reported that he did not observe any abuse and that no instances of abuse were mentioned by [Mohamed].'[18] This stalwart subsequently found fame as Witness B, when compelled to give evidence in the case brought by Binyam Mohamed against the government, a case focusing on the collusion of MI5 and MI6 in his unlawful treatment by the American authorities. In 2009 he won his case in the High Court. Witness B was referred by the Attorney-General to the Crown Prosecution Service; he went on to help the police with their enquiries. Meanwhile the Foreign Secretary (David Miliband) appealed against the High Court ruling that classified documents pertaining to the case should be made public. In 2010 the formidable trio of the Master of the Rolls (Lord Neuberger), the Lord Chief Justice (Lord Judge), and the President of the Queen's Bench Division (Sir Anthony May), who constituted the Court of Appeal, ruled that Binyam Mohamed had been subject to cruel, inhuman and degrading treatment by the American authorities – a judgement now uncontested – and overruled the Foreign Secretary, forcing the release of a seven-paragraph summary of forty-two classified CIA documents that were handed to MI5 before Witness B travelled to Karachi to conduct his see-no-evil, hear-no-evil interrogation. These documents proved that MI5 was aware that Mohamed was being continuously deprived of sleep, threatened with rendition, and subjected to other interrogations that were causing him 'significant mental stress and suffering'. In other words, they demonstrated beyond doubt that MI5 was complicit in torture.

In 2011 Binyam Mohamed received a £1 million compensation settlement from the British government.

There was a further twist. The draft judgement of the Court of Appeal contained withering criticism of MI5 (and MI6) and their 'culture', prompting the lead counsel for the government (Jonathan Sumption QC) privately to appeal to the Court to reconsider one swingeing paragraph in particular. The Master of the Rolls, who did the drafting, agreed in effect to redact the offending paragraph. After further legal representations, however, Sumption's petition was itself made public, which served helpfully to underline the points at issue. It encapsulated a devastating critique:

> The Master of the Rolls's observations, to whichever service they relate [MI5 alone, or MI5 and MI6], are likely to receive more public attention than any other part of the judgements. They will be read as statements by the Court: (i) that the Security Service does not in fact operate a culture that respects human rights or abjures participation in coercive interrogation techniques; (ii) that this in particular is true of Witness B whose conduct was in this respect characteristic of the Service as a whole ('it appears likely that there were others'); (iii) that officials of the Service deliberately misled the Intelligence and Security Committee on this point; (iv) that this reflects a culture of suppression in its dealings with the Committee, the Foreign Secretary and indirectly the Court, which penetrates the Service to such a degree as to undermine any UK government assurances based on the Service's information and advice; and (v) that the Service has an interest in suppressing information which is shared, not by the Foreign Secretary himself (whose good faith is accepted), but by the Foreign Office for which he is responsible.[19]

Official 'suppression' in this realm is endemic, though it is liable to be punctured by independent investigation. In a deposition compiled at Guantánamo, Bisher Al-Rawi had stated that he was dressed in nappies, hooded and shackled by a CIA rendition team for his transfer from Banjul to Kabul, in a military aircraft, on a Sunday in early December 2002, two or three days after the end of Ramadan. Independent inquiries by Amnesty International, Cage Prisoners and the *Guardian*, aided by some indefatigable plane spotters, established that a Gulfstream V executive jet, registration N379P, arrived in Banjul from Washington on Sunday 8 December 2002, and then flew on to Kabul via Cairo.[20] N379P, also known as the Guantánamo Bay Express, is a registration of some notoriety. It has the distinction of being the plane most often identified with known cases of 'extraordinary rendition'. For this plane alone Amnesty has a record of some 600 landings and take-offs all over the world during the period 2001–5. A detailed breakdown reveals that over 100 of these went through British airports: most often Glasgow (56) and Prestwick (33), sometimes Northolt (16), Luton (11), or Brize Norton (3). The most favoured international stopovers for N379P were Amman, Cairo, Frankfurt, Larnaca, Oporto, Prague, Shannon and Tashkent. It is impossible to know exactly how many of these 'ghost flights' should be attributed to rendition, extraordinary or otherwise, but they were plainly operated by and for the CIA.

The hallmark of rendition is deception, and perhaps self-deception. In Britain, ghost flights were by no means uncommon at airports all over the country, large and small, civil and military alike. Luton was the most popular, but the CIA and its sub-contractors also availed themselves of the facilities at Belfast, Biggin Hill, Birmingham, Bournemouth, Brize Norton, Edinburgh, Farnborough, Gatwick, Glasgow, Heathrow, Inverness, Leuchars, Mildenhall, Northolt, Prestwick, Stansted and Wick. It was difficult to believe that such activity passed unnoticed or unrecorded by the British authorities; and after some persistent Parliamentary questioning it transpired that several of these flights were familiar to the National Air Traffic Services. The government for its part spent an unconscionably long time in denial about what it knew or what it chose not to know. As late as December 2005, asked in the House of Commons when he was first made aware of the rendition flights, the Prime Minister Tony Blair replied: 'In respect of airports, I do not know what the Right Hon. Gentleman is referring to.' Two weeks later, as the controversy mounted, he told journalists: 'It is not something that I have ever actually come across until this whole thing has blown up, and I don't know anything about it.'

Hardly were the words out of his mouth than a leaked memorandum from the Foreign Secretary's private office to the Prime Minister's private office revealed that the government knew of CIA requests for British logistical support, including the use of territory and airspace, and knew also of the existence of 'interrogation centres' in third countries. The memo betrayed a characteristic mixture of complicity and anxiety, issuing in a certain defensiveness. It was couched as a series of questions and answers. Among them:

Would co-operating with a US rendition operation be illegal?

If the US were to act contrary to its international obligations, then co-operation with such an act would also be illegal if we knew of the circumstances. This would be the case, for example, in any co-operation over an extraordinary rendition without human rights assurances. Conversely, co-operation with a 'legal' rendition, that met the domestic law of both of the main countries concerned, and was consistent with their international obligations, would be legal. Where we have no knowledge of illegality but allegations are brought to our attention, we ought to make reasonable enquiries.

> How do we know whether those our armed forces have helped to capture in Iraq or Afghanistan have subsequently been sent to interrogation centres?
>
> Cabinet Office is researching this with MoD [Ministry of Defence]. But we understand the basic answer is that we have no mechanism for establishing this, though we would not ourselves question such detainees while they were in such facilities.[21]

The knowledge was an embarrassment, but still the government did not (officially) know much. There is an element of 'don't ask, don't tell' in the rather attenuated Anglo-American discourse on rendition that is itself a kind of complicity, but is also a function of the habitual agreements and understandings between British and American services and agencies that are the bedrock of the much-touted special relationship (see Chapter 8). These transactions are informal, autonomous and secret. They may be kept even from ministers. That was true of American bases in Britain during the Cold War. It may well be true of extraordinary rendition during the war on terror. When it comes to operational detail, MI5 and MI6 almost certainly know more, in-house, than the Foreign Secretary or the Prime Minister. No doubt ignorance can be convenient – deniability is always convenient – but it does not rid those responsible of their responsibility. Not knowing is no excuse. Not asking is negligence. If in truth the Prime Minister did not know that extraordinary rendition was being carried out on his doorstep, with the connivance of MI5 (and, it may be, MI6), he should have asked; more than that, he should have insisted on finding out. Tony Blair's instincts in this regard were revealed surprisingly early. In January 2002, a senior official attached to the Cabinet Office sent a lengthy memo to the Prime Minister's Foreign Policy Advisor (David Manning), naming three British citizens held in Afghanistan and noting that they were 'possibly being tortured' by the Americans at a jail in Kabul. Blair was made aware of the issue. He annotated a Foreign Office memo: 'The key is to find out how they are being treated. Though I was initially sceptical about claims of torture, we must make it clear to the US that any such action would be totally unacceptable *and v quickly establish that it isn't happening.*'[22]

The intelligence services are not above a little deniability of their own. In response to another inquiry by the ISC, 'the Security Service [MI5] made the following comments, which are shared by the SIS [Secret Intelligence Service, that is, MI6]':

> Clearly the US is holding some Al-Qaeda members in detention, other than at Guantánamo, but we do not know the locations or terms of their detention and do not have access to them. The US authorities are under no obligation to disclose to us details of all their detainees and there would be no reason for them to do so unless there is a clear link to the UK. We have however received intelligence of the highest value from detainees, to whom we have not had access and whose location is unknown to us, some of which has led to the frustration of terrorist attacks in the UK or against UK interests.[23]

Despite these lawyerly denials, the same inquiry turned up several pieces of disturbing evidence. ISC reports are carefully worded. On especially sensitive issues they are officially redacted. These suppressions are indicated by three asterisks, as if blasphemous. Ostensibly, the criterion for exclusion is anything 'prejudicial to the continuing discharge of the functions' of the agencies; actually, this can be interpreted to include anything prejudicial to the cosy relationship among the cousins, and in particular anything that might discommode the White House – accomplicity by other means. Thus, with reference to MI6 interrogation of detainees in Afghanistan:

> On 10 January 2002, the first day that the SIS had access to US-held detainees, an SIS officer conducted an interview of a detainee. Whilst he was satisfied that there was nothing during the interview which could have been a breach of the Geneva Conventions, he reported back to London his '. . . observations on the circumstances of the handling of [the] detainee by the US military before the beginning of the interview. * * *
> * * *
> * * *
> * * * '[24]

Senior officials were sufficiently alarmed by those observations to issue a general instruction to all Secret Intelligence Service and Security Service officers in Afghanistan on the appropriate treatment of detainees, reminding them of their responsibility under the Geneva Conventions and other instruments, and also of their criminal liability under British criminal law. The instruction went out the very next day. That was prompt action indeed, but it did not go far enough, as the ISC pointed out. Unsurprisingly, it was weak on reporting such matters to the American authorities ('if circumstances allow, you should consider drawing this to the attention of a suitably senior US official locally'). In London, moreover, the whole issue remained something of a sideshow, confined to the mandarinate, whispered in corners, viewed with some disdain, as a mixture of trade secret and tittle-tattle, and, perhaps, only to be expected of those clumsy oafs the Americans. 'Abuse' was kept strictly off the agenda. 'Torture' never passed their lips. A quietly devastating paragraph of the ISC's report – more devastating than they knew – tells its own story:

> We have been told that in the margins of the 31 January 2002 meeting of Permanent Secretaries, what were reported to us as being 'anecdotal reports, some second or third hand, of "undue exuberance" by American personnel at Guantánamo Bay' were mentioned. The Permanent Secretary at the FCO sought more details but the Security Service could add nothing to the original comment. No action was taken by the FCO and Ministers were not informed that the matter had been raised until June 2004.[25]

As the war widened, the reports multiplied. 'Undue exuberance' at Abu Ghraib resulted in 'numerous incidents of sadistic, blatant, and wanton criminal abuses', in the words of the American investigation into the conduct of the Military Police in that chamber of horrors. The iconic photographs of those abuses – dogs, hoods, electrodes and all – were first made public in April and May 2004. By June 2004 the scandal was in full swing. It is doubtless no coincidence that the mandarins bestirred themselves to inform their masters that same month.[26] After all the rumours of torture and abuse over the previous two years, nerves cannot have been steadied by the furtive knowledge that a British military interrogation team had been deployed at Abu Ghraib from January to March 2004. The Ministry of Defence did its best to reassure the ISC that this was 'substantially after the period in which concerns about US handling of prisoners at the facility had been identified', but that was no more than a half-truth.[27] The abuse was at its height from October to December 2003; dogs were still being used to 'fear up' detainees in January 2004, only days before the arrival of the investigators.

The Prime Minister himself tried desperately to refocus. In a set-piece speech on foreign policy delivered in March 2006, he characterized the current conjuncture not as a clash of civilizations but as 'a clash about civilization', a struggle between 'democracy' and 'violence', modernism and medievalism, light and dark, good and evil, us and them. In this binary world, *we* are traduced and *they* are exempted. 'Examine the propaganda poured into the minds of Arabs and Muslims,' he urged. 'Every abuse at Abu Ghraib is exposed in detail; of course it is unacceptable but it is as if the only absence of due process in that part of the world is in prisons run by the Americans.' He peddled the same line in his memoirs four years later.[28] There is no glimmer of recognition here of the immense damage done by Abu Ghraib; the shame felt throughout the Muslim world; the humiliation visited on the United States, on the alliance of values, on *us*. 'We translated our ignorance into their pain,' as Mark Danner remarked, of the manifold abuses revealed in the report of the US Senate Intelligence Committee on the CIA's detention and interrogation practices – an investigation unmatched on the British side.[29]

For Tony Blair, accomplice-in-chief, the lesson is for others. He is a great persuader – Dick Cheney's preacher on a tank – but he is profoundly mistaken. As Walt Whitman knew, the damage is indivisible.

> Whoever degrades another degrades me,
> And whatever is done or said returns at last to me.[30]

Where civilization is invoked, barbarism is rarely far behind. Sure enough, one of the Prime Minister's loyal placemen soon began wondering aloud whether the time had come to revisit the fusty old Geneva Conventions. 'Much has been achieved in current legal frameworks,' puffed the Secretary of State for Defence. 'But warfare continues to evolve, and, in its moral dimensions, we have now to cope with a deliberate regression towards barbaric terrorism by our opponents.' Barbaric terrorism is not cricket. This sort of talk has a long history. 'As the terrorists grew more brutalized,' explained the Secretary of State for the Colonies half a century earlier, 'their moral degradation was reflected in the characteristics of the Mau Mau oath ... the taking of the oath had such a tremendous effect on the Kikuyu mind as to turn quite intelligent young Africans into entirely different human beings, into sub-human creatures without hope and with death as their only deliverance'.[31]

Civilization, like degradation, is in the eye of the beholder. It has a curiously reversible property. 'Ah yes,' says the Magistrate in J. M. Coetzee's prophetic novel, *Waiting for the Barbarians*, 'time for the black flower of civilization to bloom.'[32] In one sense, Blair was right. 'Absence of due process,' as he delicately put it, was not confined to facilities run by the Americans. At Camp Breadbasket, near Basra, officers and men of the Royal Regiment of Fusiliers were doing much the same thing: 'Ali Baba hunting', 'beasting', sexually humiliating and snapping Iraqis.[33] There are other cases of tormenting and beating and videoing, complete with schlock commentary – 'Oh yes! Oh yes! You're gonna get it. Yes, naughty little boys. You little fuckers, you little fuckers. Die. Ha Ha' – disgraceful conduct of a cruel kind, as one of the charge sheets appropriately recorded.[34]

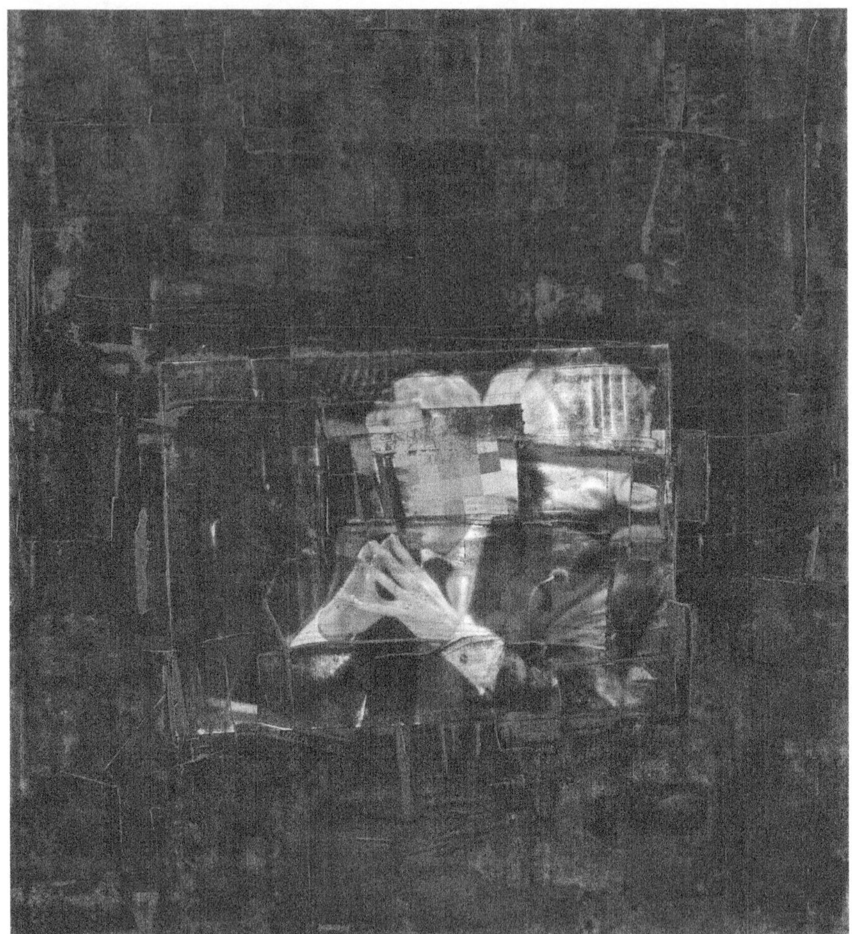

Figure 9.1
John Keane, *Figure at an Inquiry No. 5*, 2010
Oil on Linen
215 × 200 cm
© John Keane, Collection Nick Taylor

In the global war on terror, these are common-or-garden crimes. The British are small-time torturers. The template is all too familiar. 'The prisoner of war does not belong to our tribe. We can do what we want with him.'[35] A blind eye is turned to a bad apple. The crimes are disowned by the command. They are uncovered by whistleblowers or (unwittingly) by the perpetrators themselves. Scandal ensues. Internal inquiries eventuate in formal proceedings. Solemn courts martial hand down minimal sentences to Corporals and below.

Some time later, once the noise has subsided, behind closed doors the sentences are reduced.[36] Officers are conspicuous by their absence. Civil servants keep their silence. Politicians squirm and stonewall. 'As I thought on how to answer the question that was put to me at the end of my evidence to the Chilcot Inquiry,' Blair recalls in his memoirs, 'I felt sick, a mixture of anger and anguish.' The question was whether he had any regrets. It was put twice, by Chilcot himself, and on Blair's own account his answer was deliberately incomplete. He spoke of a sense of responsibility; he expressed no regrets. He seems to feel that he was set up. 'The anger was at being put in a position in an inquiry that was supposed to be about lessons learned, but had inevitably turned into a trial of judgment, and even good faith; and in front of some of the families of the fallen, to whom I wanted to reach out, but knew if I did so, the embrace would be immediately misused and misconstrued.'

There remains the anguish. 'The principal part of that is not selfish,' he continues. 'Some of it is, to be sure. Do they really suppose I don't care, don't feel, don't regret with every part of my being the loss of those who died?' Now, he says, he is beyond tears, beyond sympathy, beyond sorry. He is in a different place, a place of perpetual burden. 'Regret can seem bound to the past. Responsibility has its present and future tense.'[37] Piteous yet unrepentant, Tony Blair feels your pain.

Meanwhile, in another strange land, an old tale is being re-told, a tale of 'white rulers and non-white ruled facing off against each other like animals and keepers at a zoo'.[38] It might be a tale from the *Thousand and One Nights*.

Once upon a time, in the city of Basra . . .

Notes

1. Moazzam Begg, *Enemy Combatant* (London: Free Press, 2006), p. 254.
2. Franz Kafka, trans. Willa and Edwin Muir, *The Trial* [1925], in *The Collected Novels of Franz Kafka* (London: Penguin, 1988), p. 117.
3. Jorie Graham, 'Guantánamo', *From the New World* (New York: Ecco, 2015), pp. 270–1.
4. Begg, *Enemy Combatant*, pp. 167–8.
5. Chris Mackey with Greg Miller, *The Interrogator's War* (London: Murray, 2004), p. 292. 'Chris Mackey' is a nom de plume.
6. *English Passengers* is a historical novel of war, mutiny, shipwreck and farce by Matthew Kneale (London: Penguin, 2001); *The English* is a 'portrait of a people' by Jeremy Paxman (London: Penguin, 1999). The

intelligence services appear to be fond of instructive works. MI6 gave Paul Henderson, Managing Director of the Matrix Churchill Company, a copy of *Republic of Fear* by Samir al-Khalil (the nom de plume of the Iraqi exile Kanan Makiya) before his departure for Baghdad to spy for Britain in 1989.

7. Begg, *Enemy Combatant*, p. 387 (emphasis added).

8. See Moazzam Begg, 'The real reason behind the confiscation of my passport', 24 December 2013, and 'Syria: Britain's new War on Terror', 27 January 2014, http://www.cageprisoners.com (last accessed 10 February 2015).

9. Special Immigration Appeals Commission (SIAC) hearing, 9 May 2006.

10. The most detailed reconstruction of the story thus far is by Reprieve, drawing on evidence given at a public hearing of the All Party Parliamentary Group (APPG) on 28 March 2006, at http://www.reprieve.org (last accessed 3 May 2006). The US lawyer for the two men has compiled his own account, based on conversations with his clients and other sources: George Mickum, 'MI5, Camp Delta, and the story that shames Britain', *Independent*, 16 March 2006. Other investigations include Robert Verkaik, '"I am writing to you from the seaside resort of Guantánamo"', *Independent on Sunday*, 30 April 2006; and Cage Prisoners, 'Fabricating Terrorism: British Complicity in Renditions and Torture' (2006), case 3, at http://www.cageprisoners.com (last accessed 30 March 2006); Intelligence and Security Committee, *Rendition* (July 2007), paras 111–47. See the documentation assembled by The Rendition Project, at http://www.therendition project.org.uk (last accessed 12 February 2015).

11. Joint Committee on Human Rights, 'The UN Convention Against Torture' (UNCAT), 26 May 2006, para. 57, citing *Al-Rawi* v. *Secretary of State for Foreign and Commonwealth Affairs* (2006) EWHC Admin 972.

12. MI5 telegram, 11 November 2002, in Verkaik, 'Guantánamo'. In 2005, evidence from SIAC hearings revealed that 'association with Moazzam Begg' was used in at least two cases of 'foreign terror suspects' detained indefinitely without trial at HMP Belmarsh.

13. MI5 telegram, 1 November 2002, in Reprieve narrative, p. 2.

14. El-Banna evidence, in Reprieve narrative, p. 3.

15. El-Banna statement, 19 June 2005, in Reprieve narrative, pp. 6–7.

16. Al-Rawi to his mother, in Verkaik, 'Guantánamo'.

17. Reprieve submission to ISC, 4 December 2006, in ISC, *Rendition*, para. 99.

18. ISC, *Rendition*, paras 102–3.

19. Sumption to High Court, 8 February 2010, in *Guardian*, 10 February 2010.

20. Amnesty International, 'United States of America: Below the Radar: secret flights to torture and "disappearance"', 4 April 2006, at http://www.amnesty.org (last accessed 4 June 2015); Cage Prisoners, 'Fabricating Terrorism'; Ian Cobain et al., 'Destination Cairo' and 'Britain's role in war on terror revealed', *Guardian*, 12 September and 6 December 2005. See also Ian Cobain, *Cruel Britannia* (London: Portobello, 2013), ch. 7.

21. Irfan Siddiq to Grace Cassy, 7 December 2005, at http://www. newstatesman.com (last accessed 13 May 2006). Cf. Philippe Sands, 'Extraordinary Rendition: complicity and its consequences', Justice International Rule of Law Lecture, 15 May 2006; and Joint Committee, UNCAT, paras 148–70.

22. Blair annotation on FO memo (emphasis added), 18 January 2002, in *Guardian*, 28 September 2010.

23. ISC, *The Handling of Detainees by UK Intelligence Personnel in Afghanistan, Guantánamo Bay and Iraq* (2005), para.78.

24. ISC, *Detainees*, para. 46, quoting a letter from the SIS, 24 September 2004. A later reference makes clear that the officer 'had reported a serious potential abuse by the US military' (para. 50), one of several such incidents brought to light in the report, inadequate as it is (as the ISC itself subsequently admitted). See, for example, paras 52–5, 87, 92.

25. ISC, *Detainees*, para. 58, quoting a letter from the Security Service, 6 October 2004.

26. The ISC noted that ministers did not see the report of the International Committee of the Red Cross on the treatment of POWs and other detainees in Iraq until May 2004 – three months after its release – 'after the pictures of the abuse at the US-run facility at Abu Ghraib were made public' (para. 97).

27. ISC, *Detainees*, para. 95, quoting a letter from the Private Secretary to the Secretary of State for Defence, 13 December 2004.

28. Speech to the Foreign Policy Centre, London, 21 March 2006; Tony Blair, *A Journey* (London: Hutchinson, 2010), p. 467.

29. Mark Danner interviewed by Hugh Eakin, 'Our New Politics of Torture', *New York Review of Books*, 30 December 2014, apropos the Senate Select Committee on Intelligence, 'Committee Study of the Central Intelligence Agency's Detention and Interrogation Program' (2014). This 525-page report is in fact the (redacted) Executive Summary of a 6,000-page study.

30. Walt Whitman, 'Song of Myself', *Leaves of Grass* [1892] (Oxford: World's Classics, 1998), p. 48.

31. John Reid, 'Twenty-first Century Warfare, Twentieth-Century Rules', speech at Royal United Services Institute, London, 3 April 2006; Alan Lennox-Boyd, statement to the House of Commons on the deaths and

beatings at Hola Camp, Kenya (1959), in David Anderson, *Histories of the Hanged* (London: Phoenix, 2006), pp. 280–1.

32. J. M. Coetzee, *Waiting for the Barbarians* [1980] (London: Vintage, 2000), p. 86.

33. *Guardian*, 24 February 2005. These abuses dated from May 2003; they preceded the events at Abu Ghraib, though they became public several months after that scandal broke.

34. *Guardian*, 13 and 14 February 2006. Video and commentary from the case of the Light Infantry, in Amara, north of Basra, dating from early 2004.

35. J. M. Coetzee, *Elizabeth Costello* [1999] (London: Vintage, 2004), p. 104.

36. The sequence as described follows that of the Camp Breadbasket case. Investigators failed to find any witnesses; the court martial itself 'did not fully accept all the evidence given in the court by every officer and every warrant officer'; prison sentences ranged from 140 days to two years, subsequently reduced to eighteen months by the Army Reviewing Authority; the officers and warrant officers since promoted. *Guardian*, 26 February, 19 May and 2 June 2005. The Court of Appeal, Redress, and Public Interest Lawyers reached similar conclusions.

37. Blair, *A Journey*, pp. 371–2.

38. Maya Jasanoff, *Edge of Empire* (London: Harper, 2006), p. 308.

10

Mending the World:
Artists' Manifestos

Whoever shall set out to mend the world, and reform men's notions, as well as their manners, will certainly be the mark of much scandal and reproach.

Samuel Johnson[1]

We are from the very heart and from the very first – *accustomed to lying*. Or, to express it more virtuously and hypocritically, in short more pleasantly: one is much more of an artist than one realizes.

Friedrich Nietzsche[2]

'On or about December 1910,' according to Virginia Woolf, 'human character changed.'[3] Modernism took hold. Manifestoism can be dated a little more precisely. On or about 20 February 1909, when 'The Foundation and Manifesto of Futurism' was splashed across the front page of *Le Figaro*, manifestoing began in earnest. That celebrated document not only announced a new movement but started a new trend, effectively a new genre, an adventure in artistic expression.

Once upon a time the manifesto was the province of kings and princes. In the seventeenth century it was hijacked by the Poor Oppressed People of England, also known as the Diggers and the Levellers, the radical dissenters of their day. In 1848 Karl Marx and Friedrich Engels made it their own: *The Communist Manifesto* is the ur-manifesto of the modern period, 'the archetype of a century of modernist manifestos and movements to come'.[4] *The Communist Manifesto* was first and foremost a political manifesto – a call to arms in the service of the revolution. That was the point. Thus the famous peroration:

The Communists disdain to conceal their views and aims. They openly declare that their ends can be attained only by the forcible overthrow of all existing conditions. Let the ruling classes tremble at a Communistic

163

revolution. The proletarians have nothing to lose but their chains. They have a world to win.

WORKERS OF THE WORLD, UNITE![5]

Marx himself was deeply interested in 'the poetry of the revolution' – the forms and the phrases that would make it sing – so much so that the rhetorical strategy of *The Communist Manifesto* is as highly developed as the political analysis.[6] As Marshall Berman underlined, 'the *Manifesto* is remarkable for its imaginative power, its expression and grasp of the luminous and dreadful possibilities that pervade modern life. Along with everything else that it is, it is the first great modernist work of art.'[7] Curiously enough, Bertolt Brecht wanted to make a 'versification' of it, in hexameters, just as Sergei Eisenstein wanted to make a film of *Das Kapital*. The original seems to be proof against adaptation, but the preamble is already a kind of prose poem, the dramatic opening positively theatrical. 'A spectre is haunting Europe – the spectre of Communism. All the Powers of old Europe have entered into a holy alliance to exorcize this spectre: Pope and Czar, Metternich and Guizot, French radicals and German police spies.'[8] Much of this is proleptic, or futuristic; in 1848 the spectre of Communism haunted the pages of the *Manifesto* rather more effectively than it did the chancelleries of Europe. Its time would come. The poetry of the revolution is unforgettable.

> Constant revolutionizing of production, uninterrupted disturbance of all social conditions, everlasting uncertainty and agitation distinguish the bourgeois epoch from all earlier ones. All fixed, fast-frozen relations, with their train of ancient and venerable prejudices and opinions are swept away, all new-formed ones become antiquated before they can ossify. All that is solid melts into air, all that is holy is profaned, and man is at last compelled to face with sober senses, his real conditions of life, and his relations with his kind.[9]

These strategies – these very phrases – would be recast and recycled time and again in the artists' manifestos of the twentieth century. 'Workers of the mind, unite!' mimicked the author of the Futurist Manifesto. With artists, the life of the mind is a dazzling and voluptuous operation. A hundred years after Marx appeared in English translation, the architect Lebbeus Woods, a dedicated experimentalist, wrote a manifesto-versification of his own:

> I declare war on all icons and finalities, on all histories that would chain me with my own falseness, my own pitiful fears.

I know only moments, and lifetimes that are as moments, and forms
  that appear with infinite strength, then 'melt into air'.
I am an architect, a constructor of worlds, a sensualist who worships
  the flesh, the melody, a silhouette against the darkening sky. I cannot
  know your name. Nor can you know mine.
Tomorrow, we begin together the construction of a city.[10]

Anyone who manifestoed after Marx had the spectre of that sainted
longhair hovering somewhere near.

To manifesto is to perform. The Futurists may be described as the
original performance artists. In print, on stage, showering leaflets
from the top of the nearest tall building, their pronouncements performed their principles. The founding of Futurism was a boisterous
affair. One of its sharpest observers was Leon Trotsky, organizer of
the Russian Revolution. Trotsky had a brilliant mind and an acid
pen. 'Futurism arose,' he wrote later, 'as a protest against the art of
petty realists who sponged on life.'[11] The introduction to the Futurist
Manifesto did not disappoint:

> It is from Italy that we hurl at the whole world this utterly violent, inflam-
> matory manifesto of ours, with which we today are founding 'Futurism',
> because we wish to free our country from the stinking canker of its pro-
> fessors, archaeologists, tour guides and antiquarians.
>
> For far too long Italy has been a marketplace for junk dealers. We want
> our country free from the endless number of museums that everywhere
> cover her like countless graveyards. Museums, graveyards! They're the
> same thing, really, because of their grim profusion of corpses that no one
> remembers.[12]

The Futurist Manifesto itself was of a piece with this magniloquence.
Its author was F. T. Marinetti (1876–1944), philosopher, novelist,
playwright, poet, propagandist and self-publicist, the Napoleon of
the Futurist legions yet unborn, the Trotsky of the Futurist revolt yet
unachieved. Its tenets were a marinade of Marinetti and his influences, poetical and political, acknowledged and unacknowledged,
among them Walt Whitman's 'Song of Myself' and Émile Zola's
'J'accuse', Henri Bergson's notion of *élan vital* and Georges Sorel's
Reflections on Violence, Stéphane Mallarmé's lyrical experimental-
ism and Friedrich Nietzsche's philosophical iconoclasm.[13] Nietzsche
in particular was an inspiration, as much for the dramatic quality of
his writing as for the prophetic character of his thought. Nietzsche
is both unsettling and unsparing. His very titles send a shiver down
the spine – *Beyond Good and Evil* (1886), subtitled 'Prelude to a

Philosophy of the Future'. His aphorisms continue to goad. 'One must free oneself from the question, "What is good? What is compassionate?" and ask instead, "What is the good *man*, the compassionate man?"' 'We no longer eat a particular dish for moral reasons, one day we will no longer "do good" for moral reasons either.' His observations on artists were at once shocking and appealing:

> Artists are *not* the men of *great* passion, whatever they try to tell us and themselves. And that's for two reasons: they lack shame towards themselves (they watch themselves *living*; they spy on themselves, they are too curious . . .) and they also lack shame towards great passion (they exploit it as artistes, the avarice of their talent . . .).
>
> But secondly: (1) their vampire, their talent, usually begrudges them that squandering of force which is passion (2) their artists' *miserliness* shelters them from passion.[14]

Marinetti, a light-fingered borrower and a true original, made free with choice passages from his suggestive works, in particular, perhaps, *The Gay Science* (1882):

> I welcome all the signs of a more virile, warlike age approaching that will above all restore honour to bravery! For it shall pave the way to a still higher age and gather the strength that the latter will need one day – the age that will carry heroism into the search for knowledge and *wage wars* for the sake of thoughts and their consequences. To this end we now need many preparatory brave human beings who surely cannot spring from nothingness any more than from the sand and slime of present-day civilization and urbanization. . . . For – believe me – the secret for harvesting from existence the greatest fruitfulness and the greatest enjoyment is – *to live dangerously*! Build your cities on the slopes of Vesuvius! Send your ships into uncharted seas! Live at war with your peers and yourselves! Be robbers and conquerors as long as you cannot be rulers and possessors, you seekers of knowledge! Soon the time will be past in which you had to be content living hidden in forests like shy deer! Finally the search for knowledge will reach for its due; it will want to rule and possess, and you with it![15]

The Futurist Manifesto neatly bottles Nietzsche along with all the rest:

> 1. We want to sing about the love of danger, about the use of energy and recklessness as common, daily practice.
> 2. Courage, boldness and rebellion will be essential elements in our poetry.
> 3. Up to now, literature has extolled a contemplative stillness, rapture and

reverie. We intend to glorify aggressive action, a restive wakefulness, life at the double, the slap and the punching fist.

4. We believe that this wonderful world has been further enriched by a new beauty, the beauty of speed. A racing car, its bonnet decked with exhaust pipes like serpents with galvanic breath . . . a roaring motor car, which seems to race on like machine-gun fire, is more beautiful than the Winged Victory of Samothrace.

5. We wish to sing the praises of the man behind the steering wheel, whose sleek shaft traverses the Earth, which itself is hurtling at breakneck speed along the racetrack of its orbit.

6. The poet will have to do all in his power, passionately, flamboyantly, and with generosity of spirit, to increase the delirious fervour of the primordial elements.

And more, much more, until, finally, 'Standing tall on the roof of the world, yet once again, we hurl our defiance at the stars!'[16]

We now know that Marinetti had a plan of campaign: the Futurist Manifesto had been extensively trialled in Italy before it appeared in *Le Figaro*.[17] Its inflammatory rhetoric was not spontaneous but carefully rehearsed. No less disingenuous was the disclaimer from the newspaper's editors which prefaced it:

Mr Marinetti, the young Italian and French poet, whose remarkable and fiery talent has been made known throughout the Latin countries by his notorious demonstrations and who has a galaxy of enthusiastic disciples, has just founded the school of 'Futurism', whose theories surpass in daring all previous and contemporary schools. The *Figaro* . . . today offers its readers the Manifesto of the Futurists. Is it necessary to say that we assign to the author himself full responsibility for his singularly audacious ideas and his frequently unwarranted extravagance in the face of things that are eminently respectable and, happily, everywhere respected? But we thought it interesting to reserve for our readers the first publication of this manifesto, whatever their judgement of it will be.[18]

Futurist teaching or preaching has always been too much for the unconverted. 'Futurism, as preached by Marinetti, is largely Impressionism up-to-date,' rejoined Wyndham Lewis. 'To this is added his Automobilism and Nietzsche stunt.'[19] But the withering Wyndham Lewis was out of touch with the times. The Manifesto caused a sensation. With the beauty of speed, the French text was turned into a leaflet and all Europe leafleted. Excerpts appeared in newspapers and magazines the world over. 'Futurism' was launched. So too was the talented Mr Marinetti. Overnight, as it seemed, the artists' manifesto had come of age. For the next twenty years it was all the rage.

For Marinetti, the secret of the successful manifesto lay in its violence and its precision ('l'accusation *précise*, l'insulte bien *définie*'), to which we can add its bombast and its wit.[20] This was the Marinetti model, encapsulated in the notorious paragraph 9, with its provocative, almost gratuitous, concluding flourish: 'We wish to glorify war – the sole cleanser of the world – militarism, patriotism, the destructive act of the libertarian, beautiful ideas worth dying for, and scorn for women.'

It is interesting to find that Marinetti had a clear idea of what would do and what would not. The art of making manifestos, as he put it, called for a certain rigour, a verve (or perhaps a nerve), and a sense of style, or form, analogous to the work of art itself. A few years later, Gino Severini, one of a handful of founding Futurists but a little semi-detached, sent Marinetti the manuscript of a projected manifesto. With Napoleonic self-assurance, he replied:

I have read with great attention your manuscript, which contains extremely interesting things. But I must tell you that there is nothing of the *manifesto* in it.

First of all, the title ['The Painting of Light, Depth and Dynamism'] absolutely won't do because it is too generic, too derivative of the titles of other manifestos. In the second place, you must take out the part in which you restate the *merde* and *rose* of Apollinaire, this being, in absolute contrast to our type of manifesto, a way of praising a single artist by repeating his own eulogies and insults. Moreover . . . you must not repeat what I have already said, in *Futurism* [the Manifesto] and elsewhere, about the Futurist sensibility. The rest of the material is very good and important, but to publish it as is would be to publish an article that is excellent but not yet a manifesto. I therefore advise you to take it back and reword it, removing all that I have already mentioned, and intensifying and tightening it, recasting the whole new part in the form of a *manifesto* and not in that of a review article about Futurist painting. . . .

I think I shall persuade you by all that I know about the art of making manifestos, which I possess, and by my desire to place in *full* light, not in *half* light, your own remarkable genius as a Futurist.[21]

'The *merde* and *rose* of Apollinaire' was a reference to a manifesto composed by that astonishing figure, 'L'antitradition futuriste' (1913), as like as not solicited by Marinetti, and edited – manifestoed – according to strict Marinettian principles. Apollinaire himself, it appears, was not exempt from the treatment. 'L'antitradition futuriste' manifests a number of features common to the genre. The Marinetti model became a kind of template. Marinetti's *mots* and

Marinetti's antics resonate throughout the century. The composer Karl-Heinz Stockhausen's scandalous comment on the destruction of New York's twin towers on 11 September 2001, 'the greatest work of art imaginable for the whole cosmos', was pure Marinetti. Every art movement commander-in-chief is a mini-Marinetti. The Dadaist Tristan Tzara and the Surrealist André Breton deliberately followed in his footsteps. It was perhaps inevitable that the capo of Dadaism would fall out with the pope of Surrealism. Breton first courted Tzara ('I think about you as I've never thought about anyone') and then dumped him, finding him insupportable and ungovernable. Tzara, it has been said, was a disappointing mail-order bride. He was certainly a handful, and rivalrous to boot. Given the output of both men, there is a certain irony in the attempt of one to diminish the other by characterizing him as a mere writer of manifestos, and not a poet. 'Dada is amazed to see that it now has only a few poor devils on its side, who, huddled up in their poetry, emote like good bourgeois over the memory of its already ancient misdeeds,' wrote Breton acidly in 1922, as Surrealism came on stream. 'And what does it matter if, going his sorry little way, Mr Tzara must one day share his glory with Marinetti?' Breton had a fine line in disdain. 'It has been said that I change men the way most people change socks,' he continued. 'Kindly allow me this luxury, as I can't keep wearing the same pair for ever: when one stops fitting, I hand it down to my servants.'[22]

Novel as it seems, and self-proclaims, Apollinaire's manifesto is in fact derivative of other manifestos, notwithstanding Marinetti's strictures. The artists' manifesto is a thievish pursuit, with cannibalistic tendencies. (Inevitably, perhaps, there are Cannibalist Manifestos.) In other words, it is a highly self-conscious and self-referential form. The art of making manifestos is also the art of appropriation. If the bad poet borrows, and the good poet steals, as T. S. Eliot said, then artist-manifestoists are very good poets indeed.

It is also polarizing, or to put it more delicately, self-differentiating. Artists' movements and artists' manifestos typically define themselves *against*. Intellectually, this causes them no trouble: it is not hard to identify who or what they are against – usually their rivals and predecessors. Vicente Huidobro, for example, exponent of Creacionismo (Creationism), specialized in the art of the put-down. 'I find that Surrealism is, in fact, nothing but the violin of psychoanalysis.' As for Futurism, 'a new art for the eleven thousand virgins, but not for those who know anything about anything'.[23] In this crowded field the Futurists were unusual only in the sheer comprehensiveness of their condemnation: they were against the past.

To specify what they are *for*, on the other hand, is a good deal more difficult. Many manifestos resolve the difficulty into a crude dichotomy, or a round of name-calling, where brickbats and bouquets are tossed at the selected candidates. Apollinaire's manifesto offers an extravagant example, possibly a parody, throwing *merde* at Montaigne, Wagner, Beethoven, Poe, Whitman and Baudelaire, among many others, and *rose* at a long list of the notable and not-so-notable, beginning with Marinetti, Picasso, Boccioni, and Apollinaire himself. Wyndham Lewis's Vorticist version of this procedure was trumpeted in the very title of the journal he created, *BLAST*, which *blasts* some things, Futurist-fashion ('France, sentimental Gallic gush, sensationalism, fussiness . . .'), and *blesses* others ('cold, magnanimous, delicate, gauche, fanciful, stupid Englishmen . . .').

Artists' manifestos are strong on remonstration. 'Long live – !' and 'Down with – !' are two of its most familiar tropes. In this mood, they are at once vigorous and reductive. Other features of the manifesto, however, are sophisticated indeed. The Futurist revolt was effectively thwarted, but one thrust carried forward: 'words-in-freedom', to use Marinetti's language, and a 'typographical revolution' aimed at exploding 'the harmony of the page'. Words-in-freedom promoted an emancipatory orthography, where the old rules of spelling and syntax could be abandoned, where the typeface flips merrily from one font to another, where letters are repeated as often as you please – 'reds, rrrrreds, the rrrrrredest rrrrrrreds that shouuuuuuuut' – and there is word-play all day long in the grammatical Garden of Eden. Not coincidentally, Futurist manifestos resemble modernist poems. Ghosted or otherwise, Apollinaire's manifesto has the look of his famous 'calligrammes' or word-pictures, composed at around the same time.[24]

Word-play is not the only play involved. Some artists' manifestos are deadly serious. Some are not. In the immortal phrase of the self-styled living sculptures, Gilbert and George, 'The lord chisels still, so don't leave your bench for long.'[25] Some waver between the incendiary and the buffoonery. Some are outlandish; some are gibberish. Claes Oldenburg's 'I Am for an Art' (1961) is a glorious fusion of Whitman and Dada, a rattlebag incantation four pages long:

> I am for an art that you can hammer with, stitch with, sew with, paste with, file with.

> I am for an art that tells you the time of day, or where such and such a
>   street is.
> I am for an art that helps old ladies across the street.
> I am for the art of the washing machine. I am for the art of the
>   government check. I am for the art of the last wars raincoat.
> I am for the art that comes up in fogs from sewer-holes in winter. I am
>   for the art that splits when you step on a frozen puddle. I am for the
>   worms art inside the apple. I am for the art of sweat that develops
>   between crossed legs.
> I am for the art of neck-hair and caked tea-cups, for the art between the
>   tines of restaurant forks, for the odour of boiling dishwater.[26]

The artist as author is full of surprises. Painters in particular are often
supposed to be either stupid or vapid, and in any event inarticulate,
unable or unwilling to explain themselves. In fact, many painters
are capable writers and – whisper it softly – penetrating thinkers.
Anselm Kiefer is a great exemplar (see Chapter 6). Barnett Newman
is another. 'The artist is approached not as an original thinker in
his own medium,' noted Newman caustically, 'but, rather, as an
instinctive, intuitive executant who, largely unaware of what he is
doing, breaks through the mystery by the magic of his performance
to "express" truths the professionals think they can read better than
he can himself.'[27] Artist-manifestoists give the lie to such condescen-
sion. Making manifestos engages the thinker-practitioner; and in this
sphere the thinker-performer is by no means a contradiction in terms.
Art and thought are not incompatible after all.

It is only to be expected that the thinking is not in straight lines.
Artists' manifestos are full of quirks and foibles. Charles Jencks
proposed an arresting typology or tropology of 'the volcano and the
tablet', which might crush the fun out of them, but which captures
very well the deep-seated emotion and semi-scriptural injunction
so often on display.[28] Despite the clowning, much manifestoing is
deeply engaged. Like the face of 'the other' in the philosophy of
Emmanuel Levinas (see Chapter 1), the manifesto is a demand. It
demands something from us, and it demands it now. That something
may be no more than our attention – our full attention. Or it may
be our adherence to a certain worldview, and as like as not a certain
programme. The programme and the worldview are often political,
intensely political. Perhaps the most striking feature of the artists'
manifesto is the frequency with which it outruns art to embrace life.

Georg Baselitz's 'Pandemonic Manifesto II' (1962) concludes,
pithily, 'All writing is crap.' Baselitz has wit; at root, however, he is

deadly serious. As he has acknowledged, his work is anchored in an 'unhealthy' history – German history (and possibly his own). Like Kiefer, Baselitz is a great reader, at once an intellectual and visceral painter, who uses his head as well as his feet. 'I work exclusively on inventing new ornaments,' he insists. But these ornaments are not mere baubles. Typically they are upside-down – *Upside-Down Lenin* has recently been added to the catalogue – turned on their heads, as if to invert, or subvert, or empty out. Baselitz is an ironist. Perhaps that is the only -ist he is. Physically and psychologically, he stands outside. 'I proceed from a state of disharmony, from ugly things . . . from feet that are too big'.[29]

Baselitz's contemporary R. B. Kitaj apprenticed himself early to what he called 'the primacy of artistic craziness': passionate commitment, deep immersion, fierce self-scrutiny. Like his hallowed mentor Cézanne, his career is a monument to the dedicated artist-life; he grew crazier with each passing year. Kitaj's is a high calling, as his manifestos testify. Unfashionably, he believed that art could bear witness (see Chapter 2), and in his own inimitable fashion he bore witness to the trauma of his times – the Holocaust, the Terror, the camp, the pit. The 'First Diasporist Manifesto' (1989) is his testament: 'We learn about life and its events by uncovering ourselves. . . . The timeless [Samuel] Beckett may also be paraphrased: (Art), that double-headed monster of damnation and salvation. . . . I even suspect that art can mend the world a little.'[30]

For the manifestos of the first half of the twentieth century, especially, *the revolution* was their unavoidable preoccupation: their subtext and sometimes their pretext. Futurist manifestos raved about 'the multicoloured polyphonic tides of revolution'. The last words of Le Corbusier's influential 'Towards an Architecture' (1923) posed the question, 'Architecture or revolution?', and offered the answer, or the prayer, 'Revolution can be avoided.'[31] Others felt differently. In 1919 Raoul Hausmann and Johannes Baader 'founded' a Dada Republic by manifesto, in which they instructed the Mayor of Berlin to hand over the treasury and commanded the city's employees to obey only the orders of the joint authors. Sadly, the Dada Republic was stillborn. The quest continued. In 1938 Breton and Trotsky concluded their manifesto, 'Towards a Free Revolutionary Art' (1938), with a ringing declaration:

Our aims:
The independence of art – for the revolution.
The revolution – for the complete liberation of art![32]

In the 1960s, the Situationists gave their own rather prim expression to a similar yearning. Under the Situationist dispensation, everyone would be an artist – an artist in the construction of his own life, as they put it. Their programme was nothing if not expansive:

> Against the spectacle, the realized Situationist culture introduces total participation.
>
> Against preserved art, it is the organization of the directly lived moment.
>
> Against particularized art, it will be a global practice with a bearing, at each moment, on all the usable elements. Naturally this would tend to collective production which would be without doubt anonymous (at least to the extent where the works are no longer stocked as commodities, this culture will not be dominated by the need to leave traces). The minimum proposals of these experiences will be a revolution in behaviour and a dynamic unitary urbanism capable of extension to the entire planet, and of being further extensible to all habitable planets.[33]

The revolutionary preoccupation might be called the manifesto obbligato. It is exhilarating, even elevating, but it also tends to find them out. Trotsky himself published a devastating critique of the artist's limitations in the sphere of 'moral and social revolt'. The critique centred on the feckless Futurists and their half-baked ideas, their political posturing and their artistic shortcomings. It was an awful warning.

> The connection of the aesthetics 'revolt' with the moral and social revolt is direct; both enter entirely and fully into the life experience of the active, new, young, and untamed section of the intelligentsia of the Left, the creative Bohemia. Disgust against the limitations and the vulgarity of the old life produces a new artistic style as a way of escape, and thus the disgust is liquidated. In different combinations, and on different historic bases, we have seen the disgust of the intelligentsia form more than one new style. But that was always the end of it. This time, the proletarian revolution caught Futurism at a certain stage of its growth and pushed it forward. Futurists became Communists. By this very act they entered the sphere of more profound questions and relationships, which far transcended the limits of their own little world, and which were not quite worked out organically in their soul. That is why Futurists . . . are weakest artistically at those points where they finish as Communists. . . . That is why they are frequently subject to artistic and psychological defeats, to stilted forms and to making much noise about nothing.[34]

Revolution or no revolution, artists manifestoed, undeterred. There is something of the incorrigible optimist about the manifestoist. To make a manifesto is to imagine or hallucinate the promised land, wherever that might be. It is in its own way a utopian project. It is certainly not an undertaking for the faint-hearted. In this sense, perhaps, it is apt for the artist. The characteristic stance of the artist-manifestoist is a sort of spiritual resilience, an uprightness, amid the general flux and flex. Artists strive to make headway in a resistant medium (and a hostile environment, as it may be). With the exception of the latter-day Stuckists, who stand proudly on the wrong side of history, the Futurists and their successor-ists are in every sense forward movements. They wager on progress as they see it. Their battle cry is *towards*. The Moses of modernism for so many of these artists is Paul Cézanne (see Chapter 11), who died just as the manifesto was being conceived. As Cézanne knew, the artist's work is never finished. Nor yet the manifesto.

Beyond the catfights, therefore, artists' manifestos tap into a larger vision. An exchange in Roberto Bolaño's extraordinary novel, *The Savage Detectives*, affords a glimpse of the vision, and the movements:

> You're a Stridentist, body and soul. You'll help us build Stridentopolis, Cesárea, I said. And then she smiled, as if I was telling her a good joke but one she already knew, and she said that she had quit her job a week ago and that anyway she'd always been a Visceral Realist, not a Stridentist. And so am I, I said or shouted, all of us Mexicans are more Visceral Realists than Stridentists, but what does it matter? Stridentism and Visceral Realism are just two masks to get us where we really want to go. And where is that? she said. To modernity, Cesárea, I said, to goddamned modernity.[35]

The artists' manifesto is a passport to modernity. To goddamned modernity.

And then to post-modernity. To poor, put-upon post-modernity. And beyond.

Notes

1. Samuel Johnson, *The Works of the English Poets, from Chaucer to Cowper* (London: Johnson, 1810), p. 325.
2. Friedrich Nietzsche, trans. R. J. Hollingdale, *Beyond Good and Evil* [1886] (London: Penguin, 1990), p. 115.
3. See Peter Stansky, *On or About December 1910* (Cambridge, MA: Harvard University Press, 1996), quoting from *Mr Bennett and Mrs Brown* (1924).

4. Karl Marx and Friedrich Engels, trans. Samuel Moore, *The Communist Manifesto* [1888] (London: Penguin, 2002); Marshall Berman, *All That Is Solid Melts Into Air* (London: Verso, 1983), p. 89.

5. *Communist Manifesto*, p. 258 (translation modified).

6. 'The poetry of the revolution', an idea drawn originally from *The 18th Brumaire of Louis Bonaparte* (1852), is the master concept of Martin Puchner's penetrating study, *Poetry of the Revolution* (Princeton: Princeton University Press, 2006). The poetic qualities of *The Communist Manifesto* are also explored in a classic work by Marjorie Perloff, *The Futurist Moment* [1986] (Chicago: University of Chicago Press, 2003).

7. Berman, *All That Is Solid*, p. 102.

8. *Communist Manifesto*, p. 218.

9. *Communist Manifesto*, p. 223.

10. Lebbeus Woods, 'Manifesto' (1993), in Alex Danchev (ed.), *100 Artists' Manifestos* (London: Penguin, 2011), pp. 411–12.

11. Leon Trotsky, trans. Rose Strunsky, *Literature and Revolution* [1925] (Chicago: Haymarket, 2005), pp. 120–1.

12. F. T. Marinetti, trans. Doug Thompson, 'The Foundation and Manifesto of Futurism' [1909], in Danchev, *100 Artists' Manifestos*, p. 6.

13. Marinetti was steeped in Mallarmé, who is quoted and disparaged (sometimes in the same breath) throughout his work. He was especially fond of a line from 'The Windows': 'In the former sky where Beauty flourished', which features in at least two manifestos: see F. T. Marinetti, trans. Doug Thompson, *Critical Writings* (New York: Farrar, Straus & Giroux, 2008), pp. 43, 142. But it may be that Mallarmé is more important for what is not quoted, or admitted, for example 'The Phenomenon of the Future', a suggestive text in the celebrated collection *Divagations* (1896). See Stéphane Mallarmé, trans. Henry Weinfield, *Collected Poems* (Berkeley: University of California Press, 1994).

14. Friedrich Nietzsche, trans. Kate Sturge, *Writings from the Late Notebooks* (Cambridge: Cambridge University Press, 2003), pp. 19, 125, 181.

15. Friedrich Nietzsche, trans. Josefine Nauckhoff, *The Gay Science* (Cambridge: Cambridge University Press, 2001), pp. 160–1. For more from *The Gay Science*, see Marinetti, *Critical Writings*, p. 428.

16. 'The Futurist Manifesto', in Danchev, *100 Artists' Manifestos*, pp. 4–5.

17. See Giovanni Lista, trans. Daniel Katz, 'Genesis and Analysis of Marinetti's "Manifesto of Futurism", 1908–1909', in Didier Ottinger (ed.), *Futurism* (London: Tate, 2009), pp. 78–83.

18. In Perloff, *Futurist Moment*, p. 82.

19. Wyndham Lewis, 'The Melodrama of Modernity', in *BLAST* 1 [1914] (Santa Barbara: Black Sparrow, 1981), p. 143.

20. Marinetti to the Belgian painter Henry Maassen, c.1909–10, quoted in Perloff, *Futurist Moment*, pp. 81–2. Perloff's treatment is exemplary. See also Puchner, *Poetry of the Revolution*, ch. 5.
21. Perloff, *Futurist Moment*, p. 81 (her translation, slightly modified), dated to 1913. Cf. Gino Severini, trans. Jennifer Franchina, *The Life of a Painter* [1983] (Princeton: Princeton University Press, 1995), pp. 138–9, an account rather more favourable to the author.
22. Quoted in Danchev, *100 Artists' Manifestos*, p. 166.
23. Quoted in Danchev, *100 Artists' Manifestos*, p. 217.
24. See Guillaume Apollinaire, trans. Anne Hyde Greet, *Calligrammes* (Berkeley: University of California Press, 1980), for example 'Ocean-Letter' [1914], pp. 58–65. The manifesto pre-dates this particular example, but the earliest calligrammes were written at the turn of the year 1912–13, a few months before 'L'antitradition futuriste'.
25. Gilbert and George, 'The Laws of Sculptors' [1969], in Danchev, *100 Artists' Manifestos*, p. 380.
26. Claes Oldenburg, 'I Am for an Art' [1961], in Danchev, *100 Artists' Manifestos*, p. 353.
27. Barnett Newman, unpublished review of Thomas B. Hess, *Abstract Painting* [1951], in *Selected Writings and Interviews* (Berkeley: University of California Press, 1990), pp. 121–2.
28. Charles Jencks and Karl Kropf (eds), *Theories and Manifestos of Contemporary Architecture* (Chichester: Wiley, 2006), pp. 2–11.
29. Baselitz in Danchev, *100 Artists' Manifestos*, pp. 356–7.
30. Kitaj in Danchev, *100 Artists' Manifestos*, pp. 405–6, paraphrasing Samuel Beckett, *Proust* [1931] (London: Calder, 1965), p. 11 (where the double-headed monster is Time). To 'mend the world' is Samuel Johnson: see the epigraph to this chapter.
31. Le Corbusier, 'Toward an Architecture' [1923], in Danchev, *100 Artists' Manifestos*, p. 229.
32. André Breton, Diego Rivera and Leon Trotsky, 'Towards a Free Revolutionary Art' [1938], in Danchev, *100 Artists' Manifestos*, p. 301.
33. Guy Debord, 'Situationist Manifesto' [1960], in Danchev, *100 Artists' Manifestos*, p. 350.
34. Trotsky, *Literature and Revolution*, p. 126.
35. Roberto Bolaño, trans. Natasha Wimmer, *The Savage Detectives* [1998] (London: Picador, 2007), p. 433.

11

The Hallowed Mentor:
Cézanne by Numbers

Every great human being exerts a retroactive force: for his sake all of history is put on the scale again, and a thousand secrets of the past crawl out of their hiding places – into *his* sunshine.

Friedrich Nietzsche[1]

In every work of genius we recognize our own rejected thoughts; they come back to us with a certain alienated majesty. Great works of art have no more affecting lesson for us than this.

Ralph Waldo Emerson[2]

According to the catalogue raisonné of his paintings, his lifetime production was 954. There are over 100 still lifes, of which about half feature apples. There are at least eighty *Bathers*, almost equally divided between male and female. There are over forty Mont Sainte-Victoires. To these should be added 645 watercolours and around 1,400 drawings, most of them from eighteen sketchbooks. Many of the sketchbooks have since been broken up and dispersed. There are extant fifty-six drawings of his wife, and no fewer than 136 of his son (often asleep). The catalogue raisonné of the drawings is the work of Adrien Chappuis, a connoisseur and collector – his collection of drawings the second-largest after the Kunstmuseum Basel. When Chappuis' heirs decided to sell the remaining sixty or so drawings and watercolours from his estate, in 2002, the French state selected a single watercolour in return for an export licence for the remainder of the collection, despite the fact that there are hardly any Cézanne drawings in French national museums.

Immediately after his death, the dealers Vollard and Bernheim-Jeune jointly acquired twenty-nine 'studies' (oil paintings) for 213,000 francs and 187 watercolours for 62,000 francs from Cézanne's son, who received his first payment on 13 February 1907: cheques for 81,000 francs and 50,000 francs. Further payments followed on 15

177

March (16,000 francs), 4 April (8,000 francs), 15 June (8,000 francs) and 26 June (8,000 francs). Regular sales and regular payments continued thereafter. In 1912, for example, he received 40,000 francs for *The Feast*, otherwise known as *The Orgy*; in 1913, 100,000 francs for *The Card Players* (sold by Vollard to an American collector for ten times that figure in 1925).[3] So dissipated his inheritance.

According to Renoir, he had only to put two strokes of colour on the canvas and it was already something. According to Picasso, it took only one. 'A big thing about modern painting is this. A painter like Tintoretto, for example, starts on his canvas, and then continues, and at the end when he has filled in and worked over everywhere, only then is the picture finished. Now if we take a painting by Cézanne (and this is even more obvious in the watercolours), the painting already exists the moment he paints the first stroke.'[4] According to Manny Farber, in the watercolours, 'more than half the event is elided to allow energy to move in and out of vague landscape notations'.[5] According to Alfred Steiglitz, 'there's nothing there but empty paper with a few splashes of colour'.[6] In the watercolours on white paper, it is the white paper that organizes the watercolours. The pathos of the paper was one of his great discoveries.

According to E. E. Cummings, the watercolours speak of love.

Pausing, I lift my eyes as best I can,
Where twain frail candles close their single arc
Upon a watercolour by Cézanne.
But you, love thirsty, breathe across the gleam;
For total terror of the actual dark
Changing the shy equivalents of dream.[7]

According to Vollard, Cézanne needed 115 sittings for his portrait, before it was abandoned. According to Merleau-Ponty, 'he needed one hundred sessions for a still life, one hundred and fifty sittings for a portrait'. According to the standard translation of Merleau-Ponty, he needed *five hundred* sittings for a portrait.[8]

According to Gasquet, Cézanne said: 'One minute in the life of the world is going by. Paint it as it is!' This became one of John Berger's favourite quotations.[9] According to Émile Bernard, 'his method of study was a meditation with a brush in his hand'. Bernard was allowed to paint in one of the ground floor rooms of his studio. 'I got an idea of the slow pace of his work when he installed me in the studio outside Aix. While I worked on a still life that he had arranged for me in the room below, I could hear him pacing to and fro in the studio above; it was like a meditative walk the length and breadth of the room; also he would frequently come downstairs, go into the garden to sit down, and rush back upstairs.'[10] According to Joachim Gasquet, 20 minutes in the life of the world could go by in the interval between strokes.[11] According to Merleau-Ponty, it could be an hour. According to Merleau-Ponty's translators, it could be several hours.[12]

According to X-rays of his paintings, Cézanne the slowcoach is part of the legend. He could also paint *fast*.

According to Louis Le Bail, the still life was arranged with great care, and a trade secret: he used coins to wedge the fruit – one- or two-sou pieces – tipping them forward, as if eager for inspection. The apple, too, strikes a pose. According to the poet W. S. Di Piero, a Cézanne painting is an object offering. 'The objects are not in repose; they press themselves forward, ingenuously disposed, at once defiant and inviting. . . . In Cézanne's still lifes the canvas is a field that discloses the actual *activity* of the form-making imagination, not only the products of it. . . . He paints the action of the desirous imagination as it seeks to know its object.'[13]

According to Vollard, he thought live models expensive – especially female models – four francs per session in the 1890s, 20 sous more than before the Franco-Prussian War. According to Léontine Paulet, daughter of the gardener and card player Paulin Paulet, who was the model for the girl in the largest of the *Card Players*, she and her father were paid three francs and five francs, respectively, per session. Léontine remembered interminable sittings. To begin with, she was very scared when Cézanne stared at her, but on the day of her first Communion he gave her a two-franc piece and told her to go and buy whatever she wanted.

According to his correspondence, he used to go all the way to the Château Noir by carriage for five francs. When the coachman raised the price of a return journey to the Pont des Trois Sautets to three francs, in 1906, Cézanne dispensed with his services. After paying additional postage on a letter from Zola, in 1878, he asked his friend to economize on the number of sheets of paper in the envelope. When he wrote to the impoverished Emperaire, however, he enclosed a stamp for the reply, 'in order to save you going into town'. He also offered to send him some tubes of paint.[14] According to his niece, Marthe Conil, he always gave a five-franc piece to the beggar at the cathedral door. One day, when his nieces began to mock the beggar, Cézanne quieted them: 'But you don't know, it's Germain Nouveau, professor and poet, he was my classmate at the Collège Bourbon.'[15]

According to technical studies of his work, he used more cobalt blue in his landscapes after his father's death, in 1886, when he became financially secure. According to Marcel Provence, he considered it the height of luxury (*un luxe de nabab*) to buy his materials from a supplier to museums. 'I paint as if I were Rothschild!'[16] A vertical stripe of light on the milk jug in the late *Still Life with Milk Jug and Fruit* is a product of cadmium yellow, then very expensive, mixed with lead white. Remarkably, the highlights on the fruit emerge from underneath. Most highlights are painted last. Cézanne's highlights were painted first. He applied chrome yellow directly to the white ground; then he built up the piece of fruit. For the shadows under the plate he mixed iron oxide and red or yellow lake; it was unusual to use the lake in the mix rather than as a glaze. He knew his pigments. X-ray photography shows that the paint was applied slowly and meticulously; the lower layers are allowed to show through the upper ones. There are few changes in the composition. On the fruit, the oranges in particular, the blue paint is carefully exposed.

According to Heidegger, his philosophy was at once coherent and parsimonious. 'Cézanne was not a philosopher, but he understood all of philosophy. In a few words he summed up everything I have tried to express. He said: "Life is terrifying." ["*C'est effrayant, la vie.*"] I have been saying just that for forty years.'[17]

According to Robert Bresson, Cézanne said: 'I paint, I work, I am free of thought.'[18]

I paint, therefore I am.

According to Madame Brémond, his housekeeper, he got up at three. According to the former controller of tolls, Olivier, he was often to be seen at four, on his way to the studio. He would light the stove, make coffee, and read. According to a former apprentice of the master mason, Viguier, he would bring the artist a bottle of milk at five. Cézanne would boil the milk, have breakfast, and set to work. According to Bernard, he began painting at six. According to Le Bail, he set off to paint outdoors at seven. As like as not, he would say: 'We're going to put our absurd theories into practice.'[19]

According to the jottings in his sketchbook, he ate as follows:

Wednesday	morning	60 [centimes]	beef and kidneys
	evening	50	cutlets
Thursday	morning	75	cutlets
	evening		six sausages

Friday	morning	70	
	evening		nothing
Saturday	morning	1 [franc]	beef and kidney paid
Sunday	morning	1	beef and [?] slice
	evening	35	beef
Monday	–		
Sunday	morning	1	
Monday	morning	70	cutlet[20]

According to his granddaughter, Aline, two recipes for cutlets came down to her: lamb cutlets in breadcrumbs, and lamb cutlets with truffles – the latter perhaps not entirely to Cézanne's taste. She also had two recipes for baked tomatoes. Both of them prescribed three tablespoons of olive oil.[21]

According to the menu of the Dada-inspired dBFoundation of New York artists, 'Cézanne Salad' consists of apples, oranges and drapery.

According to his bill from the Hôtel Baudy in Giverny, in 1894, he regularly ordered a bottle of Mâcon (1.5 francs), sometimes a whisky (75 centimes), occasionally a cognac (40 centimes), and, unusually, a pair of braces (3 francs).

According to Ernest Hemingway, Cézanne's work is best seen on an empty stomach. 'I learned to understand Cézanne much better and to see truly how he made landscapes when I was hungry,' he recalled in *A Moveable Feast* (1964). 'I used to wonder if he were hungry too when he painted; but I thought possibly it was only that he had forgotten to eat. It was one of those unsound but illuminating thoughts you have when you have been sleepless or hungry. Later I thought Cézanne was probably hungry in a different way.' As a struggling writer, Hemingway went nearly every day to see the Cézannes in the Luxembourg. 'I was learning something from the painting of Cézanne that made writing simple true sentences far from enough to make the stories have the dimensions that I was trying to put in them. I was learning very much from him but I was not articulate enough to explain it to anyone. Besides, it was a secret.'[22]

According to Bernard, his palette had three blue pigments: cobalt blue, ultramarine and Prussian blue. According to Le Bail, when beginning a canvas, 'he drew with a brush of ultramarine, diluted with lots of turpentine, laying in with a will, unhesitatingly'. Asked why he was so fond of ultramarine, he replied: 'Because the sky is blue.'[23] According to Eric Rohmer, for Cézanne, 'the sky is *blue* before it is sky'.[24] According to an unpublished bill, on 18 October

1888 Tanguy supplied him with ultramarine by Guimet. According to a recently discovered letter to an unnamed colour merchant, on 14 July 1905 he ordered five tubes of Prussian blue by Bourgeois. According to technical studies of his work, Prussian blue is found only in his oils and indigo only in his watercolours; mixed greens made of cobalt blue and chrome yellow have been identified in several of the watercolours. According to Huysmans, a certain painter of the Impressionist persuasion favoured a wigmaker blue. According to Bridget Riley, the *Large Bathers* present us with a great thundering blue. According to Rilke, Cézanne used at least sixteen shades of blue. Some of them are familiar (sky blue, sea blue, blue-green), but for the most part these were no ordinary blues. Among his blues: a barely-blue, a waxy blue, a listening blue, a blue dove-grey, a wet dark blue, a juicy blue, a light cloudy blue, a thunderstorm blue, a bourgeois cotton blue, a densely quilted blue, an ancient Egyptian shadow-blue, a self-contained blue and a completely supportless blue. 'As if these colours could heal one of indecision after all. The good conscience of these reds, these blues, their simple truthfulness, it educates you; and if you stand among them as ready as possible, you get the impression that they are doing something for you.'[25] According to Bresson, there is Cézanne blue, like Breughel red. According to Octave Mirbeau, there is a blue hour in the day, which Cézanne succeeds in capturing. According to Merleau-Ponty, the phenomenologist, there is blue-being. Titian is supposed to have said that a painter needed only three colours: white, black and red. Cézanne needed blue.

According to Cézanne, 'we men experience nature more in terms of depth than surface, whence the need to introduce into our vibrations of light, represented by reds and yellows, a sufficient quantity of blue tones, to give a sense of atmosphere'.[26] According to Sergei Makovsky, editor-in-chief of the journal *Apollon*, the Russian collector Ivan Morosov determined to buy a blue Cézanne. Makovsky remembered a visit to Morosov's gallery: 'I was surprised to see a blank spot on a wall otherwise completely covered with Cézanne's works. "That place is intended for a 'blue Cézanne'", explained I. A. Morosov. "I have had my eye on it for a long time but haven't been able to make a selection."'[27] Finally, in Vollard's shop, he found what he was looking for: *Blue Landscape*, which became his favourite painting. Some years later, in 1926, Walter Benjamin had his own epiphany in front of it, in what was then the Museum of Modern Western Art in Moscow:

As I was looking at an extraordinarily beautiful Cézanne, it suddenly occurred to me that to the extent that one grasps a painting, one does not in any way enter into its space; rather, this space thrusts itself forward, especially in various specific spots. It opens up to us in corners and angles in which we believe we can localize crucial experiences of the past; there is something inexplicably familiar about these spots.[28]

Like many others, Benjamin continued to refine his Cézanne-encounter in his own work. 'The true image of the past flits by,' he mused prophetically in 'On the Concept of History' (1940), only months before he committed suicide (see Chapter 3). 'The past can be seized only as an image which flashes up at the moment of its recognizability, and is never seen again.'[29]

Bluescapes (as Fredric Jameson calls them) meet their match in bluelifes. The late watercolours continue to echo. In these rapturous still lifes, broken blue contours convey a sense of air circulating around and through objects. According to his young visitors Rivière and Schnerb, 'he did not seek to represent forms by a line. The outline existed for him only as the place where one form ended and another began. . . . In principle there is no line, a form exists only in relation to the neighbouring forms.'[30] The ubiquitous blue pot vibrates, bluishly, in sympathy with the blue fruit that keeps it company. Cézanne breaks the skin of things, in Henri Michaux's phrase, 'to show how the things become things, how the world becomes world'. According to Heidegger, what goes on in a Cézanne is 'worlding'.[31] Rilke captures it perfectly:

> Soundless living, endless opening out,
> space being used without space being taken
> from that space adjacent things diminish,
> existence almost uncontoured, like ground left blank
> and pure within-ness, much so strangely soft
> and self-illuminating – out to the edge:
> is there anything we know like this?[32]

Countless people have had a Cézanne-epiphany. According to Kenneth Clark, when he went to see a loan exhibition at the Victoria Art Gallery in Bath as a teenager during the First World War, 'the Manets meant nothing to me; and Monet's cathedrals left me as baffled then as they do now; but the Cézannes were a knock-out blow. One landscape, in particular, gave me the strongest aesthetic shock I had ever received from a picture. I could not keep away from it, and went down the hill to see it almost every day.' Samuel

Courtauld saw the same painting a few years later, in 1922, on loan to the Burlington Fine Arts Club. 'A young friend who was a painter of conventional portraits, and had been serving in the RFC [Royal Flying Corps], led me up to Cézanne's *Provençal Landscape. . . .* Though genuinely moved he was not very lucid, and finished by saying, in typical airman's language, "It makes you go this way, and that way, and then off the deep-end altogether!" At that moment I felt the magic, and I have felt it in Cézanne's work ever since.'[33]

'I could imagine someone not prepared . . . who had no experience of external ecstasy [that is, marijuana], passing in front of a Cézanne canvas, distracted and without noticing it, his eye travelling in, to, through the canvas into the space and suddenly stopping with his hair standing on end, dead in his tracks seeing a whole universe,' said Allen Ginsberg. 'And I think that's what Cézanne really does, to a lot of people.'[34] The philosopher Henri Maldiney saw *space*, in an instant, in front of the Moscow *Mont Sainte-Victoire seen from Les Lauves*, at the Cézanne exhibition in Paris in 1936. But a live canvas may not be necessary. For Robert Motherwell, it was love at first sight, at age fourteen, when he saw his first late Cézanne, in reproduction.

According to Fredric Jameson, it has become impossible to have a direct or unmediated experience of a Cézanne painting, 'because the value of Cézanne has become a functional component of the ideology of establishment modernism'.[35] We are engaging, not a canvas, but a cultural institution. 'Everyman loves everyman's Cézanne and rolls his eyes: "That paaynting! Ooo that paaynting!"' spouted Max Ernst, in his Dada phase. 'I don't give a damn about Cézanne, for he is an enormous hunk of painting.'[36] According to John Berger, consciously or unconsciously echoing Roger Fry, 'millions of words have been written in psychological and aesthetic studies about Cézanne yet their conclusions lack the gravity of the work. Everyone is agreed that Cézanne's paintings appear to be different from those of any painter who preceded him; whilst the works of those who came after seem scarcely comparable, for they were produced out of the profound crisis which Cézanne . . . half foresaw and helped to provoke'.[37] Hemingway's secret remains secret. It sometimes seems as if no advance has been made on Gertrude Stein:

The apples looked like apples the chairs looked like chairs and it all had nothing to do with anything because if they did not look like apples or chairs or landscape or people they were apples and chairs and landscapes and people. They were so entirely these things that they were not an oil painting and yet that is just what the Cézannes were they were an oil painting. They were so entirely an oil painting that it was all there whether they were finished, the paintings, or whether they were not finished. Finished or unfinished it always was what it looked like the very essence of an oil painting because everything was always there, really there.[38]

'Why do we feel a momentary completeness of being when we look at his work,' asked Di Piero, 'with all his constant self-confessed failures, his endlessly unsatisfactory "researches" . . ., the grinding habitual unhappy inadequacy of it all? Despite all that, which in Cézanne's case is to say because of it, *the all is there*.'[39] According to Van Gogh, 'you must feel the whole of a country – isn't that what distinguishes a Cézanne from anything else?'[40]

According to Rilke, his own poetry spoke for itself. 'I believe that no poem in the *Sonnets to Orpheus* means anything that is not fully written out there, often, it is true, with its most secret name,' he wrote to a friend, not entirely reassuringly. 'All "allusion" I am convinced would be contradictory to the indescribable "being-there" of the poem.' On another occasion he suggested that his most recalcitrant obscurities may require not elucidation so much as 'submitting-to'.[41]

Surely Cézanne requires submitting-to.

Yet there is an impulsion to say more. The best explanation so far has been offered by the critic David Sylvester:

> In our lives nothing troubles us more than our inability to deal with those contradictions which we recognize in ourselves, in our feelings, our desires, our consciences – our inability to accept them and reconcile them. We tend to deal with such contradictions by closing our minds to the essence of one side or another or by evading them with some feeble compromise. Perhaps it is because Cézanne's art accepts contradictions to the full and finds a means to reconcile them that we always feel instinctively that it means so infinitely more than its ostensible subject. What it means is a moral grandeur which we cannot find in ourselves.[42]

Worlding is at the same time grounding and elevating.

According to the Dadaist house journal and Surrealist incubation unit, *Littérature*, edited by Louis Aragon, André Breton and Philippe Soupault, Cézanne is more or less harmless. In 1921 the journal published approval ratings of the high and mighty throughout history – not to classify but to declassify, as they said – on a scale from $+20$ to -25, where $+20$ indicated complete approval, -25 extreme aversion, and 0 absolute indifference. Cézanne emerged with −3.36, a mild aversion, on the level of Corot (−4.90). This was far behind Baudelaire (+9.00) and Freud (+8.60), but well ahead of Delacroix (−8.54) and Debussy (−9.18). In that circle, it was a creditable achievement. The average concealed a surprisingly enthusiastic +13 from Paul Eluard, a studiously indifferent −1 from Breton, and an annihilating −25 from Tristan Tzara, the Dadaist commander-in-chief.[43]

According to Jean-Luc Godard, in *Histoire(s) du cinéma* (1988), 'there are perhaps ten thousand people who haven't forgotten Cézanne's apples, but there must be a billion viewers who will remember the cigarette lighter of *Strangers on a Train*'. For Godard, a Cézanne was a painting that you could put in the cell of a condemned man without its being an outrage. Even in his own medium, however, he underestimated the pulling power of the apples. According to Woody Allen's alter ego Isaac Davis, in *Manhattan* (1979), there are eleven things that make life worth living: 'Groucho Marx, Willie Mays, the second movement of the Jupiter symphony, Louis Armstrong's 'Potato Head Blues', Swedish movies, *A Sentimental Education* by Flaubert, Marlon Brando, Frank Sinatra, and of course those incredible apples and pears by Cézanne . . .'.[44]

According to his son, he would say: 'Politicians, there are two thousand of them in every legislature, but a Cézanne, there is only one every two centuries.'[45]

According to Roland Barthes, there is in a single painter a whole history of painting. The whole of Nicolas de Staël is in three square centimetres of Cézanne. Then he scaled it down even further. The whole of Nicolas de Staël is in one square centimetre of Cézanne.[46] According to László Moholy-Nagy, supposedly abstract formal elements in certain compositions by Kandinsky or Matisse can be conceived of as 'close-ups' or enlargements of details in Cézanne's paintings.[47]

They are all there, somewhere, in one square centimetre or another. Picasso and Braque, Matisse and Modigliani, Kandinsky and Klee, Giacometti and Morandi, Johns and Kelly, De Kooning and Lichtenstein, Gorky and Kossoff, Marden and Kitaj, Freud and Auerbach, Strand and Wall. The sublime little grimalkin is large. He contains multitudes. According to Klee, 'he is the teacher *par excellence*'. According to the writer Peter Handke, he is the teacher of mankind in the here and now.[48]

According to sages of every stripe, he was the great exemplar.[49] Asked to name the formative influences on his poetry, Rilke said that

Cézanne had been his supreme example, and that 'after the master's death, I followed his traces everywhere'. Gertrude Stein, who did not lightly confess to influences, testified that 'everything I have done has been influenced by Flaubert and Cézanne, and this gave me a new feeling about composition. Up to that time composition had consisted of a certain idea, to which everything else was an accompaniment and separate but was not an end in itself, and Cézanne conceived the idea that in composition one thing was as important as another thing. Each part is as important as the whole, and that impressed me enormously.'[50] For Cézanne there was no hierarchy of subject or genre. He once said of the mighty *Woman with a Coffee Pot* that a teaspoon teaches us as much about ourselves and our world as a woman or a coffee pot. He was a revolutionary visionary.

He was not merely influential. He has a much rarer distinction. He won for himself the kind of glory beautifully described by Paul Valéry: 'To become for someone else the example of the dedicated life, being secretly invoked, pictured, and placed by a stranger in a sanctum of his thoughts, so as to serve him as a witness, a judge, a father, a hallowed mentor.'[51] For Liliane Brion-Guerry, he was the great sustainer. She began work on her study of Cézanne as a conscious act of resistance, 'a testimony of faith in certain values', in 1943. In the black years of the Occupation, moral values and colour values coalesced.[52] For Picasso, he was the great protector: mother, father, grandfather and spiritual advisor. *Still Life with Hat*, otherwise known as *Cézanne's Hat* (1909), is a portrait of a Kronstadt hat – a characteristic tribute – impudent, rivalrous, slightly comic, deadly serious, and a dig in the ribs for brother Braque, who supplied the hat.[53] For Seamus Heaney, he was an agent of equilibration, a kind of moral spirit level:

Sitting there *sur le motif*, his grumpy contrary old back turned on us as he faces the humpy countervailing mountain. The first time I went to London I came back with a Cézanne print of the Mont Sainte-Victoire. The first art book I bought for myself was about Cézanne. When I wrote [the poem] 'An Artist' I was reading Rilke's letters about his infatuation with Cézanne and some of Rilke's words are included. What I love is the doggedness, the courage to face into the job, the generation of what Hopkins would have called 'self-yeast' – but in a positive sense: the miller gristing his own mill. This may or may not be the Cézanne known to art critics and historians, but he's the one I've lived with, the one rewarded with those incontrovertible paintings, so steady in themselves they steady you and the world – and you in the world.[54]

The pilgrimages to Aix that began in his lifetime continued after his death. They were not confined to artists. Heidegger was there in 1956, 1957 and 1958. On 20 March 1958, he prefaced a lecture on Hegel and the Greeks with a description of the way into the Bibémus quarry, to a place where the Mont Sainte-Victoire comes into sight. There, he said, he had found Cézanne's path, 'the path to which, from beginning to end, my own path as a thinker corresponds in its way'.[55] Merleau-Ponty was there in 1960, writing 'Eye and Mind'. He took his epigraph from Cézanne, by way of Gasquet: 'What I am trying to convey to you is more mysterious, entangled in the very roots of being, the impalpable source of sensations.' He concluded with a Cézannian meditation on progress and completion, the life and the afterlife:

> If we cannot establish a hierarchy of civilizations or speak of progress – either in painting or in anything else that matters – it is not because some fate holds us back; it is, rather, because the very first painting in some sense went to the farthest reach of the future. If no painting comes to be *the* painting, if no work is ever absolutely completed and done with, still each creation changes, alters, enlightens, deepens, confirms, exalts, re-creates or pre-creates all the others. If creations are not established advances, this is not only because, like all things, they pass away; it is also that they have almost all their lives still before them.[56]

His creations have colonized our consciousness. His impact on our world, and our conception of our world, is comparable to that of Marx or Freud. According to Charles Taylor, Cézanne 'brought to expression the meaningful forms and relationships which under-gird our ordinary perception, as they emerge and take shape from the materiality of things. To do this he had to forge a new language, abandoning linear and aerial perspective and making the spatial dispositions arise from the modulations of colour. He "recaptures and converts into visible objects what would, without him, remain walled up in the separate life of each consciousness: the vibration of appearances which is the cradle of things."'[57]

Cézanne is a life-changer.

Robert Bresson stopped painting and turned to filmmaking because of Cézanne. 'Painting is over,' he told an interviewer in 1996. 'There is nowhere to go. I don't mean after Picasso, but after Cézanne. He went to the brink of what could not be done.'[58] At the very same moment, after seeing a centenary retrospective at the Tate, Lucian Freud said that what affected him most was Cézanne's 'being able to do things which I thought were undoable. It's heartening.' Three years later, Freud set about painting his own version of *Afternoon in Naples* (1876–7), *After Cézanne* (2000).[59] After Cézanne, he declared his intention to paint himself to death. In 2011 he succeeded.

R. B. Kitaj persevered because of Cézanne. For Kitaj, Cézanne was the Man.

> When you fall in love with one person above all others, that love makes special claims on you. In that way, the mysterious way of love, Cézanne singles me out. Artists create their precursors, said a sage. Cézanne's last three great *Bather* pictures excite me more than any other art except Kafka's three novels. Both of these trios were left unfinished/finished at the death of their makers. Cézanne's lessons appear endless to me, encyclopaedic like, say, Shakespeare or Beethoven.[60]

The poet Francis Ponge maintained that Braque was good for him. He was surely right. Great painters are good for us. Cézanne, the hallowed mentor, shows the way.

Notes

1. Friedrich Nietzsche, trans. Josefine Nauckhoff, *The Gay Science* [1882] (Cambridge: Cambridge University Press, 2001), p. 53.
2. Ralph Waldo Emerson, 'Self-Reliance', in *Essays: First Series* [1841], in *Essential Writings* (New York: Modern Library, 2007), p. 132.
3. A century later, in 2012, one of *The Card Players* was bought by the Qatari royal family for the stupendous sum of \$250 million.
4. Hélène Parmelin, *Picasso dit . . .* (Paris: Gonthier, 1966), p. 85.
5. Manny Farber, 'Kitchen without Kitsch' [1977], in *Negative Space* (New York: Da Capo, 1998), p. 340.
6. Dorothy Norman, 'From the Writings and Conversations of Alfred Stieglitz', *Twice a Year* 1 (1938), p. 81.
7. E. E. Cummings, *Erotic Poems* (New York: Norton, 2010), p. 47.
8. Maurice Merleau-Ponty, 'Le Doute', in *Sens et non-sens* (Paris: Gallimard, 1996), p. 15; 'Cézanne's Doubt', in *Sense and Nonsense* (Evanston: Northwestern University Press, 1964), p. 9 (my emphasis).
9. Joachim Gasquet, *Cézanne*, in Michael Doran (ed.), *Conversations avec Cézanne* (Paris: Macula, 1978), p. 113, quoted by Merleau-Ponty in 'Le Doute' (p. 32), which is probably where Berger found it. See John Berger, 'Drawn to That Moment' [1976], in *Selected Essays* (London: Bloomsbury, 2001), p. 419. The same quotation is woven into his novel, *G* [1972] (London: Bloomsbury, 1996). See p. 15.
10. Émile Bernard, 'Souvenirs', in *Conversations avec Cézanne*, pp. 58, 62.
11. Gasquet, *Cézanne*, in *Conversations avec Cézanne*, p. 124.

12. Merleau-Ponty, 'Le Doute', p. 28; 'Cézanne's Doubt', p. 15.

13. W. S. Di Piero, 'Morandi of Bologna' and 'Miscellany I', in *Out of Eden* (Berkeley: University of California Press, 1993), pp. 33, 79 (his emphasis).

14. Cézanne to Zola and Emperaire, 28 March 1878 and January 1872, in Alex Danchev, *The Letters of Paul Cézanne* (London: Thames & Hudson, 2013), pp. 166, 146. The postage in question was a 25 centime stamp.

15. M.C. [Marthe Conil], 'Quelques souvenirs sur Paul Cézanne', *Gazette des Beaux-Arts* 56 (1960), p. 302.

16. Léo Larguier, *Cézanne* (Paris: Julliard, 1947), p. 93.

17. Heidegger in conversation with André Masson [1956], in Françoise Will-Levaillant (ed.), *Le Rebelle du surréalisme* (Paris: Hermann, 1976), pp. 138ff. 'C'est effrayant, la vie,' was indeed a habitual refrain.

18. Bresson interviewed by Michel Ciment [1996], trans. Pierre Hodgson, in *Projections* 9 (London: Faber, 1999), p. 3.

19. Marcel Provence notes, in Denis Coutagne (ed.), *Atelier Cézanne* (Aix: Société Paul Cézanne, 2002), p. 91; Bernard, 'Souvenirs', in *Conversations avec Cézanne*, p. 57; Le Bail to Rewald, 19 March 1935, in Rewald Papers, Box 50–1, National Gallery of Art, Washington DC.

20. *A Cézanne Sketchbook* (New York: Dover, 1985), p. II. For 'January', no date given. The sketchbook is thought to date from c.1869–70 to c.1885–6.

21. Aline Cézanne, *Le Carnet de recettes de Mamine Cézanne* (Paris: Lattès, 2006), pp. 38, 41, 48, 79. Aline was the elder child of Paul Cézanne *fils* and Renée Rivière ('Mamine'), daughter of Georges Rivière.

22. Ernest Hemingway, *A Moveable Feast* (Harmondsworth: Penguin, 1966), pp. 16, 53. Hemingway was in Paris in 1921.

23. Le Bail to Rewald, loc. cit.

24. Eric Rohmer, 'Des goûtes et des couleurs' [1956], in *Le Goût de la beauté* (Paris: Cahiers du Cinéma, 2004), p. 110.

25. Rilke to Clara, 13 October 1907, in Rainer Maria Rilke, trans. Joel Agee, *Letters on Cézanne* (New York: North Point Press, 2002), pp. 45–6.

26. Cézanne to Bernard, 15 April 1904, in Danchev, *The Letters of Paul Cézanne*, p. 334.

27. Sergei Makovsky in *Apollon* [1912], in Rebecca A. Rabinow, *Cézanne to Picasso* (New Haven: Yale University Press, 2006), p. 254.

28. Benjamin diary, 24 December 1926, in Walter Benjamin, trans. Richard Sieburth, *Moscow Diary* (Cambridge, MA: Harvard University Press, 1986), p. 42.

29. Walter Benjamin, trans. Harry Zohn, 'On the Concept of History', in *Selected Writings*, vol. 4 (Cambridge, MA: Harvard University Press, 2003), p. 390.

30. Rivière and Schnerb, 'L'atelier', in *Conversations avec Cézanne*, p. 87.

31. Maurice Merleau-Ponty, trans. Carleton Dallery, 'Eye and Mind', in *The Primacy of Perception* (Evanston: Northwestern University Press, 1964), p. 181; Julian Young, *Heidegger's Philosophy of Art* (Cambridge: Cambridge University Press, 2004), p. 157, citing 'On the Question of Being' (1955).

32. Rainer Maria Rilke, trans. Edward Snow, 'The Bowl of Roses', in *New Poems* [1907] (New York: North Point Press, 1985), p. 193.

33. Kenneth Clark, *Another Part of the Wood* (London: Murray, 1974), pp. 70–1; Anthony Blunt, 'Samuel Courtauld as Collector and Benefactor', in Douglas Cooper, *The Courtauld Collection* [1954], in Stephanie Buck (ed.), *The Courtauld Cézannes* (London: Courtauld, 2008), pp. 12–13.

34. Allen Ginsberg, 'Art of Poetry', *Paris Review* 37 (1966), p. 29.

35. Fredric Jameson, 'Towards a Libidinal Economy of Three Modern Painters' [1979], in *The Modernist Papers* (London: Verso, 2007), p. 258.

36. Max Ernst, trans. Gabriele Bennett, 'Über Cézanne' from *Bulletin D* [1919], in Lucy R. Lippard (ed.), *Dadas on Art* (Englewood Cliffs, NJ: Prentice-Hall, 1971), p. 125. 'Je m'en fous de Cézanne,' in French in the original.

37. John Berger, 'Sight of a Man', in *Selected Essays* (London: Bloomsbury, 2001), p. 225.

38. Gertrude Stein, *Lectures in America* (New York: Random House, 1935), pp. 76–7.

39. Di Piero, 'Miscellany 1', in *Out of Eden*, p. 79.

40. Van Gogh to Theo, 3 November 1889, Van Gogh Letters, no. 816, at http://vangoghletters.org/vg/letters/let816/letter.html (last accessed 15 June 2015).

41. Rilke to the Countess Sizzo and to Clara, 1 June and 23 April 1923, in Rainer Maria Rilke, trans. Edward Snow, *The Duino Elegies* (New York: North Point Press, 2001), p. xii.

42. David Sylvester, 'Still Life' [1962], in *About Modern Art* (London: Pimlico, 2002), pp. 96–7.

43. *Littérature* 18 (1921), p. 1.

44. Plus crabs at Sam Wo's and (his girlfriend) Tracy's face.

45. Rewald, *Cézanne et Zola* (Paris: Sedrowski, 1936), p. 416, citing information from Maxime Conil and Paul. According to Larguier (*Cézanne*, p. 78), 'Politicians, there are over a thousand in France, and it's shit. Whereas there's only one Cézanne!'

46. Roland Barthes, trans. Richard Howard, 'Réquichot and his Body' [1973] in *The Responsibility of Forms* (Berkeley: University of California Press, 1991), p. 229; 'Pause', *Le Nouvel Observateur*, 26 March 1979, in Roland Barthes, *Œuvres Complètes*, vol. V (Paris:

Seuil, 2002), pp. 652–3. In between, it went up to five square centimetres. 'Archimboldo ou Rhétoriqueur et magicien' [1978], in ibid., p. 505.

47. László Moholy-Nagy, trans. Daphne M. Hoffmann, *The New Vision* [1932] (London: Faber, 1939), p. 81.

48. Peter Handke, *The Lesson*, in *Slow Homecoming* (New York: NYRB, 2009), p. 176; Klee diary, 1909, in *The Diaries of Paul Klee* (Berkeley: University of California Press, 1964), p. 237. 'I am large, I contain multitudes' is from Walt Whitman, 'Song of Myself', in *Leaves of Grass*.

49. Louis Vauxcelles, 'La légende de Cézanne', *Carnet de la Semaine*, 19 January 1930; Clement Greenberg, 'Cézanne and the Unity of Modern Art' [1951], in *Collected Essays*, vol. III (Chicago: University of Chicago Press, 1993), p. 91; Merleau-Ponty, *Sens et non-sens*, p. 11.

50. Rilke to Alfred Schaer, 20 February 1924, in Heinrich Weigand Petzet, 'Foreword' to Rilke, *Letters on Cézanne*, p. ix; Gertrude Stein and Robert Haas, 'A Transatlantic Interview' [1946], in R. Bruce Elder, *The Films of Stan Brakhage in the American Tradition* (Waterloo, ON: Wilfrid Laurier University Press, 1998), p. 279.

51. Paul Valéry, trans. Stuart Gilbert, *Analects* (Princeton: Princeton University Press, 2015), p. 227.

52. Liliane Brion-Guerry, *Cézanne et l'expression de l'espace* (Paris: Albin Michel, 1966), p. 7; conversation with Denis Coutagne, 8 September 2008.

53. See Alex Danchev, *Braque: A Life* (London: Penguin, 2007), pp. 180–2.

54. Seamus Heaney interviewed by Dennis O'Driscoll, in *Stepping Stones* (London: Faber, 2008), pp. 262–3.

55. Jean Beaufret, *Dialogue avec Heidegger*, vol. III (Paris: Minuit, 1974), p. 155, gives 'J'ai trouvé ici le chemin de Cézanne, auquel, de son début jusqu'à sa fin, mon propre chemin de pensée répond à sa façon.' François Fédier, 'Voir sous le voile de l'interprétation', in Walter Biemal and Friedrich-Wilhelm von Herrmann (eds), *Kunst und Technik* (Frankfurt: Klostermann, 1989), p. 331, gives a variant of the last phrase: 'mon propre chemin de pensée en une certain mesure correspond'. Both men were present on this occasion; Fédier says that he has a copy of the text in front of him as he writes.

56. Merleau-Ponty, 'Eye and Mind', pp. 159, 190. The epigraph comes from one of his prime sources, Gasquet's *Cézanne* (and sounds more like Gasquet than Cézanne).

57. Charles Taylor, *Sources of the Self* (Cambridge: Cambridge University Press, 1989), p. 468, quoting Merleau-Ponty (after Rilke), 'Cézanne's Doubt', pp. 17–18.

58. Bresson interviewed by Ciment, *Projections* 9, p. 11.

59. William Feaver, *Lucian Freud* (London: Tate, 2002), p. 46.

60. Colin Wiggins, *Kitaj in the Aura of Cézanne and Other Masters*

(London: National Gallery, 2001), pp. 43, 47. Artists creating their precursors is Borges. Kafka's *The Castle*, *The Trial* and *Amerika* were prepared for publication by Max Brod.

12

The Vacuity of Evil:
Rumsfeld in Washington

'All There Is To Know About Adolph Eichmann'

EYES   Medium
HAIR   Medium
WEIGHT   Medium
DISTINGUISHING FEATURES   None
NUMBER OF FINGERS   Ten
NUMBER OF TOES   Ten
INTELLIGENCE   Medium
What did you expect?
Talons?
Oversize incisors?
Green saliva?
Madness?

Leonard Cohen[1]

'He's a ruthless little bastard. You can be sure of that.'

Nixon to Haldeman[2]

Donald Rumsfeld could have been a contender. In 1980 he was at the Republican National Convention in Detroit, pacing round his hotel room, waiting for Ronald Reagan to call and tell him that he wanted him to be his running mate. George H. W. Bush (the father) was in another room, awaiting the same call. Bush was chosen. His camera fixed on Rumsfeld's face, Errol Morris recalls the moment when it all slipped away:

Morris: It seems to me that if that decision had gone a slightly different way, you would have been Vice-President and a future President of the United States.

Rumsfeld: [Pause] That's possible.

He meets the camera's gaze, inscrutable. Nothing else is vouchsafed. A known unknown has been registered, not to be discussed. There will be more of those to come.

Famously the youngest and the oldest Secretary of Defense in the history of the United States, Rumsfeld is still in the ring. His complacent but disastrous tenure of that office from 2001 to 2006 under President George W. Bush (the son) is the focus of *The Unknown Known* (2014), a documentary based on thirty-three hours of interviews with its subject. Its director is in every sense an *auteur*. As filmmaker, interviewer, private investigator and blogger, Errol Morris has form. He has taken on a Secretary of Defense before, in *The Fog of War* (2003), an Academy Award-winning study of Robert McNamara; and he has tackled the grisly subject of Abu Ghraib, in *Standard Operating Procedure* (2008), at once an inquiry into the nature of the evidence and a compilation of witness testimony, out of the mouths of the perpetrators themselves.[3]

Morris has been called an erudite gumshoe. It is an apt description, as his 'Opinionator' blogs in the *New York Times* amply confirm. 'The certainty of Donald Rumsfeld', a four-part series drawing on everything from Pascal's *Pensées* to Lewis Carroll's *Alice in Wonderland*, displays his characteristic blend of intellectual voracity and professional idiosyncrasy.[4] He is deeply interested in certainty: in self-belief and self-deception. 'Believing is seeing,' as he puts it, in a neat inversion of the old saw. 'We see what we are prepared to see.'[5] He is also drawn to perpetrators, of every kind and condition. These preoccupations are what give his films their distinctive flavour. They are human interest stories – human, all too human – and also forensic investigations. Morris made his name with *The Thin Blue Line* (1988), about a murder and a case of mistaken identity, a case he solved, in effect, by interviewing the murderer.

Interviewing is his forte. In the age of the short attention span and the sound bite, his technique is almost outrageous. He asks a question (off-camera) and lets his subjects talk (on-camera). 'The idea is that if you let someone talk they're going to reveal something about themselves.'[6] Like Laura Poitras (see Chapter 5), as a documentarian Morris is remarkably abstemious in his interventions. He is seldom directive, and never confrontational. The results are extraordinary. The quality of the witness testimony in *Standard Operating Procedure* is unsurpassed. The 'bad apples' of Abu Ghraib talk and talk; they concede almost nothing, but they are marvellously self-revealing.[7] McNamara for his part appears tortured, self-critical, remorseful; he struggles to find a dignified way to make amends for his own shortcomings over the debacle of Vietnam. *The Fog of War* is the examined life laid bare, it seems, as McNamara goes to meet his maker. If it is not exactly a moral tale, it is at least an apologia. 'There is a kind of faux-redemption,' as Morris shrewdly says.[8]

In the light of this experience, and the morally dubious terrain they are bound to traverse, Morris and Rumsfeld would appear to be made for each other. Evidently Rumsfeld was a willing participant, despite the fact that he did not much care for *The Fog of War*. (In Rumsfeld's view, McNamara had nothing to apologize for, nor perhaps to agonize about.) He came to Morris; he also gave him access to his archive.[9] He seems not to have tried to set conditions or impose restrictions, as he did with Bradley Graham for the aptly titled biography *By His Own Rules* (2009), where he refused altogether to talk about Iraq, as a condition of access.[10] At the end of the film Morris asks him about his motive. 'Why are you doing this – why are you talking to me?' Rumsfeld is as genially evasive as ever. 'That is a vicious question,' he replies. 'I'll be darned if I know.'

The answer surely has to do with that fickle jade posterity. Rumsfeld is hard at work rescuing his reputation, if he can. This involves burnishing his image – his self-image – as the consummate right hand of the President and Commander-in-Chief: a counsellor, far-sighted, disinterested, worldly, wily, watchful – a cross between Clausewitz and Confucius, with a talent for plain speaking and an eye for the apothegm – and also an executant, a leader of men, a scourge of organizations, an agent of change. The overweening conceit of sage and samurai, bruiser and lion-tamer, is nicely caught, or spoofed, in *Donald*, a novel by Eric Martin and Stephen Elliott:

He is reading. The library is empty except for two limp scholars by the window. Look at their posture. How much butt would he have kicked here? The place is old, the oldest library in an old town. It's too dark but the scholars don't seem to mind. They're twenty years younger than him, but he could outwrestle them. Them and every scholar in his weight class in every library in the world. His scholarly skills are not shabby, either. He reads like lightning. His hands are always moving, wringing ideas from the page. 'Like a perv,' an assistant aide's assistant once observed, and if by that she meant the body is the mind, then fine, nice jab, he could give a rat's how it looked. There's a reason she was an assistant's assistant. A reason generals and bureaucrats waited in turn with him, turns that by well-publicized accounts were not all pleasant. But was he fair? He was so fair. He was so fair he screwed himself all the time.[11]

In a rather different register the same conceit pervades his memoir, *Known and Unknown* (2012), an 800-page monstrosity well described by Morris as a brick of a book, and variously characterized by others as 'a revenge memoir', 'a prodigious monument to human vanity', and 'a masterpiece of buck-passing and score-settling'.[12]

The memoir is all of that. The buck-passing and score-settling extends to Richard Armitage, Paul Bremer, Ted Kennedy, John Kerry, John McCain, Barack Obama, Colin Powell, Condoleezza Rice and George Tenet, among others, not to mention Generals Abizaid, Franks, Jones, McKiernan, Sanchez and Shinseki. But Rumsfeld is also keen to convey his seriousness of purpose, and to bag a place for himself in a tradition extending back through Henry Kissinger, Dean Acheson and Robert Murphy – a tradition of wise men and weighty memoirs, each of them carefully referenced. 'Tell it like it happened, Don,' Henry urges, straight-faced, when he comes to visit. 'Don't gloss things over. I didn't.' A quotation from Acheson's classic *Present at the Creation* (1971) is used as an epigraph: 'At the top there are no easy choices.' The author himself pops up, Zelig-like, in a photograph with Murphy, 'the renowned "diplomat among warriors"', a nod to the title of that celebrated memoir.[13] There is a sort of smuggled self-regard in evidence here, a startling pretension. To contemplate the disparity between Acheson and Rumsfeld as public servants and presidents' men is to take the measure of a spectacular decline. It is difficult to know what Dean Acheson's response would have been to the revelation of Abu Ghraib, but it is safe to say that it would not have been Donald Rumsfeld's: 'I didn't know you were allowed to bring cameras into a prison!'[14]

Rumsfeld presents himself as not only alert but prescient (and, incidentally, well-read). As Morris has observed, his life is book-ended by two surprise attacks: the attack on Pearl Harbor in 1941, when he was nine, and the attack on the World Trade Center and the Pentagon, sixty years later, when he was Secretary of Defense. Reflecting on the 9/11 attacks in his memoir:

> I sometimes remarked that the only thing surprising is that we continue to be surprised when a surprise occurs. In 1962, Harvard economist Thomas Schelling wrote a foreword to a book on Pearl Harbor that captured this idea perfectly. 'We were so busy thinking through some "obvious" Japanese moves that we neglected to hedge against the choice that they actually made,' he wrote. 'There is a tendency in our planning to confuse the unfamiliar with the improbable.' I was so taken with his piece that I sent

a copy to President Bush during our first month in office as well as to many members of Congress.[15]

The piece in question was Schelling's foreword to Roberta Wohlstetter's *Pearl Harbor: Warning and Decision* (1962). Rumsfeld was so taken with it that he circulated it to the Joint Chiefs of Staff in March 2001, to members of Congress in September 2001, and to the President, once more, in July 2004. In *The Unknown Known* Morris asks him why it is so important to him, and why he describes Pearl Harbor as 'a failure of imagination'.

> Rumsfeld: We didn't know we didn't know that they could do what they did the way they did it. We had people working on breaking codes. We had people thinking through, what are the kinds of things they might do? And, lo and behold, the carriers were able to – on a Sunday morning – get very close to Hawaii, launch their planes, and impose enormous destruction.
>
> Morris: Was it a failure of imagination, or failure to look at the intelligence that was available?
>
> Rumsfeld: They had thought through a great many more obvious possibilities. People were chasing the wrong rabbit. That one possibility was not something that they had imagined was likely.

For Rumsfeld, Pearl Harbor was a failure to imagine Pearl Harbor. It was a consequence of what we didn't know we didn't know. From this perspective, it takes its place as the most terrible unknown unknown in the recent experience of the United States – until the next one, the failure to imagine 9/11. Bolstered by an interview with a splendidly sceptical Schelling – not only an economist but the subtlest of strategic thinkers – Morris calls into question that dubious notion, and the equally dubious analogy with 9/11. As he has pointed out, neither Wohlstetter's book nor Schelling's foreword posits a failure of imagination, as such; they are all about a complex web of explanation, at once more sophisticated and more prosaic, and above all more systemic.[16] Schelling offers a brilliant distillation in his foreword:

> Surprise, when it happens to a government, is likely to be a complicated, diffuse, bureaucratic thing. It includes neglect of responsibility, but also responsibility so poorly defined or so ambiguously delegated that action gets lost. It includes gaps in intelligence, but also intelligence that, like a string of pearls too precious to wear, is too sensitive to give to those who need it. It includes the alarm that fails to work, but also the alarm that

has gone off so often that it has been disconnected. It includes the unalert watchman, but also the one who knows he'll be chewed out by his superior if he gets higher authority out of bed. It includes the contingencies that occur to no one, but also those that everyone assumes somebody else is taking care of. It includes straightforward procrastination, but also decisions protracted by internal disagreement. It includes, in addition, the inability of individual human beings to rise to the occasion until they are sure it *is* the occasion – which is usually too late. (Unlike movies, real life provides no musical background to tip us off to the climax.) Finally, as at Pearl Harbor, surprise may include some measure of genuine novelty introduced by the enemy, and possibly some sheer bad luck.[17]

That is a compelling anatomy of failure – as compelling for 9/11 as for Pearl Harbor. For all his admonitory activity, it is not an analysis with which Rumsfeld is prepared to engage.

Rumsfeld's verbiage – it is tempting to say Rumsfeld's shtick – has served to bring him a degree of double-edged fame (or notoriety) as wise man, wordsmith and wit. He revels in this, of course, and trades on it. The most celebrated example of this shtick, the one for which he will probably be remembered, is embodied in the title of his own memoir and reprised in Morris's film. As set out in a compilation of 'The Existential Poetry of Donald H. Rumsfeld', it runs as follows:

As we know,
There are known knowns.
There are things we know we know.
We also know
There are known unknowns.
That is to say
We know there are some things
We do not know.
But there are also unknown unknowns,
The ones we don't know we don't know.[18]

How profound is this? Not very. Indicatively, perhaps, it transpires that the wordsmith himself is unsure whether it is the known unknowns or the unknown unknowns that signify 'the things that you think you know that it turns out you do not'. This makes for a cherishable moment in the film, but it does not inspire confidence in the philosophy. Rumsfeld's shtick is part rodomontade, part smokescreen.

What does Rumsfeld know? What does he really think? What does he have to say? Morris tries hard to draw him out. At one point in the film he invites the former Secretary of Defense to read out a list of 'enhanced interrogation techniques' that he approved in December

2002. It is a long list. Such techniques were divided into three categories. Category I were the most commonplace and the least aggressive (direct questioning; standard rewards and deceptions; yelling, but not in the ear). Category III went much further. Rumsfeld approved one of these: 'Use of mild, non-injurious physical contact such as grabbing, poking in the chest with the finger, and light pushing.' On legal advice, other Category III techniques were disallowed, among them 'use of a wet towel and dripping water to induce the misperception of suffocation,' otherwise known as waterboarding. Category II became the benchmark:

1. The use of stress positions (like standing), for a maximum of four hours.
2. The use of falsified documents or reports.
3. Use of the isolation facility for up to 30 days.
4. Interrogating the detainee in an environment other than the standard interrogation booth.
5. Deprivation of light and auditory stimuli.
6. The detainee may also have a hood placed over his head during transportation and questioning. The hood should not restrict breathing in any way and the detainee should be under direct observation when hooded.
7. The use of 20-hour interrogations.
8. Removal of all comfort items (including religious items).
9. Switching the detainee from hot rations to MREs [Meals Ready to Eat].
10. Removal of clothing.
11. Forced grooming (shaving of facial hair, etc.).
12. Using detainees' individual phobias (such as fear of dogs) to induce stress.[19]

Rumsfeld reads in a monotone. When he gets to the end he looks up at Morris, blinks, and exclaims, 'Good grief, that's a pile of stuff.' It is almost as if he is seeing the list for the first time. In fact he is intimately familiar with it, not only because this is one of the seminal texts of the global war on terror, but also because his approval became a kind of *cause célèbre* in the bureaucratic politics of torture (as he well knows), and a touchstone of his very personal involvement in what his crony Dick Cheney is pleased to call 'the dark side' of that doomed enterprise. His personal involvement in the 'special interrogation plan' for Mohammed al-Qahtani, the so-called twentieth hijacker, is well-documented. More recently, the publication of Mohamedou Ould Slahi's *Guantánamo Diary* (2015) has served to reveal another rather similar case (see Chapter 2).

When he signed the memorandum of approval, Rumsfeld could not resist inserting a scribbled addendum: 'However, I stand for 8–10 hours a day. Why is standing limited to 4 hours?' Those words came back to haunt him. He returned to the subject in his memoir:

> My offhand comment was a statement of fact. I used a stand-up desk and spent much of the day on my feet. The note received enormous attention when detainee abuse became a major public issue. It was a mistake to make that personal observation to my General Counsel [who drafted the memorandum]. It certainly was not a signal to the Department that it would be okay to stretch the rules, as some have suggested.[20]

As for who is doing the suggesting, Rumsfeld cites a later work by the international lawyer Philippe Sands, *Torture Team* (2008). There were isolated individuals in high office who suggested as much at the time. Alberto Mora, General Counsel of the US Navy, understood well enough that Rumsfeld's offhand comment could be construed as a jest, a throwaway line. He also feared that it could become an argument for the defence in any prosecution of terrorist suspects; and furthermore that it could be read as an encouragement to exceed the limits officially prescribed by the Secretary of Defense himself, 'a written nod-and-a-wink to interrogators . . . that they should not feel bound by the limits set in the memo, but consider themselves authorized to do what was necessary to obtain the necessary information'. Colonel Lawrence Wilkerson, Chief of Staff to the Secretary of State, Colin Powell, had a similar reaction when he saw the addendum. Wilkerson was in no doubt about what it meant. 'It said, "Carte blanche, guys." That's what started them down the slope. You'll have My Lais then. Once you pull this thread, the whole fabric unravels.'[21]

For the most part, however, the addendum went unremarked. Mischievous or heinous, it was a perfect expression of the banality of the Bush Administration, the moral blindness of the principal policy-makers, the hubris of the neo-con cocoon, the signature mixture of arrogance and incompetence that led to the crushing loss of moral authority suffered by the United States and its accomplices in their prosecution of their war. It might almost be described as a failure of imagination.

At which point Morris launches a surprise attack of his own. Pursuing the question of the enhanced interrogation techniques, which were originally requested and approved for use at Guantánamo, he puts to Rumsfeld 'a claim that the interrogation rules used at Guantánamo migrated to Iraq, where they led to incredible abuse'. The plant here is the word *migrated*. Rumsfeld seizes on it with self-righteous indignation:

> The evidence is to the contrary. There were twelve investigations that looked at these issues – some by civilians, distinguished people like Dr Harold Brown and Dr James Schlesinger, former Secretaries of Defense, others by military officials. To suggest that procedures from Guantánamo migrated over to Iraq is to suggest that the procedures at Guantánamo would have encouraged the kind of unbelievably bad, illegal, improper behaviour that took place at Abu Ghraib. And there was nothing that would have permitted anything like that. Anyone who reads the investigative reports knows that's not the case.

Whereupon Morris produces the relevant passage from the Schlesinger Report and reads it out to Rumsfeld:

> As already noted, the changes to DoD [Department of Defense] interrogation policies between December 2, 2002, and April 16, 2003, were an element contributing to uncertainties in the field as to which techniques were authorized. Although specifically limited by the Secretary of Defense to Guantánamo, and requiring his personal approval (given in only two cases), the augmented techniques for Guantánamo migrated to Afghanistan and Iraq where they were neither limited nor safeguarded.[22]

There is a significant pause.

'Yeah,' says Rumsfeld, 'I think that's a fair assessment.'

This is the crux of the film, the clinching moment for director and spectator alike. We have witnessed a memorable exchange, at the same time gripping and frustrating. Plainly, Rumsfeld has been found out, or caught red-handed. It was he who commissioned the Schlesinger Report; he quotes from it (selectively) in his memoir; he could not but be aware of its principal findings, spelled out in the Executive Summary. Yet he concedes nothing, not even the glaring contradiction. So far from acknowledging it, he seems blandly to embrace it. He offers nothing more.

Uncharacteristically, Morris persists:

> Morris: Are you saying stuff just happens?[23]

> Rumsfeld: Well, we know that in every war there are things that evolve that hadn't been planned for or fully anticipated, and things that occur that shouldn't occur.

Morris: Wouldn't it have been better not to go there at all?

Rumsfeld: Well, I guess time will tell.

Morris is getting nowhere. Rumsfeld has slipped into the third-person passive once removed, as Colin Powell used to call it, evading every probe.[24] He is not merely unreconstructed, he is self-delighted. He is not merely unrepentant, he is ebullient. This time there will be no redemption, faux or otherwise.

Recantation is out of the question. That may be no surprise. Reflection, however, is another matter. The singular revelation of Errol Morris's film is that Rumsfeld has nothing to say. 'Is he hiding something?' Morris asked himself. 'Is he playing with me? Or is there really nothing there?' As the director observes regretfully of his own movie, 'it often seems like an excursion to nowhere'. For Morris, Rumsfeld emerges as 'deeply vapid and crazy'.[25] It is a sympathetic characterization. As the afflicted are profoundly deaf, so Rumsfeld is profoundly vacuous. What Morris has laid bare is the vacuity of evil.

There is something of Eichmann in Rumsfeld. Allowing for the difference in the enormity of their crimes, Rumsfeld in Washington echoes *Eichmann in Jerusalem*, Hannah Arendt's celebrated 'report on the banality of evil':

> Eichmann was not Iago and not Macbeth, and nothing would have been farther from his mind than to determine with Richard III 'to prove a villain'. Except for an extraordinary diligence in looking out for his personal advancement, he had no motives at all. And this diligence in itself was in no way criminal; he certainly would never have murdered his superior in order to inherit his post. He *merely*, to put the matter colloquially, *never realized what he was doing*. . . . In principle he knew quite well what it was all about, and in his final statement to the court he spoke of the 'revaluation of values prescribed by the government'. He was not stupid. It was sheer thoughtlessness – something by no means identical with stupidity – that predisposed him to become one of the greatest criminals of that period. And if this is 'banal' and even funny, if with the best will in the world one cannot extract any diabolical or demonic profundity from Eichmann, that is still far from calling it commonplace.[26]

This cuts close to a fundamental truth about Rumsfeld. He is thoughtless. 'I stand for 8–10 hours a day' is the quintessence of thoughtlessness. 'It is indeed my opinion now that evil is never "radical", that it is only extreme, and that it possesses neither depth nor any demonic dimension,' Arendt explained to Gershom Scholem.

'It can overgrow and lay waste the whole world precisely because it spreads like a fungus on the surface. It is "thought-defying", as I said, because thought tries to reach some depth, to go to the roots, and the moment it concerns itself with evil, it is frustrated because there is nothing.'[27]

With Rumsfeld, nakedly, there is nothing. That is Errol Morris's experience. Thanks to Morris, it is ours too.

'Evil always appeared to me as embodied evil,' reflected Zbigniew Herbert, 'always *with a human face.*'

The practicality of that point of view:

(a) It is easy to recognize,
(b) It is easy to point out and consequently to choose what is good and reject what is evil. Moral life is a set of practical problems, not theoretical ones,
(c) Whoever grumbles about the difficulty of choosing, stimulates and plays up an intellectual malaise while in fact he lacks character, the ability to make a choice according to one's moral being. That being is, as it were, given by nature, it connects us to the structure of the universe and in particular the world of human beings and animals.

'This much in brief, but by God and the truth, there is no need to go on about it or write fat tomes; one must exercise good will, for that way we spare ourselves and our neighbours much suffering.'[28]

Notes

1. Leonard Cohen, 'All There Is To Know About Adolph Eichmann', in *Flowers for Hitler* [1964], collected in *Stranger Music* (London: Cape, 1993), p. 53.
2. Nixon Tapes, conversation number 464-012, 9 March 1971, http://millercenter.org/presidentialclassroom/exhibits/nixon-and-bob-haldeman-on-donald-rumsfeld (last accessed 5 June 2015). See *The Haldeman Diaries* (New York: Putnam, 1994), p. 169.
3. See Alex Danchev, *On Art and War and Terror* (Edinburgh: Edinburgh University Press, 2011), ch. 9.
4. Errol Morris, 'The Certainty of Donald Rumsfeld', *New York Times*, 25–28 March 2014, at http://opinionator.blogs.nytimes.com (last accessed 27 May 2014). *Believing is Seeing* (New York: Penguin, 2014), a collection of his earlier blogs, includes two substantial investigations of Abu Ghraib, 'Will the real hooded man please stand up' and 'The most curious thing'.
5. Morris, 'Certainty', part 3, p. 6.

6. Errol Morris Q and A, following a preview of *The Unknown Known* at the Institute of Contemporary Arts, London, 19 March 2014.

7. Some of this talk is recorded in Philip Gourevitch and Errol Morris, *Standard Operating Procedure* (London: Picador, 2008).

8. Morris Q and A at the ICA.

9. Rumsfeld's archive of declassified (sometimes redacted) documents is available online at http://www.rumsfeld.com. It is extensive but partial. Much of it issues from Rumsfeld himself. As Secretary of Defense he was in the habit of writing or dictating a memorandum at any moment: admonitions to his staff or to the Department as a whole (the famous 'snowflakes'); personal reflections; notes for the record. Some of these documents have a self-protective or self-exculpatory cast. See, for example, 'Nightmare' and 'List of Steps', 10 and 20 May 2004, in the wake of the Abu Ghraib scandal, at http://library. rumsfeld.com/doclib/sp/1192/2004-05-10%20re%Nightmare.pdf and 1198/2004-05-20%20to%Pete%20Geren%20re%20List%20of%20 Steps.pdf (last accessed 27 May 2014).

10. Bradley Graham, *By His Own Rules* (New York: PublicAffairs, 2009), p. 12. In their final interview, in late 2008, he relented and 'addressed a number of aspects of the war'. It is clear that he was not very forthcoming.

11. Eric Martin and Stephen Elliott, *Donald* (San Francisco: McSweeney's, 2011), p. 5. The novel imagines him getting a taste of his own medicine: he is abducted, rendered, and imprisoned in a black site beyond reach.

12. Donald Rumsfeld, *Known and Unknown* (New York: Penguin, 2012); Morris Q & A. The other characterizations come from reviews by Gwen Ifill in the *Washington Post*, 8 February 2011; Colonel Lloyd J. Matthews in *Parameters*, Spring 2011; and Max Boot in *The New Republic*, 17 March 2011.

13. Rumsfeld, *Known and Unknown*, pp. 205–6, 554 and photograph 20.

14. Andrew Cockburn, *Rumsfeld* (London: Verso, 2007), p. 194, quoting an official who was present.

15. Rumsfeld, *Known and Unknown*, p. 334, quoting Thomas C. Schelling, 'Foreword' to Roberta Wohlstetter, *Pearl Harbor: Warning and Decision* (Stanford: Stanford University Press, 1962), pp. vii–viii. He is also fond of quoting Schelling's lovely phrase, 'a poverty of expectations': 'The danger is not that we shall read the signals and indicators with too little skill; the danger is in a poverty of expectations – a routine obsession with a few dangers that may be familiar rather than likely.' But the conclusion he draws is by no means self-evident, and its application to Pearl Harbor (or 9/11) very doubtful. Cf. *Known and Unknown*, pp. xvi–xvii.

16. Morris, 'Certainty', part 3. See also Mark Danner, 'Donald Rumsfeld Revealed', *New York Review of Books*, 9 January 2014. Typically,

Morris scoured Wohlstetter's text for any treatment of 'failure of imagination'. The best he could find was a passage relating to a certain conception of naval operations, or cultural assumptions: 'Even in the Congressional hearings, as late as 1945, with the evidence of six carriers before them, naval witnesses often refer to four carriers because it was beyond the reach of imagination that any naval power would risk its entire heavy carrier strength in one operation. Even if we had played out a Japanese war game, we might not have been able to project the daring and ingenuity of the enemy' (*Pearl Harbor*, p. 355).

17. Schelling, 'Foreword', p. viii.

18. Hart Seely (ed.), 'The Unknown', in *Pieces of Intelligence: The Existential Poetry of Donald H. Rumsfeld* (London: Simon & Schuster, 2003), p. 2. From a Department of Defense news briefing on 12 February 2002. On the etymology, Rumsfeld may well know Confucius, as quoted by Thoreau: 'To know that we know what we know, and that we do not know what we do not know, that is true knowledge.' See Henry David Thoreau, *Walden* [1854] (Oxford: Oxford University Press, 1997), p. 12. Cf. Rumsfeld, *Known and Unknown*, pp. xv–xvii, and Morris, 'Certainty', part 2.

19. General Counsel memorandum, 'Counter-Resistance Techniques', 27 November 2002 (approved 2 December 2002), in Karen J. Greenberg and Joshua Dratel (eds), *The Torture Papers* (New York: Cambridge University Press, 2005), p. 236.

20. Rumsfeld, *Known and Unknown*, p. 579. Graham's treatment of this episode is exiguous in the extreme: *By His Own Rules*, p. 375.

21. Jane Mayer, *The Dark Side* (New York: Anchor, 2009), ch. 9; Philippe Sands, *Torture Team* (London: Allen Lane, 2008), ch. 16. Rumsfeld or his people can hardly have missed Mayer's account, first published as 'The Memo' in *The New Yorker*, 27 February 2006, which is also the prime source cited by Sands. Wilkerson was referring to a notorious killing spree by US Army soldiers in the Vietnamese hamlet of My Lai, in 1968, during a search and destroy mission in a Vietcong stronghold known as Pinkville. The story was broken by the young Seymour Hersh, who played a key part in bringing to light the systemic nature of torture and abuse in the war on terror. See his *Chain of Command* (London: Penguin, 2005).

22. The Schlesinger Report, officially the Final Report of the Independent Panel to Review DoD Detention Operations (2004), is published in full in *Torture Papers*, pp. 908–75. The point about migration is underlined in the Executive Summary: see pp. 914–15. On the investigative reports and the question of what Rumsfeld knew, see Danchev, *On Art and War and Terror*, ch. 8.

23. A reference to another of the famous news briefings. This is exactly what Rumsfeld was saying about the war in Iraq and its consequences.

Asked about looting in Baghdad, on 11 April 2003, he replied: 'Freedom's untidy, and free people are free to make mistakes and commit crimes and do bad things. They're also free to live their lives and do wonderful things. And that's what's going to happen here. Think what happened in our cities when we've had riots, and problems, and looting. Stuff happens!' Rumsfeld blames media misrepresentation: *Known and Unknown*, pp. 475–8.

24. Bob Woodward, *Plan of Attack* (New York: Pocket, 2004), pp. 182–3. 'To Powell,' he adds, 'it seemed almost that Rumsfeld was wearing rubber gloves, not wanting to leave fingerprints on policy recommendations.'

25. Morris Q & A. Cf. Toby Lichtig, 'A pile of stuff', *Times Literary Supplement*, 4 April 2014.

26. Hannah Arendt, 'Postscript' to *Eichmann in Jerusalem* [1963] in Peter Baehr (ed.), *The Portable Hannah Arendt* (London: Penguin, 2003), p. 379.

27. Arendt to Scholem, 24 July 1963, in *The Portable Hannah Arendt*, p. 396. Arendt's original formulation, the conclusion of *Eichmann in Jerusalem*, was 'the fearsome word-and-thought-defying *banality of evil*'.

28. Zbigniew Herbert, trans. Alissa Valles, 'Evil' [1998], in *The Collected Prose* (New York: Ecco, 2010), pp. 662–3.

Index